MW00786192

SCALING YOUR STARTUP

MASTERING THE FOUR STAGES
FROM IDEA TO $10 BILLION

Peter S. Cohan

Apress®

Scaling Your Startup: Mastering the Four Stages from Idea to $10 Billion

Peter S. Cohan
Marlborough, MA
USA

ISBN-13 (pbk): 978-1-4842-4311-4   ISBN-13 (electronic): 978-1-4842-4312-1
https://doi.org/10.1007/978-1-4842-4312-1

Library of Congress Control Number: 2019930174

Copyright © 2019 by Peter S. Cohan

This work is subject to copyright. All rights are reserved by the Publisher, whether the whole or part of the material is concerned, specifically the rights of translation, reprinting, reuse of illustrations, recitation, broadcasting, reproduction on microfilms or in any other physical way, and transmission or information storage and retrieval, electronic adaptation, computer software, or by similar or dissimilar methodology now known or hereafter developed.

Trademarked names, logos, and images may appear in this book. Rather than use a trademark symbol with every occurrence of a trademarked name, logo, or image we use the names, logos, and images only in an editorial fashion and to the benefit of the trademark owner, with no intention of infringement of the trademark.

The use in this publication of trade names, trademarks, service marks, and similar terms, even if they are not identified as such, is not to be taken as an expression of opinion as to whether or not they are subject to proprietary rights.

While the advice and information in this book are believed to be true and accurate at the date of publication, neither the authors nor the editors nor the publisher can accept any legal responsibility for any errors or omissions that may be made. The publisher makes no warranty, express or implied, with respect to the material contained herein.

Managing Director, Apress Media LLC: Welmoed Spahr
Acquisitions Editor: Shiva Ramachandran
Development Editor: Laura Berendson
Coordinating Editor: Rita Fernando

Cover designed by eStudioCalamar

Distributed to the book trade worldwide by Springer Science+Business Media New York, 233 Spring Street, 6th Floor, New York, NY 10013. Phone 1-800-SPRINGER, fax (201) 348-4505, e-mail orders-ny@springer-sbm.com, or visit www.springeronline.com. Apress Media, LLC is a California LLC and the sole member (owner) is Springer Science + Business Media Finance Inc (SSBM Finance Inc). SSBM Finance Inc is a **Delaware** corporation.

For information on translations, please e-mail rights@apress.com, or visit www.apress.com/rights-permissions.

Apress titles may be purchased in bulk for academic, corporate, or promotional use. eBook versions and licenses are also available for most titles. For more information, reference our Print and eBook Bulk Sales web page at www.apress.com/bulk-sales.

Any source code or other supplementary material referenced by the author in this book is available to readers on GitHub via the book's product page, located at www.apress.com/9781484243114. For more detailed information, please visit www.apress.com/source-code.

To Robin.

Contents

About the Author

Peter S. Cohan is Lecturer of Strategy at Babson College. He teaches strategy and entrepreneurship to undergraduate and MBA students at Babson College. He is the founding principal of Peter S. Cohan & Associates, a management consulting and venture capital firm. He has completed over 150 growth strategy consulting projects for global technology companies and invested in seven startups—three of which were sold for over $2 billion. Peter has written 13 books and writes columns on entrepreneurship for Forbes, Inc, and The Worcester *Telegram & Gazette*. Prior to starting his firm, he worked as a case team leader for Harvard Business School professor Michael Porter's consulting firm and taught at MIT, Stanford, and the University of Hong Kong. Peter earned an MBA from Wharton, did graduate work in computer science at MIT, and holds a BS in Electrical Engineering from Swarthmore College.

Acknowledgments

This book has benefited greatly from the help of many people.

I could not have embarked on this project without the enthusiastic support of Nan Langowitz, who chairs the Management Division at Babson. My Babson colleagues Alana Anderson, Renee Graham, Alexandra Nesbeda, and Sam Hariharhan provided helpful suggestions.

Without Apress this book would not exist. I am most grateful to Shivangi Ramachandran for her enthusiastic support of the idea for this book and for the outstanding editing and project management help from Laura Berendson and Rita Fernando Kim.

Finally, I could not have completed this book without the help of my wife, Robin, who patiently read and commented on many of the chapters and my children, Sarah and Adam, who always make me proud.

Introduction

I wrote this book because there is nothing more important to startup success than a leader's ability to scale it. I came to this realization while writing *Startup Cities* (Apress, 2018) where I saw that what makes the difference between the few startup hubs and the many that aspire to be is the relatively high proportion of CEOs who can turn a business idea into a large company. More specifically, I noticed that cities vary in their mix of three kinds of business leaders:

- Amblers (who start and run businesses that employ friends and family),

- Sprinters (who can turn a business idea into a company that grows fast and is bought by a larger firm), and

- Marathoners (who turn an idea into a huge, fast-growing, publicly-traded company that supports the creation of local startups).

While there are a few marathoners with no prior startup experience, such as Amazon's Jeff Bezos or Facebook's Mark Zuckerberg, who reach this pinnacle, most sprinters and marathoners learn their leadership skills through a series of corporate and startup jobs that help them gain the skills they need to turn an idea into a large company. What's more, within those categories there are finer gradations of leadership skills. More specifically, startups go through distinct stages in their growth from an idea into a large company, whether they are acquired or go public. The three kinds of business leaders relate differently to the four scaling stages. Amblers are not interested in scaling and are happy to sustain themselves at stage 1. The sprinter wants to get to stage 3 and then do other things, and the marathoner wants to participate in stages 1 to 4.

But regardless of how leaders define these stages, quite frequently, the founders of these startups cannot lead the company through each stage. In most cases, founders swallow their pride, realizing that they can either remain CEO and not raise the capital their company needs to survive, or they can give up the top job. Sometimes those founders leave the company when a new CEO joins and sometimes they stick around as chief technology officer and report to that new CEO. Often such deposed founders learn from the experience, either by role modeling from the new CEO or by consulting mentors about what they could have done more effectively, so they become better leaders. If that happens, they might become a CEO of another company where their newfound know-how can help them achieve a successful exit.

Simply put, scaling skills are important and they are in big demand among entrepreneurs, investors, and cities. As a teacher of entrepreneurship, I need good material on how to scale effectively to prepare students for the real world. As we'll see later in this book, there is good material on parts of the scaling process, such as how a startup can win its first customers. However, there is no comprehensive framework that explains all the stages and tools available to leaders seeking to turn an idea into a large company. Creating such a framework is the goal of this book.

Who Will Benefit From This Book

Scaling is of primary importance to entrepreneurs, employees, customers, partners, and capital providers and of secondary interest to government policymakers and universities. Here are the reasons for scaling's importance to each group:

- **Entrepreneurs**. Founders want to turn their ideas into companies that change the world. They also want the economic benefits that come with owning a substantial piece of a very valuable company. Both goals can only be realized if the company's CEO is capable of scaling it.

- **Employees**. A startup's employees are generally enthusiastic about its vision, want to learn from outstanding leaders and peers, and according to my interviews with Silicon Valley executives and investors, are increasingly impatient about cashing in on their stock options. These outcomes can only be achieved if the company scales.

- **Customers**. A startup's customers may have a mixed attitude towards scaling. If the startup can lower its costs and boost the value of its products for customers, then customers are likely to benefit from the startup's effective scaling. Moreover, if the company grows to the point where it can go public, then the customer may benefit since the capital provided will increase the odds that the startup will survive. Scaling could have a downside for customers if it keeps the startup from developing new products and delivering excellent service.

- **Partners**, particularly suppliers, may benefit as a startup scales. In general, the bigger the startup, the more supplies it will purchase. If the supplier can satisfy the growing demand and become more efficient in the process of scaling, then it may pass along some of the cost savings to the startup in the form of lower prices. On the other hand, if the supplier becomes too dependent on the startup for its revenues, the startup may use its bargaining power to force the supplier to slash prices.

- **Capital providers** can only realize a return on their investment if a startup scales to the point where it is acquired or goes public. If the acquirer has a record of boosting the sales of acquired startups' products, the investor may be better off accepting the acquirer's stock. However, if the startup's CEO has the potential to be a marathoner, capital providers will be better off if the startup can keep scaling after its IPO.

- **Universities** can benefit from developing courses about startup scaling, particularly if they already sponsor incubators and startup competitions or teach entrepreneurship. If universities can provide scaling skills to more graduates, their alumni may achieve greater career success. This would burnish the university's reputation and potentially enrich its endowment (if the successful entrepreneurs donate to the university).

- **Government policymakers** may benefit if more of their local entrepreneurs became sprinters or marathoners, an outcome that would be more likely if local founder were better at scaling.

Scaling Research

To gain a deeper understanding of how to scale successfully, I set out to answer the following questions:

- Are there specific traits typical of CEOs who will become sprinters or marathoners?

- How do such CEOs define the revenue tiers that their startup will reach as it scales? (My interviews with CEOs revealed that each CEO has different revenue tiers. Therefore, I reframed the question to focus on the principal business goals of each scaling stage.)

- How should CEOs create and sustain a culture that helps their startup to scale?

- What growth trajectories are most likely to turn an idea into a large company?

- What are the best sources of capital for each of a scaling startup's revenue tiers and how do the most effective CEOs persuade these capital providers to invest?

- How do effective CEOs redefine jobs as their startups scale?

- How do they decide whom to hire, promote, and let go at each revenue tier?

- How do effective CEOs set goals as a startup scales and hold everyone accountable for achieving those goals?

- How do CEOs change the way they coordinate processes as their startup scales?

- How do CEOs decide whether they should continue to lead their company as it scales?

To investigate these questions and refine my scaling model, I interviewed 88 CEOs and 6 venture capital investors in Boston/Cambridge, Silicon Valley, Tel Aviv, and Munich. I sought founders and investors who could describe their experience with the seven startup scaling levers. For each lever, I looked for successful and unsuccessful case studies at each of the four scaling stages.

The Scaling Roadmap

This book presents the findings of this research in two sections.

Part I. Exploring the Scaling Model

Chapters 2 through 8 examine more deeply each of the seven startup scaling levers: creating growth trajectories (Chapter 2), raising capital (Chapter 3), sustaining culture (Chapter 4), redefining job functions (Chapter 5), hiring, promoting, and letting people go (Chapter 6), holding people accountable (Chapter 7), and coordinating processes (Chapter 8).

For each of these chapters, Section I covers the following topics

- Definition of the startup scaling lever

- Summary of the chapter's key takeaways

- Case studies of successful and less successful efforts to use the startup scaling lever at each of the four scaling stages

- Lessons learned from the cases about what to do and what to avoid

- Questions to spur action

- Conclusion

Part II. Implications for Leaders

This second section of the book consists of its concluding chapter which summarizes the key insights from the preceding chapters to help leaders decide whether they should continue as CEO and if so, what they should do to take it to the next staging scale. Chapter 9

- Presents the seven principles of scaling

- Describes how founders can assess their company's readiness to scale by calculating its scaling quotient

If you want to turn your idea into a $10 billion company, read on.

Exploring the Scaling Model

Introduction

Scaling is how leaders transform a business idea into a large company. Leaders accomplish this transformation by positioning the company to capture growth opportunities while reinventing the company as it grows.

A startup draws resources from outside stakeholders, and the relationships with those stakeholders vary depending on the startup's stage of development. This is depicted in Figure 1-1.

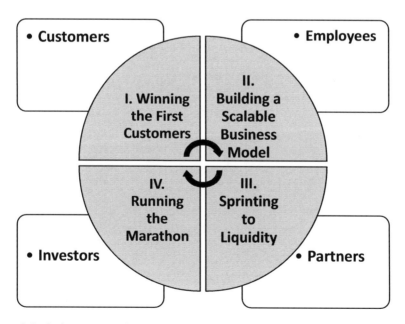

Figure 1-1. Scaling stages and startup stakeholders

© Peter S. Cohan 2019
P. S. Cohan, *Scaling Your Startup*, https://doi.org/10.1007/978-1-4842-4312-1_1

Before describing how startup's relationships with these stakeholders evolve as it scales, it is worth exploring the seven levers available to a startup CEO seeking to hurdle each of the stages, as depicted in Figure 1-2.

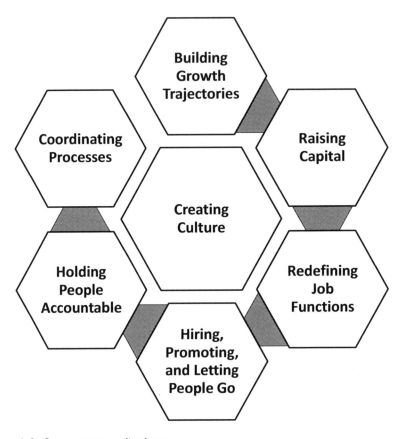

Figure 1-2. Seven startup scaling levers

Startup scaling works most effectively if each of these processes changes as the company grows. To be sure, some of the processes must change more radically than others. For example, if the founder remains CEO, a startup's culture, which infuses the other processes, remains largely unchanged. And what changes as the company grows is how the CEO keeps the culture alive. However, the other six processes must be uprooted and transformed at each scaling stage. What follows is a description of each process:

- **Creating culture:** Culture is what a company's CEO and leadership team value most and how the company uses those values to select, motivate, reward, and let go people who work there. Companies that scale successfully reward employees who take responsibility for building and sustaining customer relationships as technology, customer needs, and the competitive landscape evolve. By contrast, companies that do not scale either have the wrong culture or fail to sustain the right one. For example, when a company is small, its first employees implicitly understand the culture and are in frequent communication. When a company starts to grow and hire new people, the culture will only survive if the CEO takes time to formalize it by explicitly defining the company's values, telling stories about each value, communicating the stories to the company, and using the values to hire, reward, and let go people. While the company's culture is likely to stay the same as long as the CEO remains in place, the process of sustaining its culture requires the CEO to formalize and communicate it in a disciplined way as the company scales.

- **Building growth trajectories:** As I wrote in my 2017 book, *Disciplined Growth Strategies*, companies seeking to sustain their growth must build growth trajectories. Leaders create growth trajectories by creating chains from five dimensions of growth: customer group (current or new), product (built or acquired), geography (current or new), capabilities (current or new), and culture (current or new). Companies that scale successfully excel at planning to jump on a new growth curve in a new dimension even as their current source of growth is peaking. By contrast, startups that fail to scale wait too long to invest in a new dimension, pick the wrong one, or are simply unsuccessful when they attempt to expand because their skills do not enable them to win new customers there.

- **Raising capital:** Once a startup has figured out its growth trajectory, the CEO is better positioned to persuade capital providers to invest. But as I wrote in my 2012 book, *Hungry Start-up Strategy*, the source of startup capital varies depending on its stage of development, which corresponds to the next revenue tier it aspires to reach. During the prototyping stage, when a company is trying to fit the features of its product to a specific unmet customer need, CEOs may want to seek out financing from founders, friends, family, or possibly crowdsourcing. In the customer base stage, when a company is seeking to reach revenues of $25 million to $50 million by adding many new customers, angel investors may be the best source of capital. And in the expansion stage, where the startup may be seeking to reach $100 million in revenue, venture capitalists may be the best source of funding. CEOs who can raise capital from the right sources at each stage of development often scale successfully, while startups with CEOs who lack this ability often run out of money before they scale.

- **Redefining job functions:** As startups grow, leaders must change their organizations to adapt to the evolving needs of customers, employees, partners, and investors. Leaders do this by adding new jobs, changing existing ones, and eliminating others. For example, when a startup has a team of 10 or 20 people, they have a clear idea of the startup's mission and take it upon themselves to perform many job functions. As the company grows, leaders define jobs more narrowly, for example, by separating the role of the head of human resources into more specific jobs for recruiting, benefits administration, and compliance, and adding a chief people officer role staffed by someone who excels at leading people in these specific jobs. Successful CEOs anticipate how job functions must change as a company scales while less effective leaders wait until a crisis hits before recognizing the need to change.

- **Hiring, promoting, and letting people go:** As startups scale, leaders must fit the right individuals into these evolving job functions. To do this well, leaders must hire talented people who have succeeded in these roles before or promote current employees into these jobs. At the same time, leaders must part ways with people who no longer fit within the redefined organization, which can be particularly painful for founders who must let go people with whom they have worked for years. Successful CEOs constantly monitor how well people are performing in their evolving roles, are actively engaged in recruiting and training key talent, and firing those who no longer fit, while less effective leaders resist the need to evaluate how well people are performing and are reluctant to replace long-time colleagues.

- **Holding people accountable:** As a company adds business functions, it becomes more difficult for a leader to give each person specific goals and hold them accountable for achieving those goals. For example, to scale a startup, the CEO may seek to increase its revenues in a given year from $25 million to $50 million. And while it may be easy to assign a portion of that desired revenue growth to each sales person, it is more challenging to determine the specific goals for people in product development, human resources, customer service, and other non-revenue-generating functions. Successful CEOs establish and apply rigorous processes that hold all people accountable for contributing to the startup's growth goals. Such processes assure that each person is willing to strive toward their goals, and the CEO must be confident that achieving the targets will boost the startup's scale. Less successful leaders lack such formal processes or do not implement them rigorously. As a result, their startups are at higher risk of stagnation.

- **Coordinating processes:** CEOs organize people into departments by function and hold them accountable for corporate goals. While such functional specialization boosts efficiency in each department, it can also motivate leaders of each function to gain more resources by taking them from other departments. Unless CEOs create and manage processes to encourage departments to work together, the disadvantages of specialization can overwhelm the advantages. Simply put, leaders make the best use of a company's talent by first differentiating and then integrating. And to scale their companies, the most successful CEOs achieve corporate goals through business processes such as adding new customers, increasing revenue per customer, hiring and motivating top talent, and scaling the culture globally. Less successful leaders struggle to create such formal processes as their companies scale, which makes their companies less efficient and slower to adapt to change.

Let's examine now how startups use the seven scaling levers to interact with stakeholder at each stage.

Stage 1: Winning the First Customers

Every startup begins with an idea, and the best startup ideas alleviate customer pain better than any other product available to those customers. In this first scaling phase, the founder has no employees, investors, or partners and may have brought on a cofounder or two from among the pool of potential employees. To boost the odds for success, the founder should bring on cofounders who complement their strengths, performing well the specific activities that are important to the venture's growth but are not the founder's strengths.

Once a startup has an idea, it should seek its first customer. To do that, the founder must build a prototype, share it with potential customers, get feedback, build a better version, and repeat the process until the first customer finds the product worth buying. Once the startup has its first customer and customer research suggesting that more will buy, the founder should

- **Develop a growth trajectory and raise capital** by seeking out seed investment, possibly from the founder's capital, friends, family, or crowdfunding. To raise capital, the founder must articulate a growth trajectory and develop and execute a capital-raising strategy.

- **Create a culture, define job functions, and develop a hiring process.** Once raised, the founder should use the capital to hire employees with skills in fields such as product development, sales, and marketing. Before hiring those employees, the founder must articulate the firm's culture, define general job functions, and create a process for hiring and motivating talent.

Stage 2: Building a Scalable Business Model

In Stage 2 of the scaling process, the founder seeks to generate tens of millions of dollars' worth of revenue by selling the first product to many customers while developing repeatable processes that will lower the startup's costs and increase the company's value to customers as the startup grows. To do this, the founder must

- **Refine the company's growth trajectory.** The founder must next develop a more specific growth trajectory, making clear choices about its revenue and market share goals. The founder should decide which customer groups the startup will target; how it will make, sell, and service its product; and how it will identify and manage supply and marketing partnerships. Finally, the founder must estimate how much capital the startup will need to achieve its goals.

- **Raise more capital.** The founder must gather additional capital from investors who have achieved success in industries similar to the startup's and are eager to help prepare the company for rapid growth.

- **Articulate culture.** Since the company will begin hiring many new employees, the CEO, who may still be the founder, must articulate and communicate the culture more formally.

- **Define specialist jobs.** In addition, the CEO must define all jobs more specifically, recognizing that the company is transitioning from mostly generalists to more specialists.

- **Refine hiring processes.** The CEO must assess and improve the hiring process to keep the company competitive in the battle for talent.

- **Set and monitor goals companywide.** The CEO should create processes and systems that encourage people to agree to meet and measure goals, the achievement of which will help the company grow.

- **Introduce coordinating processes.** Finally, the CEO must create processes that coordinate the work of specialized functions such as product development, marketing, selling, service, and order fulfillment in a way that boosts efficiency and increases customers' perception of the value of the startup's products as the company scales.

Stage 3: Sprinting to Liquidity

In Stage 3, the CEO seeks to reach at least $100 million in revenue and a valuation of over $1 billion, which can generally give the startup's investors an exit through acquisition, if the CEO is a sprinter, or going public. To expand rapidly, the CEO must be confident that the startup's positioning and processes will lower its costs and boost the value of its products to customers as the company accelerates. To that end the CEO must

- **Build a global growth trajectory.** To achieve rapid expansion, the CEO must next develop a growth trajectory that sets specific revenue goals and makes clear choices about sources of revenue from current and new customer groups, current and new geographies, built and acquired products, and current and new capabilities.

- **Raise more capital.** The global growth trajectory should help the CEO develop an investor pitch deck which includes revenue and market share goals; choices about sources of revenue; how the company will make, sell, and service its product; how it will develop and manage supply and marketing partnerships; how much capital the startup will need to achieve its goals; and how it will provide a return for investors. The CEO should meet and pitch venture capital investors who embrace the CEO's vision and can offer capital, contacts, and advice to help achieve the vision.

- **Articulate its culture.** When the company goes global, it must pick a global language for communicating and then articulate the culture in that language while telling stories that global employees find compelling.

- **Define global jobs.** The CEO must focus on hiring and motivating global general managers and help them to define the mix of specialist and generalist jobs that will be needed to achieve the startup's goals in each country. As the company adds new products, the CEO must hire people to build those products and/or acquire companies that have done so already.

- **Refine global hiring processes, set and monitor goals globally, and introduce global coordinating processes.** The CEO must adapt the company's processes for hiring, setting, and monitoring the achievement of goals, and coordinating work to satisfy the cultural and other differences across each country in which the startup operates.

Stage 4: Running the Marathon

In Stage 4, the CEO seeks to keep the company growing rapidly after it goes public. For the CEO to be a marathoner like Jeff Bezos, rather than a founder like Snap's CEO Evan Spiegel, whose company struggled following its IPO, the CEO must

- **Build a high-speed growth trajectory.** To continue to expand rapidly after its IPO, the CEO must set ambitious growth goals and chain together growth trajectories including current and new customer groups, current and new geographies, built and acquired products, and current or new capabilities. Often such growth trajectories depend on capabilities and culture that lead to high customer retention coupled with adding adjacent products that loyal customers want to buy and expanding into new customer groups.

- **Raise more capital.** By going public, a company will have easier access to the capital it needs to build its growth trajectories; it will be able to sell more stock if needed or borrow money to finance acquisitions.

- **Formalize its culture.** As Jeff Bezos has done with Amazon, CEOs must define clearly their company's values and apply formal processes for key activities ranging from hiring, rewarding, and firing people to structuring meetings in order to motivate employees to act according to the company's values. Because a public company has so many employees, the CEO must hold meetings virtually through electronic, video, and one-to-many dialogues.

- **Create and manage cross-functional teams.** To keep a public company growing, the CEO must create dozens of cross-functional teams to take charge of specific business challenges, such as developing new products, sustaining high customer satisfaction, expanding into new countries, integrating acquisitions, and recruiting and motivating top talent. To keep growing, a public company needs functional experts who can lead the execution of key repeatable processes such as closing sales and creating financial reports.

- **Lead formal planning and reporting processes.** The CEO must adapt the company's processes for hiring, setting, and monitoring the achievement of goals and coordinating work to satisfy the cultural and other differences across each country in which the startup operates. To that end, CEOs must lead long-term strategic planning processes that encourage teams to buy into the company's financial targets and strategic initiatives; to prepare annual budgets; to meet quarterly to compare actual progress with budget results; and to take corrective action where needed.

Case Study: ThoughtSpot Grows to Over 250 People

This scaling model seems to be applicable to real startups. An example is Palo Alto, California-based ThoughtSpot, a provider of operations information to help companies cut costs and boost revenues. ThoughtSpot CEO Ajeet Singh has the distinction of founding another company, Nutanix, a publicly traded information storage company, and his 4% stake was worth $280 million as of March 6, 2018, the day I interviewed him. As we'll see in Chapter 3, such success is very helpful for a founder's efforts to raise capital for a new startup.

In 2012, Singh started ThoughtSpot "to help him realize his vision to deliver analytics at human scale to 20 million users by 2020." ThoughtSpot grew quickly. In the 12 months ending in November 2017, its customer count grew 227%, including 32 Fortune 500 companies and 12 Fortune 100 companies. Customers willing to share publicly that they worked with ThoughtSpot included Amway, De Beers, Chevron, Miami Children's Hospital, Bed Bath & Beyond, and Capital One. ThoughtSpot's headcount increased 67% to over 250 and it opened new offices in Seattle and Bangalore to add to its headquarters in Palo Alto and its EMEA headquarters in London. At the time, ThoughtSpot was continuing to grow. As Singh said in a March 2, 2018 interview, "We exceeded our plan for the year ending January 30 and we're growing at an excellent rate. We are selling well with the largest 5,000 global companies, who make up 70% of the spend on analytics and business intelligence technology."

The secret to ThoughtSpot's growth was that Singh thought in terms of four revenue growth tiers that stepped up by a factor of 10. And reaching the next tier was such an ambitious undertaking that many aspects of the company needed to be rethought. "I think in terms of four growth tiers: from $0 to $1 million in quarterly revenue; from $1 million to $10 million per quarter; from $10 million to $100 million per quarter; and from $100 million to $1 billion per quarter." To scale ThoughtSpot, Singh followed six principles:

- **Maintain a growth culture but change the way it is communicated.** If a company achieves initial success, there is value in maintaining its culture as it scales. Singh believes that the founders' values determine a company's culture but as the company grows, new employees will not intuitively grasp those values unless the company communicates those values in a systematic way.

- **Change the mix of people as you scale.** Early in a company's development it needs builders—people who are willing to take on many different roles and are eager to do whatever necessary to get the company off the ground. At some point, such people are no longer useful because they resist formal processes, so the CEO must replace some of them with scalers or formal process experts. As Singh said, "In the $1 million to $10 million growth tier, a company needs builders. But as it goes from $10 million to $100 million, the company needs a mixture of builders and scalers. And as it goes from $100 million to $1 billion, it needs more maintainers who help keep customers happy."

- **Replace generalists with specialists.** Along with changing the mix of people, companies must hire more specialists as they grow, while encouraging them to team up to make decisions and take action. "Some generalists can specialize. But usually they have to be replaced by executives with specific functional expertise. For example, the executive in charge of Administration may need to be replaced by a VP of Finance, VP of Human Resources, and a CFO," said Singh.

- **Make functions accountable for growth.** When a company sets its sights on the next growth tier, different functions must figure out how their contribution to the goal should be measured. "It is easy for different functions to have metrics but not get to the right place. You need to ask how each function can contribute to the growth target. For example, customer service might set specific customer retention targets, sales will have revenue goals, and country managers will have their own metrics," said Singh. "And functions should have leading indicators, such as the sales pipeline or leads generated by marketing. It's important to be realistic about how each function can contribute to the goal. It is so easy to have a bad metric."

- **Stay connected to global team members.** To grow from, say, $10 million to $100 million and beyond, companies must expand into new countries. And to make those country leaders effective, the CEO must keep them feeling connected. As Singh said, "You have to empathize with them and realize that it's a lonely job. You should give them the flexibility to optimize locally. And you should set a time for an all-hands meeting that works for the schedules of those around the world."

- **Keep being CEO if you love the job.** It is rare that a CEO can keep running a company as it scales beyond its initial public offering. Such marathoners, who can keep a company they founded growing after it goes public, are more valuable to a region and to investors than sprinters who take an idea and build it into a company that gets acquired. Marathoners like Jeff Bezos keep learning. As Singh said, "You have to maintain your intellectual curiosity and be willing to ask for feedback. The key questions I ask myself are: 'Do I feel bogged down or not? Am I having fun? Do people respect me or are they following orders? Are we hitting our goals? Are good people staying and doing well?' Every six months I ask for anonymous feedback on these questions."

What Is Different About the Startup Scaling Model?

Due to the benefits of scaling, recent research suggests that the ability to do it well is of great interest to entrepreneurs. While many venture capitalists, consultants, and academics have written about scaling, a comprehensive framework for scaling remains to be created.

Consider the results of a May 2018 CNBC survey of its Disrupter 50 companies. The survey found that about 30% of respondents said that scaling the company was their biggest entrepreneurial challenge. The same percentage found that hiring qualified talent was the biggest challenge. Sadly, the survey did not define what these CEOs meant by scaling, nor did it examine why scaling was such a challenge or what scaling levers and practices they found most useful or most prone to failure.

My interviews with academic experts on scaling reveal a heavy focus on managing culture, organization, operations, and process as a company grows and a relative neglect of strategy and capital raising. Yet several academics concur with the idea that there is a need for a comprehensive framework for helping founders who want their companies to scale successfully. Here are several examples:

- **Tom Eisenmann,** Harvard Business School's Howard H. Stevenson Professor of Business Administration, defined scaling as what happens after a company reaches the product/market fit stage. He said that practitioners such as Eric Reis and Steve Blank have provided effective ways to think about how to reach that stage. As he said, "There is remarkably little good stuff written about scaling. I see the need for a framework." Eisenmann argued that once a company achieves product/market fit, it is in a stronger position to seek out resources that it previously did not control so the CEO can acquire, organize, coordinate, and manage more resources. Noting that 60% of founders do not survive their startup's Series D round of funding, Eisenmann highlighted various ways that founders fail to scale. They cannot

    - Win customers outside their core market profitably.

    - Tell customers, employees, and investors the truth when their ambitious goals prove out of reach.

    - When creating a new business, let go of formal processes designed for the core.

- Resolve cultural battles between subgroups such as the old guard and new employees.

- Be realistic about growth depending on "a cascade of miracles" such as many uncontrollable factors all going well.

- **Gad Allon,** the Jeffrey A. Keswin Professor and Professor of Operations, Information, and Decisions, and the Director of the Management and Technology Program at the University of Pennsylvania, offered key insights about the importance of designing a business model that enhances a startup's competitive advantage as it scales. For example, Allon explained, "The most successful founders are good at product, organization, or in rare cases both. Zuckerberg, Evan Spiegel (Snap), and Reid Hoffman (LinkedIn) focus on product. Organization was not always top of mind or their greatest skill. So they brought in others to help with organization. Zuckerberg hired Sheryl Sandberg and Hoffman hired Jeff Weiner." Bezos is the rare individual who can do both. "Bezos was always thinking both about how to develop products and how to build an organization. For example, with Amazon Fresh, Bezos wanted to start small, trying to optimize the logistics of grocery delivery work in Seattle before expanding to San Francisco where he realized that he needed to organize by zip code." Allon argued that companies should scale only after the CEO has built a business model that will yield lower costs and greater customer value as the company gets bigger. He highlighted three key principles:

  - **Supply-side economies of scale:** "Before scaling, companies must figure out how to lower their cost of acquiring and servicing customers as they grow. For example, Amazon achieved economies of scale by building a massive infrastructure and pooling inventory in a small number of locations," he said.

  - **Demand-side economies of scale:** Startups should also capture what he called demand-side economies of scale. "To scale efficiently, companies must tap into network effects that make their product more valuable to customers and more difficult for competitors trying to lure away their customers for every new one they add to their network."

- **Hot cause, cool solution:** Another scaling challenge is creating a compelling corporate culture and effective performance measurements. "Effective scaling also depends on having a hot cause (a purpose that talented people find compelling) and a cool solution (an effective set of performance metrics that drive people to realize the company's goals)," he said.

- **Bob Sutton**, a Professor of Organizational Behavior who has a courtesy appointment at Stanford Business School and tenure at Stanford's School of Engineering, provided useful insights into how culture and process can help leaders to manage a growing organization:

  - **Use culture to get work done the right way.** A company like Amazon with a strong culture can scale because smart people can decide without getting top management's input. As Sutton said "Mindset is the agreement about what is good and bad behavior. When I meet with companies, I ask two questions: 'What's sacred?' and 'What's taboo?' When I asked those questions at Amazon everyone instantly agreed: the customer is sacred and wasting money is taboo (Amazon is really, really cheap)."

  - **Do more with less.** To manage growing teams, he thinks companies ought to be vigilant about subtracting processes that impede organizational effectiveness. As he said, "The best leaders treat it as a problem of more and less—they are always looking for things to subtract that don't work any longer, that never worked, and that are getting in the way." For example, in 2013 Dropbox sent out a companywide email entitled "Armeetingeddon has landed," which eliminated all regularly scheduled meetings.

  - **Slow down before speeding up.** "When [traffic app] Waze raised a $35 million Series B round, its CEO Noam Bardin noticed that only 5% to 6% of the people who downloaded the app were still using it. He focused everyone on figuring out what was wrong with the software and what needed to be fixed. You can't scale excellence if you don't have excellence to scale," said Sutton.

- **Jeffrey Rayport,** Harvard Business School Senior Lecturer, suggested that the most successful CEOs combine excellence in creating a compelling vision and in getting into the details of strategy execution. Rayport, who met Jeff Bezos in the 1990s, noticed that he was unique among the most successful founders in combining both attributes and that he was a voracious learner. Rayport also offered keen insights on several topics including the following:

  - **Scaling culture:** As he said, "Culture is not about being nostalgic about the good old days when there were no formal meetings and no HR department. It's not one and done. As a company goes from 10 to 100 to 200 to 1,000 people, you might have the same values, such as integrity, transparency, teamwork, accountability, passion, and energy. But those are all outputs. For the culture to scale, you need to know what management levers you can pull to get people to act according to those values. For example, Bezos has physical, tangible rituals, such as leaving an empty chair at meetings for the customer and asking everyone to read a six-page memo prepared for a meeting before it begins."

  - **Strategy changes with scale:** "It's smart to look at the stages as relating to the different funding rounds, such as seed, Series A, B, and so on. The first stage is before you have product/market fit, at which point you are trying to raise seed capital from angel investors. Once you have product/market fit, which means customers are willing to pay for your product and you can scale up with profitable unit economics, you should capitalize to get big fast," said Rayport.

- **Shikhar Ghosh,** HBS Professor of Management Practice, believes that as startups get bigger, their leaders must change how they manage the organization. He noted that these break points occur at powers of three, for example, 30, 90, 270, or 810 employees. Effective leaders must

  - **Manage the tension between process and culture.** According to Ghosh, "Managers come into the company and they want to create formal processes. But processes work for activities like accounting and not so well for creative work where it is better to set goals and let people figure out how to get there. Size often demands more formal processes, which is at odds with the history and mythology of the company, such as the idea that everyone worked 24 hours a day for a week before the end of a quarter in order to meet goals."

- **Let go to go further.** When a company gets bigger, the leader has to accept that new talent will do things differently—and make mistakes. But if the leader does not let go, the company will not be able to scale. As Ghosh said, "If the founder continues to be the chief problem solver, the people he hires to run, say, an operation in a new city will never become effective leaders. Instead, the founder should accept that as you create a new subgroup, there's a V-curve. You will initially get less efficient. But after the subgroup makes mistakes and learns, it becomes more efficient and reaches a limit. If you intervene, you do worse."

- **Make a common purpose stronger than chaos.** As a company scales, the leader should make sure that the centripetal forces are stronger than the centrifugal ones. "As a company grows, it gets more specialized. Specific business functions want to optimize themselves, which pulls the company apart. The only way to keep functions like engineering, finance, sales, and so on together is to continuously remind everyone of the company's purpose, mission, values, and desired behaviors," he said.

- **Ranjay Gulati,** Jaime and Josefina Chua Tiampo Professor of Business Administration at Harvard Business School, argued that scaling can only happen if leaders add structure and processes and formalize culture, According to Gulati, "Firms must hire functional experts to take the enterprise to the next level, add management structures to accommodate increased head count while maintaining informal ties across the organization, build planning and forecasting capabilities, and spell out and reinforce the cultural values that will sustain the business. This approach to scaling will make a firm more efficient and help it find and exploit new opportunities."

- **Bill Aulet,** Managing Director of the Martin Trust Center for MIT Entrepreneurship, offered insights on three topics:

  - **Specify the founders' ambitions.** Aulet said that the founders must decide whether their idea is "(1) a feature, (2) a product, or (3) a company." What's more, they should recognize that the risk, opportunity, resources required, and management challenges all rise with the founder's ambition.

  - **The importance of culture.** He considers culture a "silent supervisor" and advocates that a CEO must explicitly define the company's core values and "then make them visible through stories, the personnel appraisal process, public relations, incentives, real estate, hiring policies, and articulating clear reasons why the world is a better place because the organization exists."

  - **How jobs change with scale.** As he said, "At first you need change agents and leaders to create new markets but then you must add managers who know how to optimize, control risk, and make more predictable results without losing the innovation brought by the change agents. The [change agents and managers] must coexist and be respectful of each other. But as you get bigger, you have more to lose and the managers become more and more important but can't dominate."

This book's scaling model draws on many of the insights developed by these professors, recognizing the importance of redefining organizational roles, formalizing culture, creating processes for setting goals and measuring their achievement, and creating a business model that will create supply and demand economies as the company grows.

However, unlike these approaches, this book places scaling in the context of a startup's stakeholders, including investors and partners. Although others place emphasis on important stakeholders such as employees and customers, investors and partners are not a key focus of their approaches. To that end, the book adds two important scaling activities which are not addressed extensively by other models: building growth trajectories and raising capital. This book's scaling model also defines four stages of scaling and provides a structure that CEOs can use to reinvent the company as needed to keep it growing.

Creating Growth Trajectories

To help in thinking about scaling, Chapters 2 through 8 will examine two layers of scaling:

- **The mission and strategy layer**, which consists of three scaling levers that relate to defining the company's purpose and formulating and raising capital for its growth strategy.

- **The execution layer**, to be examined more closely in Chapter 5, in which leaders implement the strategy by managing four scaling levers: redefining jobs; hiring, firing, and letting people go; holding people accountable; and coordinating processes.

Figure 2-1 depicts the three scaling levers that founders can pull to define their startup's purpose and strategy.

© Peter S. Cohan 2019
P. S. Cohan, *Scaling Your Startup*, https://doi.org/10.1007/978-1-4842-4312-1_2

Figure 2-1. The mission and strategy layer

At the execution layer, leaders must manage the interaction of three scaling levers:

- **Creating growth trajectories:** As we'll see below, growth trajectories articulate a startup's current and potential sources of revenue growth by making clear choices about the markets in which the startup will compete and how it will gain share.

- **Raising capital:** As a startup scales, founders must persuade different kinds of investors to provide capital. Those investors will invest, in part, depending on their confidence in the startup's growth trajectories.

- **Sustaining culture:** By defining the startup's values, the founder articulates the startup's enduring purpose, which helps motivate potential and current employees and helps to attract the right kinds of investors.

Growth Trajectories

Any company's growth comes from winning new customers and selling more to existing ones. For a startup to grow, its CEO must spend a significant amount of time, particularly in the first scaling stage, winning customers. To do that effectively, the startup must plan and execute a *sustainable growth trajectory*, which is the sequence of *growth vectors* that the company will target over time along with the *growth levers* it will pull to generate revenue from those vectors. These growth vectors are depicted in Figure 2-2.

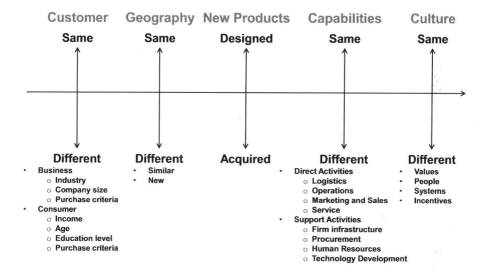

Figure 2-2. Five dimensions of growth

These dimensions, which when chosen by the CEO become growth vectors, can either be the same as those in a company's existing practices or reflect new and different parameters.

- **Customer groups:** Customers are grouped differently depending on whether they are businesses or individuals. Businesses are grouped based on attributes such as industry, size, purchase criteria, or level of interest in buying a company's product. Consumers can be grouped based on age, income, and the other factors illustrated.

- **Geographies:** This refers to the regions in which the company sells its products.

The growth levers include the following:

- **Products** must be renewed or expanded because of customer needs and technology changes and competitors adapting their strategies in order to take share from a company's successful product. Products can be built internally or acquired,

- **Capabilities** are a company's business functions, such as product development, sales, and customer service.

- **Culture** means the company's values and the specific practices used to hire, promote, and motivate people so everyone will act according to the values. Capabilities and culture can be both a source of growth and a means of achieving growth.

How can growth levers be pulled to gain market share? To gain market share, startups must convince customers to buy. And to do that, the company must outperform rivals on the customer's *ranked purchase criteria* (CPC), factors such as quality, price, and product variety, and *deploy capabilities*, such as product development, sales, and customer service, that enable the startup to win on those CPC consistently.

To illustrate the concept of outperforming rivals on ranked customer purchase criteria, consider the case of Berlin Packaging, a $900 million (2014 sales) distributor of plastic, glass, and metal containers and closures for the food and beverage, household, personal care, and healthcare markets. Berlin Packaging grew over 10 times faster than the $55 billion packaging industry for the decade ending in 2014, at a 22.6% annual rate in an industry that grew at a 1.5% to 2% annual rate. Table 2-1 illustrates that Berlin grew faster than the industry, thus taking market share. It matched or beat competitors on the "table stakes" for becoming a strong contender for a contract by matching rivals on price but doing better on reliability of supply and product quality. But it won the business by giving away services that helped potential customers to boost their cash flow, defined as Earnings before Interest, Taxes, Depreciation, and Amortization (EBITDA).

Table 2-1. Customer perception of Berlin Packaging on ranked purchase criteria

Purchase Criteria	Berlin Relative Performance	Basis for Assessment
Price	Matching	Berlin seeks to match the price customers require, as do its rivals.
Reliability of supply	**Superior**	As of April 2015, "for the last 131 months in a row we have delivered 17,000 shipments a month 99% on time; that is better than the industry," according to Berlin.
Product quality	**Superior**	Products conform to customers' quality standards more frequently than rivals, says Berlin.
Increase customer EBITDA	**Superior**	Berlin gives customers services that boost their EBITDA in exchange for long-term contracts.

For a company to win the battle in the customer's mind for superior performance on ranked CPC, the company must create and improve capabilities. For a startup CEO, this imperative raises difficult questions: Which capabilities will have the most positive influence on each purchase criterion? How do competitors perform each capability? How can the startup perform those capabilities in ways that enable it to win consistently? Table 2-2 illustrates how five critical capabilities influence a company's ability to win on the ranked purchase criteria and Berlin Packaging's strength in those capabilities relative to rivals.

Table 2-2. Berlin Packaging's relative performance on critical plastic bottle capabilities and importance to winning in customer purchase criteria

Capability	Evaluation Criteria	Assessment and Rationale
Purchasing	Importance to purchase criteria	Economies of scale in purchasing helps Berlin to lower its costs, thus enabling it to match price demands.
	Berlin relative performance	**Superior.** Berlin designs its own packaging and contracts out the manufacturing to 700 suppliers around the world.
Outbound logistics	Importance to purchase criteria	Efficient outbound logistics helps Berlin to maintain high shipping reliability.
	Berlin relative performance	**Superior.** Berlin uses tight control of outbound logistics to ship the right packages to the right destinations on time.

(continued)

Table 2-2. (*continued*)

Capability	Evaluation Criteria	Assessment and Rationale
Human resources management	Importance to purchase criteria	Human resources management enables Berlin to attract and motivate people who boost Berlin's EBITDA.
	Berlin relative performance	**Superior.** Berlin uses a psychological contract with its employees, paying them more than the industry standard to boost Berlin's EBITDA.
Firm infrastructure	Importance to purchase criteria	Firm infrastructure is applied to customers to boost their EBITDA.
	Berlin relative performance	**Superior.** Berlin gives away services to customers in exchange for long-term contracts. It lends customers money to buy productivity-enhancing machines at zero interest, helps customers to install enterprise resource planning and lean manufacturing techniques, works with them to get International Standards Organization-quality certified, and helps customers to analyze weaknesses in their competitors' product lines and develop products to exploit those weaknesses.

A sustainable growth trajectory makes choices about which customers that startup should target and how it will win on the CPC, and which capabilities it will build in order to perform well consistently. Consider the case of the automated external defibrillator (AED) market, a device used to revive the victim of sudden cardiac arrest (SCA). Years ago, I worked on a project to help a maker of such devices sell its product to consumers living in apartments. Table 2-3 suggests the way that a startup CEO might summarize such a growth trajectory. Such trajectories must be developed at a minimum for each scaling stage, and it if a stage lasts longer, leaders should adjust the growth trajectory each year.

Table 2-3. Home AED growth trajectory

Dimension	Choice
Target customer	SCA candidates living in U.S. apartments
Winning on CPC	High quality product sold at lowest price in the industry ($500)
Manufacturing	Outsource to China
Distribution	Express mail from warehouse
Marketing	Internet and radio advertising
Sales	Call on cardiac care centers

Takeaways for Stakeholders

What should a startup's stakeholders do differently as they exercise the first scaling lever, creating a sustainable growth trajectory? The answers vary by stakeholder, as follows:

- **Startup CEO**
  - Solve an important problem of potential customers in a unique way.
  - Interview potential customers to understand the factors that drive their purchase decisions.
  - Build inexpensive prototypes, get feedback from earliest customers, and improve the prototype until customers are willing to buy.
  - Keep looking for new customer groups who will buy the product.
  - Adjust marketing, sales, and service processes to create high customer retention and repurchase.

- **Customers**
  - Consider working as a design partner with a startup that aspires to solve your most painful problems.
  - If you are highly satisfied with the startup's product and support, consider recommending the startup's product to others in your professional network.

- **Investors**
  - Seek out startups that fit with your firm's skills and provide them capital and advice that helps them build sustainable growth trajectories.

Growth Trajectories Success and Failure Case Studies

In this section, I offer case studies of growth trajectories used by successful and less successful startups at each scaling stage, analyze the cases, and extract principles for helping founders to create sustainable growth trajectories at each stage.

Stage I: Winning the First Customers

For a startup to win its first customers, it must bridge the gap between its initial product idea and receipt of payment from them. To do this, the CEO must develop the foundation for a longer-term growth trajectory along the lines illustrated in Table 2-2. A startup CEO should develop this foundation by taking the following steps:

- **Pick the right pain point.** Identify unmet customer needs that are important to potential customers, ideally based on the CEO's own experience and skill.

- **Find design partners.** Find two or three potential customers who are so eager for a solution to this pain point that they are willing to collaborate with the startup to help develop the product.

- **Build and get feedback on prototypes.** The startup should develop an inexpensive version of its product with the features that are most important to these design partners. The startup should observe how the design partners use the prototype, get feedback on what works, what is missing, and what needs to be fixed, and then repeat the process until the customer is eager to purchase the product.

- **Develop a sales strategy.** Once the startup gets its first customer, it should identify a group of customers that is most likely to want to purchase the product and create a process that will introduce the product to an enterprise or consumer, encourage the right people to try it, and ultimately pay for the product.

Successful Case Study: Platform.sh Wins Its First Customers After Careful Development and Extends Its Lead

Introduction

Platform.sh, a San Francisco-based application platform as a service supplier, was very successful at winning its first customers and expanding from there. Founded in 2010, Platform.sh described itself as "an automated, continuous-deployment, high-availability cloud hosting solution that helps web applications scale effortlessly and serve the most demanding traffic. Developers can develop, test, deploy, and maintain their applications faster and more consistently." Before joining Platform.sh, as CEO in July 2014, Fred Plais founded or co-founded three other businesses (Commerce Guys, the software vendor behind Drupal Commerce; af83, a digital agency operating in Paris and San Francisco; and Infoclic, a natural language search engine in 2000).

Case Scenario

To win initial customers, startups must identify customer pain and develop a product that relieves that pain. Platform.sh clearly passed this initial stage of the scaling process. By June 2018 it had 650 customers including GAP, the Financial Times, Stanford University, and Adobe Systems. Platform.sh spent years fitting its product to what it saw as a big unmet need. As Plais said, "We launched Platform.sh in 2014 after taking three years to build it. We saw that companies were experiencing two problems: they needed to develop and deploy business-critical web applications in response to rapid changes in the marketplace and they had to make the transition from developing to deploying these applications without crashing their production sites." Platform.sh's initial customers were developers who worked for retail companies. As Plais explained, "We got really good traction by selling to developers who were making the transition from building applications on laptops to the cloud. We went from retailers to media, including the Financial Times, Slate, Le Temps, and Hachette as well as social networks. Our business model was to offer a free trial for a month followed by two paying options: the developer and enterprise offerings."

There was more to winning the first customers than simply building a product that customers loved. If the startup's product was made for business customers, the startup needed a carefully considered and well-executed sales process to win those initial customers. Platform.sh did so through a marketing strategy that built on strong relationships with developers. "We have won customers because we focus our marketing on how well our service solves their pain points. While developers lack the budgets for our product, they work through the layers of the organization to convince those who do have budgets, such as the vice presidents of engineering or chief technology officers, to buy our product," said Plais.

Case Analysis

Platform.sh did an excellent job of developing a sustainable growth trajectory that enabled it to win initial customers and extend its reach to new ones. Platform.sh's growth trajectory illustrates three specific principles that could be helpful for entrepreneurs:

- **Focus on an important source of customer pain.** Platform.sh picked the right problem: the expanding need for companies to develop new business applications without interrupting their existing operations.

- **Invest heavily in a product that relieves that pain effectively.** What's more, Platform.sh took three years to develop a solution to this problem that worked well for retail customers who were feeling this pain most acutely.

- **Develop and execute an efficient sales strategy.**
  Finally, Platform.sh was able to persuade companies to pay for its product by giving it away to developers who quickly recognized the product's value and acted as internal ambassadors for introducing the company to the higher-level executives who controlled budgets for its product.

Less Successful Case Study: harmon.ie Takes Its Time Winning Customers

Introduction

harmon.ie, a Boston-based software maker that organized corporate data by topic to make workers more productive, was founded in 2008. harmon.ie described its product as "a suite of user experience products that empower the digital workplace." A global company serving thousands of enterprise customers, harmon.ie helped information workers focus on getting work done, rather than on using a multitude of tools. harmon.ie helped Microsoft customers to "increase their adoption and return on investments in SharePoint, Office 365 and other Microsoft collaboration products." harmon.ie CEO Yaacov Cohen was a Paris native who graduated with a degree in computer engineering from Haifa, Israel's Technion. In 1994, he joined Mainsoft, a Tel Aviv-based maker of application porting software, where he eventually rose to CEO, after relocating the company to San Francisco in 2000. In June 2008, he relaunched Mainsoft in Boston as harmon.ie, offering "an enterprise collaboration and digital workplace company. He brought in new venture capital, a new management team, and a new product line to humanize the digital experience by aggregating multiple cloud services into business users' comfort zone: the email client."

Case Scenario

harmon.ie won customers, but after Cohen's 24 years of involvement with the company (including his time at Mainsoft), took its time scaling the company. As Cohen explained, "We started harmon.ie in 2008 with the idea of making enterprise software as easy to use as consumer applications. From no revenue in 2008, we reached $10 million in annual recurring revenue in 2017. We have self-funded since 2009." Cohen rejected both the Silicon Valley and Israeli models of entrepreneurship. As he said, "We loved the energy and passion for changing the world in Silicon Valley and saw that the goal of Israeli companies was to get acquired by a big U.S. company. They looked at people as pairs of eyeballs, They don't respect my soul." harmon.ie sees itself as more humanistic. "Social networks are destructive, competing for attention. I believe in focus and mindfulness, committing to something bigger than you.

It is impossible for you to concentrate when your iPhone is constantly interrupting you. To make it easier for you to concentrate, harmon.ie organized information by the most important topics to each of its users, the five things you care most about, rather than by app," said Cohen.

harmon.ie depended heavily on Cohen's personal salesmanship to develop its customer base and found its first customers in government. "Our first customer was the Missouri Department of Transportation. I spent lots of time flying from customer to customer. I met with the chief information officer of Missouri and offered advice on whether Missouri should trust Gartner's roadmap for Microsoft. The CIO said, 'I feel I should do business with you and I think you care about money.' Missouri bought $260,000 worth of software from us."

Case Analysis

harmon.ie won initial customers very slowly, suggesting that it did not follow the principles that Platform.sh exemplified. Indeed, harmon.ie seems to have followed different principles that worked out less well for the company, including

- **Offer customers a vitamin, rather than a drug.** In the context of winning customers, a vitamin is a product that sounds like it should be useful but is not a drug (a must-have cure for urgent pain). harmon.ie's idea of organizing information by topic struck me as a vitamin rather than a drug. Since the company won customers, some organizations found it worth buying. Yet the very slow pace of harmon.ie's scaling hinted that its product was not a drug. In short, harmon.ie seems to have picked the wrong problem.

- **Put the CEO on the road making all key sales calls.** Depending too heavily on the CEO to bring in all new customers impedes a company's growth. Indeed, as Cohen said, he spent 20 years flying from Tel Aviv to the U.S. twice a month. To his credit, Cohen recognized the need to hire sales people and give them more of the responsibility for bringing in customers. However, harmon.ie's slow pace of building and training a sales force (Cohen hired actors to play customers in Tel Aviv as part of the company's sales training) suggests that the company would not become more efficient as it grew.

Principles

Founders seeking to win initial customers through sustainable growth trajectories should bear in mind the following dos and don'ts:

- **Do**
    - Focus product development on relieving intense customer pain.

    - Collaborate with early customers you already know to develop and deliver a better product that relieves customer pain.

    - Sell to a customer group that feels this pain more intensely than others.

    - Use a sales strategy that has the potential to scale efficiently.

- **Don't**
    - Build the initial product around a "vitamin."

    - Cold call potential customers before doing research to identify groups who will need the product the most.

    - Sell the product through a long, CEO-led consultative process.

Stage 2: Building a Scalable Business Model

For a startup to build a scalable business model, it must create a sustainable growth trajectory that will generate positive cash flow as the company grows. To do this, the CEO must make the following strategic decisions:

- **Target customers.** Choose which customers to target as the firm grows based on a combination of growth vectors such as customer group or geography. Typically, startups focus on a single customer group in Stage 1 and either add new customer groups or expand geographically within the same customer group(s).

- **Product line.** Develop the product that the company will sell initially and identify adjacent ones, such as complementary products that are natural extensions of the initial product.

Successful Case Study: Threat Stack Grows Rapidly and Plans to Follow the Same Six-Vector Growth Trajectory as Industrial Defender

Introduction

Boston-based Threat Stack was a cloud security service provider whose CEO previously founded Industrial Defender, a cybersecurity firm that protects industrial control systems for the electrical grid and oil, gas, and chemical companies, which Lockheed Martin acquired in 2014. The CEO of both companies, Brian Ahern, earned an electrical engineering degree from University of Vermont and started Industrial Defender in 20012 with help from an unnamed angel investor who "bet on people heading in the right direction." Ahern oversaw rapid growth at Threat Stack. He took over as CEO of Threat Stack in May 2015 and it grew from 11 employees to about 100 in September 2017, and he expected to add 86 more in 2018. Between 2016 and 2017, its annual recurring revenue was up 187% and in the 12 months ending March 2018 that growth rate accelerated to 342%.

Case Scenario

Ahern proposed his own model, breaking down the challenge of scaling into three stages based on funding levels: Early (during which a company raises seed, Series A, and B funding), Growth (Series C and D), and Later (Series E to IPO). Ahearn expected to follow the same approach with Threat Stack as he did with Industrial Defender, whose growth trajectory evolved along six vectors. Specifically, as it grew, Industrial Defender shifted from selling its initial built product targeted at an initial customer group; expanding to new customer groups and then to new geographies; and finally to unserved customers in those groups through channels and partners.

Threat Stack intended to follow a similar path. As Ahern explained, "Initially, we built a great product that we are selling to middle market customers; next, we are expanding from the middle market to Fortune 500 customers. We will then invest in leveraging partnerships and channels to expand our reach within served markets; followed by an investment in geographic expansion from North America to Europe and eventually Asia Pacific. And finally we will transcend our served markets from the commercial sector to the government sector. In March 2018, we were in the first phases of our build strategy, continuing to build a great product selling to mid-market." However, Ahern's geographic expansion strategy cost jobs for some Threat Stack employees. In October 2018, Threat Stack announced that "in support of its refined strategy, we have made a strategic decision to reallocate resources" which would cost the jobs of "less than 10% of [its 150 as of May 2018] employees. Threat Stack said it planned to fill 17 open positions, which would leave its headcount unchanged.

Case Analysis

Industrial Defender achieved some success with its growth trajectory, although it was acquired for an undisclosed amount after 12 years, so it is difficult to evaluate how successful. To be fair, Threat Stack was growing rapidly, albeit from an unknown base of revenue. It is also likely that Ahern gained considerable insights into building sustainable growth trajectories from his Industrial Defender experience and was likely to apply them to Threat Stack. One key principle that emerges from these cases is that in the first stage of scaling a startup should seek to win customers within an initial market segment and in the second stage it should expand into a different group of customers. Ahern wanted next to target larger companies and ultimately tried to mop up the remaining customers in those segments through channel partnerships. In the third stage of scaling, Ahern believed in geographic expansion within many of the same customer groups. To that end, Threat Stack wanted to replace employees who did not fit its strategy with those who could help implement it.

Less Successful Case Study: Actifio Struggles to Shift into a New Customer Segment

Introduction

Waltham, Mass.-based Actifio, founded in July 2009, provided company data storage as a service. According to Actifio, its service "replaces siloed data management applications with a radically simple, application-centric, service-level-agreement-driven approach that lets customers capture data from production applications, manage it more economically, and use it when and where they need. The result is enterprise data available for any use, anytime, anywhere, for less."

In October 2012, my interview with Actifio's founder and CEO, Ash Ashutosh, reflected optimism for an initial public offering by the end of 2013. Ashutosh was an expert in storage; before he started Actifio, he was Vice President and Chief Technologist for Hewlett Packard's storage business and was a partner at Greylock Partners. But he left there in 2008 and decided to open Actifio soon thereafter with the idea of making "copy data management (CDM) radically more efficient."

What is CDM? Companies make many copies of the same electronic data to analyze and share it and also to protect themselves if their computing infrastructure crashes due to a blackout or to comply with record retention policies. These copies are produced by different people in different departments. In the past, these copies were stored in different ways, including magnetic tapes, hard disks, and even on paper hived away in boxes. Storing so many different copies of the same data was inefficient. Ashutosh saw clearly that several recent trends could make it possible for companies to obtain the perceived benefits of all those copies at a much lower cost. For example, the growing popularity of virtualization, a way to store and retrieve data with less hardware, coupled with the rising share of hard disk as the primary medium for data storage meant that CDM could get much more efficient. And that meant that companies could have only one copy of their "production data" instead of "between 13 and 120." And companies could "reuse that golden copy multiple times for multiple applications." Fixing CDM was a $34 billion opportunity in Ashutosh's estimation, one that no other companies were addressing.

Ashutosh started Actifio in July 2009. Between the April 2010 introduction of its Protection and Availability Storage (PAS) product, an "appliance" consisting of a cluster of servers and software that cost companies anywhere from $50,000 and $1.2 million depending on their data volumes, and October 2012, Actifio grew at "500% year-over-year, faster than any enterprise storage company ever." Starting with four people, it had won 170 customers by October 2012. Behind that growth was a boost in efficiency that Actifio customers got when they installed its product. According to Ashutosh, Actifio's product could cut by 95% the "data footprint" that companies created in their CDM process while reducing by 75% the amount of "network bandwidth" required to move it around their data centers.

That October, Ashutosh painted a bright picture of Actifio's future. It planned to add 80 people in 2013 as it expanded globally, hiring sales and marketing people and product developers. He expected Actifio to grow from 200 to 800 customers by the end of 2013 and was targeting the end of 2013 or early 2014 for an initial public offering. But managing a rapidly growing company loomed as a challenge. As Ashutosh explained, "2012 is our break point." By that, he meant that the company was "going from startup to grown up." And that meant he was talking to his employees about how important it was "to consolidate our focus on quality when we release, sell, and service our products." He expected that another such break point would occur after Actifio's IPO. By then, it would have revenues "between $100 million and $150 million and will control 10% of the market."

Case Scenario

Six years after that bullish projection, Actifio was still private and had not raised new capital since March 2014 when a $100 million round of funding valued the company at $1.1 billion. At the core of this stall out was a failure to build a sustainable growth trajectory when it shifted its focus onto a new customer group from large companies to small and medium-sized enterprises (SMEs). In February 2015, Actifio had been growing for years by selling its product to very large companies. But as Ashutosh told me then, he was thinking about finding a way to add more predictable cash flows to Actifio's income statement. To that end, the company created a service called Actifio One, a "business resiliency cloud" that would deliver the company's technology to

SMEs via the cloud using a Software-as-a-Service (SaaS) model that would yield monthly cash flows for Actifio and would be sold and serviced to SMEs through distribution partners.

He envisioned that ActifioOne would be targeting a huge market opportunity worth $580 billion, which was the amount Ashutosh said SMEs spent on IT. As he explained in a July 2016 interview, he thought that it would be much more efficient to sell to distribution partners who sold to SMEs. "With big companies, it takes us 83 days to convince them that we can generate business value. But it can take six to 14 months for their procurement departments to qualify us and pay us as a first-time supplier. Working with distribution partners who sell to SMEs, the procurement process is shorter: 20 to 80 days."

Sadly for Actifio, it took about six months for the company to realize that this strategy would not work. As Ashutosh said, "We spun out a separate group across the street. After one-and-a-half quarters we realized that the logic was right but the reality was that we had the organizational DNA of working closely with large enterprises, developing technology solutions to work with petabytes of data." Actifio then realized that it lacked the capabilities to sell successfully to SMEs. "One of the biggest differences in working with SMEs was how we needed to run finance. Whereas big companies might make three to five big payments during a contract, SMEs would pay monthly. To bill and collect from them we needed to add 20 people and be (Payment Card Industry) PCI-compliant so we could accept credit cards from them. Also, we were uncomfortable not having a direct relationship with the end users of our product," he said. Actifio decided to scrap its separate subsidiary and instead license its technology to bigger "service providers," companies that deliver an array of IT services to SMEs. As Ashutosh explained, "We license our technology to 5 of the 10 largest service providers that deal with SMEs. Like large organizations, they make a smaller number of large payments. And they may have 100 to 600 SME customers within a region. To sell to them, we need to show that our technology will help their SME customers to cut capital expenditures and achieve operational excellence."

A year later, Actifio was cutting back to achieve profitability and an IPO was off the table.

In July 2017, he said that an IPO was not a current possibility and that Actifio was "on track for its third consecutive profitable quarter, although it went into the black partly because of staff reductions." As he said, around the end of 2016, "we started hearing from our customers. They told us, 'Hey guys, we want to choose you as a strategic platform, but you better be able to survive long term.' That meant we either had to be profitable or we had to go public. Getting to profitability became our imperative. We did what was required. We got out of geographic markets where we only had a few customers. We got out of other vertical industries that didn't really help us create a scalable business. Yes, we reduced the number of people, but we also have hired new people for different geographies and different verticals. We brought in 87 new people last year [who] had different skill sets. We brought in people with cloud capabilities that we didn't have 18 months ago. Our head count was about 360 then. We are at 346 now."

Nevertheless, Actifio had thousands of customers and was growing in two market segments: DevOps and the hybrid cloud. As Ashutosh said, "We have more than 2,200 customers and add an average of about 100 new customers every quarter. Most of our customer base is within large enterprises that spend on average between $200,000 and several million dollars with us per transaction. We just closed deals with one of the largest retail organizations, one of the largest organizations in healthcare [and] pharma, and with the fifth-largest bank. In all cases, they were saying, 'Hey, I have thousands of developers and I can't afford to have them twiddling their thumbs while they wait for data.' Hybrid cloud storage is one of the fastest-growing [trends] with many of our large customers. Hybrid cloud is about 6% of our business now. It was zero three quarters ago."

Ashutosh's persistence paid off in 2018. That August, Actifio raised another $100 million, valuing the company at $1.3 billion. Ashutosh said that its customer base topped 3,000 including five of top 20 global financials, four of the top 10 energy companies, three of the top 10 healthcare providers, six of the top 10 service providers, and four of the top 20 global retail organizations. By November 2018, it remained unclear whether Ashutosh, who said Actifio had become a multi-cloud data-as-a-service company targeting a $50 billion market, could use its latest investment to go public or be acquired.

Case Analysis

Actifio is a good example of a company that received a large infusion of cash for expansion without having developed a scalable business model. More specifically, in March 2014, when Actifio received its first $100 million investment, investors were eager for fast-growing companies targeting large markets and they were happy to subsidize the price-cutting and operating losses that accompanied the growth. In 2015, the investment climate changed after the weak performance of venture-backed initial public offerings. Venture capitalists told their companies that they would not get any more money from them and that they should focus on becoming profitable. Actifio tried to do that through its SME-strategy but failed. So it was heavily dependent for growth on selling to large companies with long and expensive sales cycles. Actifio's failure to grow in the SME segment highlights three important principles:

- **Don't confuse a market's size with its profit potential.** When Actifio targeted SMEs, Ashutosh estimated that there was a $680 billion market opportunity. That figure seemed to me to be much higher than the addressable market for Actifio's services but given that SMEs have smaller IT budgets it seemed that pricing would be lower than for large companies. The lesson here is to do detailed market research before launching a new growth vector to gain deeper insight into the market's profit potential.

- **Don't assume you will gain market share unless you have a competitive advantage.** As I discussed at the beginning of this chapter, to gain market share, a company must deliver superior performance on CPC and deploy capabilities in a way that enables it to outperform its rivals. Ashutosh discovered soon after launching its SME strategy that Actifio could not outperform its rivals in working with channel partners because its culture was based on close collaboration with customers, a collaboration that was impossible to achieve when selling through channels that maintain those relationships. If Actifio had done the right research, it would have known this before launching the strategy.

- **Don't pursue new growth opportunities unless you can scale.** Many companies go public with rapid revenue growth and significant net losses. This gives some CEOs the hope that they can do the same thing. Yet the experience of Actifio and many other companies that sell to businesses is that lengthy sales cycles and winning by offering customers the lowest price is not scalable. As I discussed in Chapter 1, startups should not "pour gasoline" on their business until they can get more efficient at selling as they grow. Actifio does not appear to have figured out how to do this. After four years of struggle, perhaps Actifio's August 2018 capital infusion was a sign that its business model had finally become scalable.

Principles

Founders seeking to build a scalable business model through sustainable growth trajectories should bear in mind the following dos and don'ts:

- **Do**
  - Target new growth vectors with significant profit potential.
  - Research whether the startup's product can outperform rivals on the new growth vector's CPC.
  - Win market share by applying capabilities at which the startup excels.
  - Market, sell, and service customers in the new growth vector in ways that lower the cost of those activities as the startup scales.

- **Don't**
  - Assume that a large market opportunity means big potential profits for the startup.
  - Assume that the startup's ability to win market share in its core market will lead to similar gains in the new market.
  - Grow in existing markets through higher marketing, sales, and service costs and lower prices.

Stage 3: Sprinting to Liquidity

For a startup to sprint to liquidity, it must create a sustainable growth trajectory that will enable the company to generate enough revenue to be acquired or to go public. While the revenue levels required to do this vary by industry, for IT-related startups, CEOs should set a goal of at least $100 million in revenue and 30% to 40% annual growth. To do this, the CEO must make the following strategic decisions:

- **Target customers:** Often startups that are sprinting to liquidity seek to do so by selling to the same customers as they have in the past, but to find those customers in new geographies. For example, startups seeking to go from $25 million to $100 million in revenue might attempt to do so by entering, say, 50 countries where it currently does not operate.

- **Product line:** The injection of capital that often kicks off this stage of growth can be used to adapt a startup's core product to the specific requirements of customers in new geographies and to add to the company's product line, often through acquisitions of companies that have built products that the company can sell to its current and potential customers.

- **Partnerships:** The third scale of staging often demands that CEOs form partnerships with companies in the new countries in which the startup hopes to expand. The terms of such partnerships could require investment in the partner, sharing in marketing and service costs, and splitting revenue generated through the partnership.

Success Case Study: Looker Sprints to a 2019 IPO

Introduction

In October 2017, Looker, a Santa Cruz, California-based supplier of analytics tools for businesses such as business intelligence (BI) and data visualization was planning a 2019 IPO. According to Gartner, the $18 billion market for data analytics was expected to grow at a 7.6% compound annual rate to about $22.8 billion by the end of 2020. Looker's CEO, Frank Bien, who joined the company as president in 2013, grew up in a family of technology entrepreneurs and did not want to follow in their footsteps. But apparently, he could not resist. He ended up helping three startups get to the point where they were acquired by other companies. Bien was "a punk rock kid in LA in the 80s and never had a master plan for running a company." But he was an executive at four startups that grew and were later acquired: Vignette bought Instraspect Software for $20 million in 2003, KEYW bought SenSage in 2008 for about $35 million; EMC acquired Greenplum in 2011; and VMWare bought Virsto in 2013.

Case Scenario

Looker had grown rapidly under Bien's leadership. As Bien said in a May 2018 interview, "In the last 22 quarters we've grown from under 20 employees to about 500 and from a few customers to 1,500 including Amazon's Retail Group, Fox Networks Group, Square, trivago, CrossFit, and Five Guys." Looker had raised $180 million in funding, was growing revenue at 85% a year, and had boosted the size of its average contract by 75% since 2015. While Looker's vision had not changed, its customers did. "Technology companies were our first customers: people out of investment banks and Google want the most sophisticated tools. The next group of customers was Facebook users. After that our product was adopted by Fortune 200 companies like Cigna and State Street. 20% of our customers are in Europe, the Middle East, and Africa doing GDPR stuff [General Data Protection Regulation, meaning the right to be forgotten]. We built our growth trajectory around our financial model. There are between 100,000 and 500,000 potential customers in the world and if our customer acquisition cost is $100, we will not be able to scale. We defined our metrics around specific customer acquisition costs and lifetime value of the customer ratios. We figured out how to make our model scalable by pouring through the financial statements of our competitors and examining what we can do to modify our operations to be effective. We also track how customers are using our product. And if customers stop using the product, we will find ways to keep them engaged."

Case Analysis

While it is difficult to be sure absent audited financial information, Looker appeared to have a sustainable growth trajectory that would enable it to go public in 2019 if market conditions permitted. (Indeed Looker raised an additional $103 million in December 2018 to sustain its growth). The key principles underlying Looker's sprint to liquidity include the following:

- **Target a large, rapidly growing global market.** A company seeking to reach $100 million must target a market that is well over $1 billion in revenue because the maximum market share it could achieve is likely no more than 10%. A much larger market leaves room for error. Looker's decision to target a $20 billion market is helpful in its efforts to reach liquidity.

- **Shift growth vectors as you scale.** Looker set ambitious quarterly growth goals and met them consistently. One key to achieving this is for leaders to recognize that their current growth vector is likely to slow down; therefore, in order to keep growing rapidly, a startup must target new growth vectors before the old ones mature. In its transition from serving investment banks to Facebook users to Fortune 200 financial services firms to Europe, Looker has been able to sustain its rapid growth.

- **Invent a scalable business model.** In Stage 3, startups should operate so that their selling costs drop and the value of their product to customers rises as the company grows. Looker's CEO is very conscious of this goal and appears to be using a disciplined financial model to keep the company on a path to profitability. If Looker does go public, it will become apparent whether he succeeded.

Less Successful Case Study: Snowflake Computing Grows Fast, But Is Losing Money

Introduction

San Mateo, California-based data warehousing cloud service provider Snowflake Computing was valued at $1.5 billion when it raised a whopping $263 million in January 2018. That trend was good for Snowflake, which offered data warehousing as a service through Amazon's AWS. Demand for

Snowflake had been spiking; its customer count for the year ending January 2018 was up 300% (including Capital One and Nielsen) and investors had plowed $473 million into the company since its 2012 founding. Companies use data warehousing to store and analyze their data to find useful insights such as from machine learning algorithms. Snowflake's CEO, Bob Muglia, was a 20-year Microsoft veteran who was responsible for its $16 billion Windows Server, SQL Server, System Center, and Azure products. Muglia said "it's a $15 billion market, according to IDC, but the big data portion that uses open source database Hadoop is only $1 billion to $2 billion. That segment is limited because customers find it difficult to work with."

Case Scenario

In June 2018, Muglia spoke with me about how Snowflake had grown in the four years since he joined as CEO. And a key reason for that growth was Snowflake's compelling value proposition to companies; in a nutshell, the product did more of what customers wanted at a small fraction of the price of competing products from Oracle and SAP. Snowflake was growing rapidly by displacing incumbents with a service that did more and cost less. An example was Capital One (which also invested in Snowflake). According to Muglia, "Capital One was way ahead of the crowd. In 2013, its CEO decided to move its entire IT operation into the cloud and that process is likely to be complete this year. The CEO wanted to change the culture of the company. He thought that technology was so meaningful that Capital One needed to be more integrated into Silicon Valley." Amazon and Microsoft both offered data warehousing, but Capital One picked Snowflake. "They don't take full advantage of the cloud and Capital One was looking for a shift forward. They concluded that Teradata could not take them into the cloud. And they picked Snowflake because it could run 250 concurrent data analysis queries, compared to 60 for Teradata, at a much lower price (25% to 30% of what Teradata charges)."

Snowflake saw itself as sprinting to liquidity, "We are definitely at Stage 3. Since I joined in June 2014 we have grown from 34 people to 450 and we are on track for $100 million in 2018 bookings. We have been tripling every year. Stages 1 and 2 overlapped. We were working on our product and business model simultaneously." Snowflake maintained a consistent approach to winning customers. "Our sales strategy is direct: we let customers evaluate and sign up for the service online followed by a capacity purchase, when a sales person encourages customers to make a 24-month purchase if they are happy following the product evaluation," he explained. Snowflake's growth came from different groups of customers as it became larger. "Three years ago our customers were already using AWS—companies in the entertainment, media, online gaming, and technology industries. Later we began to focus on traditional enterprise customers—companies in financial services, manufacturing, oil and gas, and retail—that were converting from on-premise to the cloud. They were switching to Snowflake from Netezza (which was acquired by IBM) and Teradata boxes," Muglia explained.

Even though Snowflake said it was in Stage 3, it remained to be seen whether it could make a profit, suggesting to me that Stage 2 was a work in process. As Muglia said, "We have positive gross margins but our sales and engineering costs make us unprofitable. And when we hire new sales people, it takes time for them to bring in new customers. As sales territories mature and we get bigger, our cost of goods sold and cost of sales will decline and we will be on a path to profitability."

By November 2018, it was clear that investors were happy to invest in Snowflake despite the absence of a scalable business model. In October 2018, Snowflake raised $450 million, bringing its 2018 total capital raised to $713 million. Between January 2018 and October 2018, Snowflake's valuation soared from $1.5 billion to $3.5 billion. CFO Thomas Tuchscherer said that the increased valuation was "driven by the growth numbers of almost quadrupling the revenue and tripling the customer base."

Case Analysis

Snowflake was growing rapidly and had raised a significant amount of capital. Its growth trajectory had evolved as it scaled. So why was it a less successful case? Muglia said that the company was generating negative cash flow due to its high marketing and other operating expenses. This raised the possibility that Snowflake was keeping its prices below the competition's yet was not achieving efficiencies in key processes such as marketing, selling, service, and product development as it grew. What's more, Snowflake appeared to be dependent for growth on hiring new salespeople who were expensive to train, took time to reach full productivity, and tended to leave their employers, creating the need to hire new sales people to replace them. By November 2018 it was unclear whether Snowflake would be able to go public without being profitable. However, the month before, its investors sent a strong signal that rapid growth, not profitability, was what mattered most.

Principles

Founders seeking to sprint to liquidity through sustainable growth trajectories should bear in mind the following dos and don'ts:

- **Do**

    - Set aggressive growth targets and employ disciplined operating strategies to meet them consistently.

    - Recognize that current growth vectors may mature quickly and therefore keep investing in new growth vectors.

    - Experiment with sales, marketing, service, and product development approaches that will cost less as the company grows.

- **Don't**
  - Pour gasoline on a business model that does not scale efficiently.

Stage 4: Running the Marathon

For a startup to run the marathon, it must meet the demands of public investors while investing in new growth opportunities as it did when it was private. Very few public companies can do this well, and the best of them are run by a tiny handful of entrepreneurs such as Jeff Bezos and Reed Hastings, who are still at their helms. The challenge these CEOs face is that as they grow to generate tens or hundreds of billions in annual revenue, it becomes increasingly difficult to maintain an annual revenue growth rate of at least 20%. To do this successfully, CEOs must make the following strategic decisions:

- **Exceed quarterly investor expectations.** Public companies are graded every quarter. If they exceed revenue and profit growth targets and raise their forecasts for these variables, what I call "beat and raise," investors applaud. Otherwise, the stock price can take a nasty hit. CEOs must manage their communications with investors and employees so that they predictably beat and raise. And that comes from carefully developing and executing a sustainable growth trajectory that yields results for which the entire company is accountable.

- **Invest in future growth.** Founders are typically much better at identifying and investing in new growth opportunities than public company CEOs. Conversely, most such CEOs have little experience successfully creating new businesses from scratch. To run the marathon, founders must develop the skills needed to beat and raise while enhancing the scale at which they exercise their ability to identify and profit from new growth opportunities.

Success Case Study: Amazon's Value Surges from $0 to $825 Billion in 24 Years

Introduction

In 1994, Seattle-based Amazon was an idea in the mind of a hedge fund executive. 24 years later it was a $178 billion (2017 annual revenue) company worth $825 billion, with a stock price that had risen at a 37.6% average annual rate between its May 15, 1997 IPO price of $1.96 a share to $1,710 by July 6, 2018. By 2017, Amazon had broadened its product and geographic scope from the online book selling service to become far more diversified. "Online product and digital media content sales accounted for 61% of net revenue in 2017; followed by commissions, related fulfillment and shipping fees, and other third-party seller services (18%); Amazon Web Services' cloud compute, storage, database, and other service offerings (10%); Prime membership fees and other subscription-based services (6%); product sales at Whole Foods and other physical store retail formats (3%); and advertising/cobranded credit cards (3%). International segments totaled 33% of Amazon's non-AWS sales in 2017, led by Germany, the United Kingdom, and Japan."

Amazon's founder and CEO, Jeff Bezos, the son of a teenage mother, loved gadgets as a child, was his high school valedictorian, a graduate of Princeton, and a hedge fund star who quit to start an online book seller in Seattle. Bezos "showed an early interest in how things work, turning his parents' garage into a laboratory and rigging electrical contraptions around his house." He was valedictorian of his Miami high school class, graduated from Princeton summa cum laude in 1986 with a degree in computer science and electrical engineering, and worked at several Wall Street firms. In 1990, he became the youngest senior vice president at the investment firm D.E. Shaw. In 1994, he quit to start Amazon. As he said, "The wakeup call was finding this startling statistic that web usage in the spring of 1994 was growing at 2,300% a year. You know, things just don't grow that fast. It's highly unusual, and that started me about thinking, 'What kind of business plan might make sense in the context of that growth?'" After making a list of the top 20 products that he could potentially sell on the Internet, he decided on books because of their low cost and universal demand.

Case Scenario

Despite minimal profitability, a key to Amazon's success has been its growth trajectory. Between 1995 and 2018, that trajectory brought Amazon into new customer groups, new products (both built internally and acquired), new geographies, and new capabilities. For example, Amazon started selling books online; broadened its online product portfolio; turned its internal computer systems into a service (Amazon Web Services); made its own hardware devices such as the Kindle and Echo; developed its own video content; acquired a leading grocery store chain; and through acquisitions and a joint venture targeted the markets for health care and pharmaceuticals retailing.

Amazon used the capabilities that enabled it to succeed with selling books online to selling other products there. Amazon moved into selling electronics, which caused consumers to try out the products at retailers liked Circuit City before purchasing them on Amazon, and extended its product line to home goods and shoes (it paid

$850 million to acquire Zappos in 2009) among many others. In the early 2000s, Amazon decided to extend its own computer systems to offer other companies its AWS cloud service. Once people started developing apps for the iPhone, AWS became the place to host these apps. AWS became a nearly $20 billion business that generated much of Amazon's profit. AWS also formed the basis of its advertising technology business that helped other shops identify potential customers. Amazon also built its own hardware, including the Kindle e-reader, which launched in 2007; it entered the tablet market with the Amazon Fire HD in 2012; the video and audio streaming marketing in 2014 with the Amazon Fire TV; and in 2015 Amazon launched its digital home assistant device, the Amazon Echo. Amazon created its own content through Amazon Studios, which launched in 2010. By 2017, one of its movies, Manchester by the Sea, won two Oscars. Amazon made dozens of acquisitions including Twitch, which enabled Amazon to compete with YouTube. Amazon got started in the grocery delivery business in 2007 through AmazonFresh, which spent six years working out logistical problems in a Seattle suburb before launching in Los Angeles and San Francisco. In 2017, Amazon acquired Whole Foods for $13.7 billion. In 2018, Amazon, through a partnership with JP Morgan and Berkshire Hathaway, started a venture to reduce corporate health care costs and spent about $1 billion acquiring a startup PillPack, dedicated to lowering the price consumers pay for drugs.

Case Analysis

In 2018, Amazon was the most successful company still being led by its founder. An important element of Amazon's success was its ability to sustain growth that exceeds 20% per year even as it approached $200 billion in annual revenue. A key reason for its sustained high growth rate was its ability to produce quarterly revenue gains that exceeded investor expectations while investing in new businesses through a combination of internal product development, partnerships, and acquisitions that tapped into large market opportunities. Moreover, Amazon's growth trajectory led to gains in its market share because Amazon offered customers greater value than its rivals and it performed activities to deliver that value consistently at global scale.

Less Successful Case Study: Blue Apron Stock Plunges As It Burns Its Cash Pile

Introduction

Manhattan-based Blue Apron, founded in 2012, assembled and delivered "meal kits:" prepared ingredients and a recipe that consumers could follow to make at home. It offered two delivery options: a two-person meal plan (all the fixings for three meals for two people for $59.94) and a family plan. Blue

Apron shares fell 64% between July 6, 2018 and the stock's trading debut in June 2017, and 29% of its shares were sold short as of May 31, 2018. While Blue Apron's revenues had grown at a 124% annual rate since 2014 to $881 million in 2017, its negative free cash flow had soared from $21 million to $277 million and it had a mere $204 million in cash as of March 2018 and $125 million in long-term debt.

Matt Salzberg founded the company and took it public. In high school and college (Harvard), Salzberg aspired to be an entrepreneur. He worked three years at Blackstone before entering Harvard Business School. Salzberg joined Bessemer Venture Partners after HBS to learn more about startups. During a happy hour for Boston-based sales analysis software provider Insight Squared, Salzberg met a technical consultant named Ilia Papas. They started a crowd-funding platform for research scientists that raised $800,000 in seed funding from Bessemer and failed. While working together, Papas came to work after spending hours buying and cooking Argentinean-style steaks. "Wouldn't it be awesome if someone delivered you the ingredients in the right amounts?" he asked Salzberg. This is how they said they founded Part & Parsley which later changed its name to Blue Apron. Salzberg raised a $3 million Series A investment round led by Bessemer and First Round Capital. Blue Apron went public in June 2017 but in November 2017 Salzberg was replaced as CEO by a finance expert, Bradley Dickerson, who was then Blue Apron's Treasurer (since January 2017) and its Chief Financial Officer since February 2016. Before Blue Apron, Dickerson was Under Armour's CFO from December 2014 to February 2016.

Case Scenario

Blue Apron's financial performance suggested that there was a gap between its belief about the profit potential of its market and its ability to capture that value through its growth trajectory. Blue Apron believed that its market opportunity was broad due to "the quality of our product, the meaningful experiences we create, and the deep, emotional connection we have built with our customers; this positions us well to grow in the dynamic and high-profile category in which we operate." In February 2018, Blue Apron believed it participated in the global grocery and restaurant industries. Blue Apron estimated that the U.S. grocery market was $780 billion and the global grocery market was "more than eight times larger." And the company estimated that the annual U.S. restaurant market totaled $540 billion and the global restaurant market was "almost five times larger."

Blue Apron struggled to retain customers and to get those customers to keep using its service after they signed up for it. The company warned of this problem and gave an example of how it affected its results. According to the company,

"If we are unable to retain our existing customers, cost-effectively acquire new customers, keep customers engaged, or increase the number of customers we serve, our business, financial condition, and operating results would be materially adversely affected. For example, the number of our customers declined to 746,000 in the three months ended December 31, 2017 from 879,000 in the three months ended December 31, 2016, and our revenue declined to $187.7 million from $215.9 million in those periods."

Blue Apron's financial results suggested a company that poured gasoline onto a business model that was not scalable and remained so after it went public. According to its IPO prospectus, Blue Apron ended March 2017 with almost $62 million in cash, having burned through $20 million that quarter, suggesting that it would not have made it through 2017 without its IPO. The first mistake Blue Apron made was that its service did not address a source of significant customer pain: for most subscribers, deciding what to make for dinner, shopping for the ingredients, and cooking them was not a problem they were desperate to solve every week for the rest of their lives. To be sure, Blue Apron sales soared 10-fold between 2014 and 2016 to $795.4 million while its net loss increased 16% from 2015 to $54.8 million in 2016. Sadly, its growth did not lead to lower costs. For example, its marketing expenses, spent on television, digital and social media, direct mail, radio, and podcasts, soared 10-fold to $144.1 million between 2014 and 2016. And as it grew, its ingredients and other costs of goods sold rose as a percent of sales, resulting in a decline in its gross margin from 35% to 31% between the first quarter of 2016 and 2017.

If these diseconomies of scale and potentially high costs were not bad enough, Blue Apron's business lacked what Warren Buffett called a moat. Blue Apron's idea attracted competition from rivals including HelloFresh, Sun Basket, and "the vegetarian-focused Purple Carrot," according to the New York Times. Perhaps this competition was a factor in its slowing growth. After all, as the Times noted, "Its average order value for the first three months of 2017 shrank slightly from the same period a year ago, to $57.23. Both the number of orders per customer and the average revenue per customer also fell slightly in the first quarter of this year compared with the first quarter of 2016."

Blue Apron's inability to deliver what customers ordered on time seemed to have contributed both to its loss of customers and the replacement of Salzberg as CEO. In August 2017, Blue Apron's stock lost 17% of its value after a disappointing financial forecast for the second half of 2017. Blue Apron's warehouse inefficiencies cascaded into unhappy customers who quit the service and marketing challenges also hurt its revenues. Specifically, Blue Apron encountered "unexpected complexities" in transitioning from its previous New Jersey warehouse to "a new, highly automated" one. Salzberg laid the blame on "over 5,000 employees who are all being trained in new processes and new systems that are more advanced than the systems that they are used to working with. The training produces costs [since people being trained] are not doing day-to-day proactive work." The result was a deterioration in the percentage of orders that arrived on time and with all the correct ingredients (in full), the *company said. Failed first orders caused more customers to leave the service, which meant that the company wasted marketing dollars. And Blue Apron's plan to reduce its marketing expense as a percent of revenue from 20% to 15% required the company to slash its revenue forecast from $421 million in revenue in the second half of 2016 to between $380 million to $400 million for the second half of 2017. By November 2, 2018, Blue Apron's stock had fallen to $1.41 a share and it was hoping that an October 2018 partnership to distribute its products with Jet.com, a Walmart subsidiary, would help the company survive.*

Case Analysis

Blue Apron's failure to build a scalable business model makes it difficult to know whether it can survive as an independent company. Indeed, the loss of nearly two-thirds of its stock market value in about a year suggests that investors were skeptical of Blue Apron's ability to create a sustainable business model. Its challenges suggest four general principles that Blue Apron has violated in scaling Stage 4:

- **Solve an important customer pain point.** One way that startups can boost their odds of success is to solve a problem that customers find important. More specifically, startups should solve a problem that is so painful that customers would gladly pay for its solution, that other companies are not addressing, and that the startup is uniquely skilled at solving. Blue Apron's first mistake was deciding to offer customers a vitamin—a solution to a relatively unimportant problem.

- **Outperform rivals in satisfying CPC.** Once startups have picked the right problem, they must investigate the factors that customers will use to decide whether to purchase the startup's product and deliver a product that wins on those CPC. Blue Apron has grown revenues rapidly, suggesting that customers are willing to try its service. Yet its declining profitability reflects the high cost of customer churn coupled with the pressure to lower its prices thanks to rival services.

- **Lower costs and boost customer perception of value as you scale.** As I discussed earlier, companies should master the second stage of scaling, lowering their costs and boosting the value to customers of their product as they get bigger. Blue Apron skipped Stage 2 and went on to Stage 3. In Stage 4, it is visibly failing to master the complex challenge of fulfilling hundreds of thousands of orders correctly, leading customers to quit and revenues to decline.

- **Invest in capabilities to retain customers as you scale.** To keep customers happy, companies must build capabilities that make customers loyal and excited to recommend the company to others. Blue Apron failed in building the right capabilities such as an effective and efficient supply chain. Thus, it suffered a decline in accurately fulfilled orders. It remains to be seen whether the company can solve these operational problems and prove to investors that it can grow profitably.

Principles

Founders seeking to run the marathon through sustainable growth trajectories should bear in mind the following dos and don'ts:

- **Do**
    - Solve an important customer pain point.
    - Consistently outperform rivals in satisfying CPC.
    - Invest in capabilities that enable high customer loyalty.
    - Beat and raise each quarter.
    - Invest in new growth opportunities as you scale.

- **Don't**
    - Do the opposite of these five principles.

Growth Trajectories Success and Failure Principles

As a startup scales, it must win new customers, keep them happy and willing to buy more products, and do the same with new customers. The eight case studies presented in this chapter highlight specific dos and don'ts for leaders seeking to build sustainable growth trajectories at each scaling stage, which are summarized in Table 2-4.

Table 2-4. Summary of growth trajectory principles

Scaling Stage	Dos	Don'ts
1: Winning the first customer	Focus product development on relieving intense customer pain. Collaborate with early customers you already know to develop and deliver a better product that relieves the customer pain. Sell to a customer group that feels this pain more intensely than others. Use a sales strategy that has the potential to scale efficiently.	Build the initial product around a vitamin. Cold call potential customers before doing research to identify groups who will need the product the most. Sell the product through a long, CEO-led consultative process.
2: Scaling the business model	Target new growth vectors with significant profit potential. Research whether the startup's product can outperform rivals on the new growth vector's CPC. Win market share by applying capabilities at which the startup excels. Market, sell, and service customers in the new growth vector in ways that lower the cost of those activities as the startup scales.	Assume that a large market opportunity means big potential profits for the startup. Assume that the startup's ability to win market share in its core market will lead to similar gains in the new market. Grow through higher marketing, sales, and service costs and lower prices.
3: Sprinting to liquidity	Set aggressive growth targets and employ disciplined operating strategies to meet them consistently. Recognize that current growth vectors may mature quickly and therefore keep investing in new growth vectors. Experiment with sales, marketing, service, and product development approaches that will cost less as the company grows.	Pour gasoline on a business model that does not scale efficiently.
4: Running the marathon	Solve an important customer pain point. Consistently outperform rivals in satisfying CPC. Invest in capabilities that enable high customer loyalty. Beat and raise each quarter. Invest in new growth opportunities as you scale.	Do the opposite of these five principles.

Are You Doing Enough to Create Sustainable Growth Trajectories?

Creating sustainable growth trajectories is the critical first step in turning your idea into a large company that changes the world. Here are three questions that will help you know whether you are doing this properly:

- Is your startup solving a problem that is so painful that potential customers would be willing to pay for an effective solution?

- Do you know which growth vectors your startup will follow to get big and keep growing at each of the stages of scaling?

- Does your company continue to invest in new growth opportunities to sustain its rapid growth at each stage?

Conclusion

Creating and executing sustainable growth trajectories is essential to keep a startup growing from an idea into a large publicly-traded company. To do this successfully, leaders must be prepared to follow the principles outlined in this chapter to reinvent their growth trajectories as the company gets bigger. At the core of effective growth trajectories are strategic decisions about which customers to serve and how to build, market, sell, and service those products so that the startup can win customers, keep them buying over time, and attract new customers who remain loyal as the company grows. In Chapter 3, I will tackle one of the most challenging and time-consuming jobs of a startup CEO: how to raise the capital needed to fund growth.

Raising Capital

Capital-raising strategies vary at each scaling stage. My research and experience investing in startups suggest that a startup's success at raising capital is directly connected to the other six staging levers. More specifically, investors are eager to invest in a startup that solves a painful problem facing potential customers that could become a large market opportunity. To solve that problem, the startup's CEO must produce tangible results such as rapid growth in revenue from new customers, high customer satisfaction and retention, and efficient marketing to new customers. And to do that well, the CEO must conceive and execute a growth trajectory that can only be done well if the startup manages the other staging levers well. To plan and execute strategies for raising capital at each scaling stage, a startup CEO should follow the approach depicted in Figure 3-1. To succeed with these strategies, CEOs must take the following steps at each scaling stage, two of which (source of capital and investment criteria) are included in Figure 3-1:

- **Estimate amount of capital needed.** The first step in raising capital is to estimate how much money the startup needs. The amount required will vary depending on the startup's industry, business model, and scaling stage. The estimate should be based on a detailed analysis of all the costs the startup will incur to achieve its objectives for that stage, and typically it makes sense to consider doubling that bottoms-up estimate to provide a cushion for unexpected outcomes.

© Peter S. Cohan 2019
P. S. Cohan, *Scaling Your Startup*, https://doi.org/10.1007/978-1-4842-4312-1_3

- **Identify potential sources of capital.** The sources of capital vary by scaling stage. One key factor that affects the CEO's choice of capital source is whether the founder and management team have previously achieved successful outcomes for investors. For example, if a CEO has already enriched venture capital investors in a previous startup, those investors will be far more willing to invest early in that CEO's next venture.

  - **Stage 1:** A first-time entrepreneur will need to approach friends and family, and seek grants, angel investors, or crowdfunding. A previously successful founder will be able to self-fund or go to venture capitalists at this initial stage. Indeed, depending on the amount of time it takes to generate initial revenues from first customers, startups may end up seeking capital from seed stage, Series A, and possibly Series B venture capital providers.

  - **Stage 2:** Many startups do not make it past the first stage. But those that do, whether they are run by serial or first-time founders, will seek capital for this round from venture capital firms that are comfortable with later-stage investing. Moreover, many startups continue to receive funding without having a scalable business model because investors are convinced that the company can go public due to its rapid growth, despite requiring enormous amounts of capital to fund their losses.

  - **Stage 3:** When a startup has proven it has a scalable business model and a large untapped market opportunity, it will have an easier time raising capital from venture capitalists and institutional investors who envision a relatively risk-free path to high returns from an IPO within the next year or two.

  - **Stage 4:** Following a company's initial public offering, CEOs usually have a much easier time raising new capital, either by selling stock, borrowing from banks, or selling bonds.

- **Understand investor decision criteria.** Investors decide whether to invest depending on specific factors that vary by stage.

  - **Stage 1:** As illustrated in Figures 3-2 and 3-3, investors' decision criteria at Stage 1 are the least tangible. Before the company has generated any revenue, investors will assess whether the startup is targeting a market that has the potential to get big quickly and whether its founder could be a great CEO. As a startup gains a handful of early customers, investors will conduct in-depth due diligence by asking the early customers how satisfied they are with the company and its product, how likely they are to buy more from the company, and whether they see the company's solution as broadly useful for many potential customers.

  - In **Stage 2**, investors seek signs that the company has a scalable business model that will enable the startup to grow quickly while its incremental costs for marketing, selling, and servicing customers drop, and the profit generated by each customer relationship grows because those customers buy more of the startup's product and keep buying over time.

  - At **Stage 3**, investors provide funds based on the size of the market opportunity; the demonstrated ability of the company to scale efficiently, as measured by a declining cost of customer acquisition; a high customer retention rate; the startup's ability to sell more to existing customers; and its previous record of setting and exceeding quarterly business objectives.

  - At **Stage 4**, investors will purchase the company's stock if it persistently exceeds revenue and earnings expectations while raising its forecast and investing successfully in future growth trajectories to sustain rapid revenue growth.

- **Develop and deliver investor presentation.** CEOs generally communicate with potential investors using a pitch deck, usually a series of PowerPoint slides. CEOs seek feedback on their presentations from mentors before delivering them to potential investors. And the topics addressed in these presentations are intended to address the investment decision criteria of potential investors at each scaling stage.

- **Negotiate and finalize deal structure and valuation.** If the startup satisfies investors' questions, it is likely to receive offers to invest. The founder and the investors will tussle over specific deal terms including the structure of the investment, generally some form of convertible preferred stock that pays a quarterly dividend and at maturity is converted into a specific number of common shares; the valuation of the company prior to the investment, which determines what percent of the company the investors will receive in exchange for their money; liquidation preferences, which specify how the proceeds of a sale of the company will be divided; and how many board seats the investor will receive.

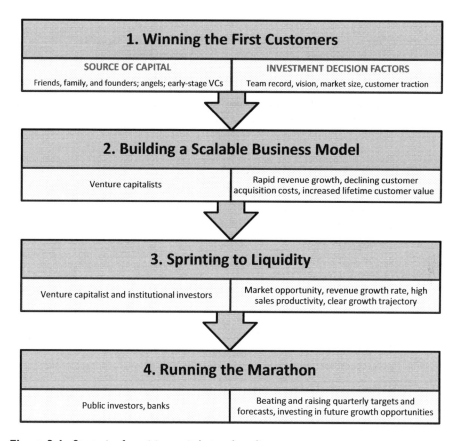

Figure 3-1. Strategies for raising capital at each scaling stage

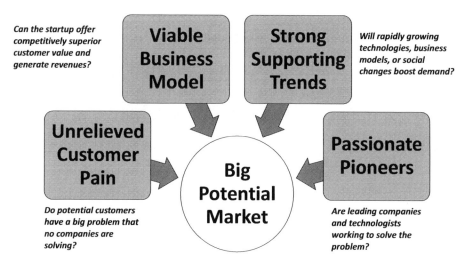

Figure 3-2. Stage I investment criterion: big potential market

Figure 3-3. Stage I investment criterion: great CEO

Takeaways for Stakeholders

What should a startup's stakeholders do differently as they exercise the second scaling lever (raising startup capital)? The answers vary by stakeholder, as follows:

- **Startup CEO**

    - Target a market opportunity with the potential to enable the startup to get large quickly.

    - Seek out design partners that suffer acutely from the problem your startup seeks to solve.

    - Build, sell, and service a product that customers are eager to purchase.

    - Provide service and new products that keep customers wanting to purchase more.

    - Find potential investors who can help the startup grow by providing capital and advice that will help the startup grow.

    - Set and exceed ambitious quarterly performance goals as the startup scales.

- **Investors**

  - Assign a partner to the startup's board who can advise the CEO on how to realize the startup's vision and meet shorter- term growth milestones.

  - Help the startup exercise scaling levers, particularly assisting with hiring key executives, finding customers and partners, and raising sufficient capital.

Capital-Raising Success and Failure Case Studies

In this section, I offer case studies of capital-raising strategies used by successful and less successful startups at each scaling stage, analyze the cases, and extract principles for helping founders to raise growth capital at each stage.

Stage I: Winning the First Customers

It is difficult for a founder to raise capital to keep a startup afloat while it tries to win its first customers. There are three ways to make that process much easier, but these paths are difficult for most entrepreneurs to follow:

- **Customer profitability:** Offer customers a product that is so valuable to potential customers that they are willing to pay enough money upfront to make the company profitable.

- **Founder's funds:** Create a founding team that can fund the early stages of the company from their own funds, possibly due to previous startup success or from borrowing.

- **Previous VC-backed exit:** As mentioned, an entrepreneur seeking to raise seed capital for a new venture could receive funding from a VC firm if the CEO has already enriched that VC thanks to a prior successful sale or IPO.

Absent these paths, the CEO will likely need to try to persuade the capital sources mentioned above (such as friends and family, crowd-funders, business plan competitions) that it is worth taking a risk on funding the startup's first stage of scaling.

The cases that follow highlight successful and less successful handling of the challenges such a CEO must overcome.

Success Case Study: As JASK Wins Customers, It Raises Capital from Kleiner Perkins

Introduction

Founded in 2016, San Francisco and Austin, Tex.-based JASK helped organizations analyze threats to their IT operations. JASK (a contraction of "Just Ask") "fuses collected data with alerts from existing security solutions and applies AI and machine learning to automate the correlation and analysis of threat alerts. JASK Insights deliver the most high-priority threat incidents for streamlined investigations and faster response times, guiding the security operations center (SOC) analyst to the most critical tasks and freeing them to proactively identify new threats." By July 2018, JASK had raised $40 million in capital as it aspired to reach $10 million in 2018 revenue. In March 2018, Greg Martin, the CEO of JASK, told me that the company was winning business from HP, IBM, and Splunk in 30% of its deals and expected that share to grow. Martin was an ex-FBI, Secret Service, and NASA hacker. As he explained in a March 2018 interview, he led the SOC for ArcSight, which went public in 2008 before HP acquired it in 2010 for $1.5 billion. Martin also founded cyber threat intelligence company ThreatStream in 2012, now known as Anomali (it's raised over $96 million). Martin started JASK in January 2016 to fix the flaws in products from IBM, HP, and Splunk that show security officers "thousands of alerts—think of them as dots—but failed to connect them. To deal with the volume, SOCs threw more bodies at the problem and suffered from wasted time to connect the dots from thousands of alerts that machines are now capable of handling."

Case Scenario

In 2018, JASK was gaining share of a growing market which had eased, though not eliminated, all the challenges of raising $40 million of capital in its first stage of scaling. JASK and its rivals were vying for a $5 billion market—expected to reach $6 billion by 2023—for security intelligence and event management (SIEM) software that tracked and analyzed cyberattacks. JASK was in the first stage of scaling. As Martin explained in a July 2018 interview, "We are at the product/market fit stage where we want to win 50 to 100 customers. We typically want to win $100,000 per contract and are not focused at all on Stage 2. We pay out all of our revenues to our sales team, which is not sustainable." JASK won its first customers from companies that its founders knew well before they started the company. "You can't afford to try a bunch of experiments; you have to spray and pray. We tried to sell to five to 10 customers that were friends and family, marquee names that we hoped could become reference customers. The earliest customers happened to be in finance and health care, and we expanded into those verticals," he said.

Customers bought from JASK because they believed the product would help them solve current and future problems and due to JASK's meticulous customer support. According to Martin, "Our first 20 customers bought because we offer a future-proof platform that meets their needs now and will continue to do so in the future. These days 80% of Chief Information Officers see the value of the public cloud because of the cost savings to them. And we offer world-class support, letting customers talk to the people who developed our product." JASK's sales process is based on both inside and outside sales. As he said, "When we sell to companies with fewer than 15,000 employees, we can use our inside sales people who are based in Austin. For larger clients, we have outside sales representatives in eight regions around North America." In mid-2018, JASK won its biggest contract, worth $2 million over three years, from a "Fortune 100 company." As Martin said, "We came in late in the process, competing against Splunk and FireEye. HP ArcSight had been there for 10 years. The company wanted the next generation. They had used Splunk, which was proposing an $8 million, eight-year contract, but an internal advocate for JASK added us late in the process. We wrapped ourselves around the customer and addressed their transition process. There was a vote of all the people involved and the Chief Information Officer and Chief Information Security Officer finally signed off."

JASK had a relatively easy time raising nearly $40 million in capital. Indeed, in June 2018, it raised a $25 million Series B round led by Kleiner Perkins and in 2017, it raised a $12 million Series A round led by Dell's venture arm and TenEleven Ventures. Battery Ventures provided its initial $3.4 million in funding. As Martin explained, "It took four months using a PowerPoint presentation to raise the initial round from Battery, which was much easier because of our prior track record of success. We had a team with a strong background; our team brings together decades of experience solving real-world SOC issues from ArcSight, Carbon Black, Cylance, Netflix, Cloudera, and the U.S. counter intelligence community, and a novel approach to a large addressable market. Our Series A round raised a relatively large amount of money—such rounds range from $6 million to $12 million—due to strong competition among investors. We had product/market fit and 10 customers." The Series B round was quite challenging. "The bar of success is raised high for collecting the $15 million to $30 million provided by a Series B. Investors expect revenue of $1 million per quarter and annual recurring revenue of $2 million to $3 million, with few exceptions. The investors talk to at least six customers and partners to find out why they purchased." Whatever Kleiner Perkins found in its due diligence made it want to put its General Partner, Ted Schlein, on the JASK board. As Schlein said, "Through advanced AI and machine learning, JASK frees security analysts from onerous data review to focus on investigating and responding to the most critical threats, improving efficiency, and reducing organizational risk exposure."

Case Analysis

To succeed at raising capital during the first stage of scaling, it helps to give investors what they are looking for. More specifically, founders seeking outside funding at this stage should follow four principles:

- Field a successful founding team.
- Focus on unresolved customer pain.
- Hire people with expertise and passion for solving the problem.
- Design, deliver, and service a product that customers love.

Less Successful Case Study: With $37 Million in Capital, OmniSci Gradually Gets Its Product Up to Speed

Introduction

Founded in September 2013, San Francisco-based OmniSci (which changed its name from MapD in October 2018), provided a database that helped companies analyze and visualize huge amounts of data very quickly. OmniSci had taken about five years to reach the end of the first stage of scaling and as of July 2018 had gradually raised $37 million to fuel its growth. OmniSci described itself as "the extreme analytics platform used in business and government to find insights in data beyond the limits of mainstream analytics tools. The OmniSci platform delivers zero-latency querying and visual exploration of big data, dramatically accelerating operational analytics, data science, and geospatial analytics."

OmniSci's cofounder and CEO, Todd Mostak, started programming in his early teens but ended up with a degree in economics and anthropology from UNC, earned a Masters' degree in Middle Eastern Studies from Harvard, and became fascinated with analyzing the locations from which Egyptian tweets emanated during the Arab Spring. He spent 2013 as a researcher at MIT's Computer Science and Artificial Intelligence Lab where he wowed his professors with the demo he developed for a database that could visualize billions of points on a map. P&G, a company participating in MIT's Industrial Liaison Program, was impressed and wanted to buy the product. The company was an MIT spinout started because its product targeted a real point of customer pain. As Mostak said in a July 2018 interview, "The demo was not ready for production but the fact that it fit a major need made me think I should work on it. In September 2013, I spoke with a friend from Harvard Law School and decided to leave MIT and start the company, which I did in January 2014."

Case Scenario

OmniSci's gradual growth paralleled the pace of its capital raising. To be sure, OmniSci was targeting a large addressable market. Adding up all the segments in which it competed in July 2018 yielded $70 billion worth of revenues from three markets: $40 billion from analytics databases, $25 billion from business intelligence, and $5 billion from geographic information systems. But OmniSci took its time turning the demonstration version of the product that Mostak had developed at MIT. By July 2018, OmniSci had grown to between 75 and 80 employees and "gotten decent customer traction," competing against big companies like IBM (Netezza), Oracle, SAP, and Vertica, which HP sold to Microfocus, to win "50 to 100 customers." OmniSci's victorious battles resulted from unique capabilities such as real-time analysis of 5 to 100 billion records and rendering capabilities that enable users to pinpoint specific data points on a map, which customers valued. OmniSci's customers fell into three industries. "We have 8 to 10 telecommunications customers around the world who are using our product to find out why calls are dropped. They are slow to move, but offer us significant revenues," he said. In addition to defense department and intelligence clients, companies also use its product to analyze real-time purchases to pick winning investments. "We have hedge fund and investment banking clients that use OmniSci to analyze stock ticker data and credit card transactions. They analyze 10% to 30% of all transactions in real time to see which companies are enjoying upticks in purchases. Our product lets them refresh their analysis every 30 minutes instead of daily."

Its journey to that end was impeded by several factors: the company's founder had never started a company before, the product was technically complex, and its earliest customers were cautious in their collaboration with the company. Initial money came from family and a business plan competition. As Mostak said, "We got loans for between $5,000 and $10,000 from our parents. My family was questioning why I was doing this instead of working for the man. They would have pushed me to take a real job if we had not succeeded. But we won a $100,000 early stage challenge from Nvidia during a period when big data was hot." Between 2014 and 2017, OmniSci raised more money. "In June/July 2014, we raised $2 million more from Nvidia; after endless meetings they decided to give us more money to develop our product. In March 2016, we raised a $10 million Series A led by Vanedge, a Vancouver, BC-based fund, which was tricky because we were still trying to get product/market fit with potential customers like Verizon. And in February 2017, we raised a $25 million Series B, at which point we had double-digit numbers of customers, some of whom paid over $1 million." By October 2018, OmniSci had raised a $55 million Series C round of funding led by hedge fund Tiger Global Management. "It was clear that [Series C investors] held a strong thesis around the massive market opportunity in front of our company and were fully aligned with our vision of the disruptive power of GPU-accelerated analytics," Mostak wrote.

Case Analysis

OmniSci's gradual approach to the first stage of scaling not only paralleled its slow path to building its product and winning its first customers, it also highlights the challenges facing a first-time founder. More specifically, such founders must convince investors that

- Their startup's product will address real customer pain.

- They can turn an idea into a product that will produce tangible benefits for which customers will pay.

- The market for that product will be worth billions of dollars.

- They can build and run an organization that can design, build, market, sell, and service products for a growing collection of customers.

To OmniSci's credit, it was able to overcome the first three challenges, succeeding despite significant obstacles to raise enough capital to keep the company going until it could begin to generate revenues. And in October 2018, it raised a significant Series C round, indicating that investors found its vision compelling.

Principles

Founders seeking to raise capital to fuel the process of winning initial customers should bear in mind the following dos and don'ts:

- **Do**

    - Focus on a source of unrelieved customer pain that is so high that potential customers would pay for a product to alleviate it.

    - Form design partnerships with early customers who feel this pain most intensely.

    - Build a team that cares passionately about building such a product and has the skills needed to make that product a market leader.

    - Demonstrate that the product targets a large market opportunity.

    - Seek capital from sources that will care most about contributing to your Stage 1 success.

- **Don't**
    - Assume—without talking to dozens of potential customers—that your unresolved pain is shared at all or, if it is shared, is intense enough to make potential customers pay to relieve it.
    - Seek to raise capital without conducting in-depth research with potential customers that provides strong evidence that there could be a big market for your product.
    - Assume venture capitalists will invest in you if your company has a founding team without a track record of turning ideas into large companies or lacks relevant industry expertise.

Stage 2: Building a Scalable Business Model

If a startup passes the first scaling stage, as measured by its ability to generate revenue of at least $10 million by selling to an initial set of customers, the CEO will often need to raise additional capital to fuel the company's growth. At this point of a startups' development, the CEO should be able to provide potential investors, usually venture capital firms at this stage, with evidence that will make them willing to invest, including

- **Reference customers:** Investors want to conduct in-depth interviews with a startup's happiest customers who know the company well and have benefited significantly from its products. Based on these interviews, investors should be convinced that your startup's reference customers will keep buying more from you and will happily help you win more customers;
- **Evidence of a large potential market:** Investors will also want to be convinced that the market for your product is, or is quickly growing to be, at least $1 billion. Such evidence can come from research reports from analyst firms such as Gartner or IDC. If your company is creating a new product category, such research may not be available, in which case the CEO should provide an estimate of the size of the addressable market based on the number of potential users, the expected purchase frequency, and an estimated purchase price.

- **Team with strong functional skills:** Potential investors will also assess the strength of a startup's team to reach a conclusion about whether its key functional executives (e.g., Chief Marketing Officer, Chief Technology Officer, and Chief Sales Officer) have a prior track record of building an organization that can boost the efficiency of their functions as the company grows to $100 million in revenue.

- **Potential for improved efficiency:** Investors at this stage will try to assess whether a startup has the potential to grow quickly to $100 million without spending too much money. For example, if the startup's revenues increase at 200% annually, investors will look for the company to achieve that growth while increasing the number of employees more slowly, say by 50%. To persuade investors that this is possible, a startup should track metrics such as the cost to acquire a new customer, the customer retention rate, the company's net promoter score, the cost to filter qualified leads from inquiries, the coefficient of virality, and the lifetime value of customers. Moreover, the CEO should have ideas on how to improve the startup's performance on these measures as the company grows.

Absent these paths, the CEO will likely need to try to persuade the capital sources mentioned above (such as friends and family, crowd-funders, business plan competitions) that it is worth taking a risk on funding the startup's first stage of scaling.

The cases that follow highlight successful and less successful handling of the challenges such a CEO must overcome.

Success Case Study: Varsity Tutors Raises $107 Million to Target $1 Trillion Market Opportunity

Introduction

A first-time entrepreneur with a knack for turning problems into opportunities was able to tranform an idea into a company that was growing rapidly thanks to his ability to solve difficult operational problems and to keep finding new growth opportunities. The company in question was St. Louis and Seattle-based Varsity Tutors, "a live-learning platform that in minutes connects students with vetted tutors and offers Instant Tutoring that matches students in 15 seconds with tutors in over 100 subjects." By July 2018, Varsity Tutors had grown from an idea in 2007 to a service with about 500 employees, some 40,000 tutors, and 100,000 customers who could be tutored in 1,000 subjects. Students paid between $60 and $70 per hour, and as of February 2018, the company had facilitated 3 million hours of tutoring, yielding about $200 million in revenue since 2007.

CEO Chuck Cohn discovered the value of good tutoring in high school. As he said, "I had a range of experiences with tutoring—from the incredible experience of raising my honors geometry grade from an F to an A thanks to a great tutor, to working with a French tutor who couldn't speak English and couldn't help me, to failing to find a qualified biology tutor in time for a big test despite looking online, asking for referrals, and calling local colleges." One night in college, I was studying for a Calculus 2 test and I was really struggling with a few key concepts. I was on the verge of failing the exam and probably the class. Thanks to two good friends who explained the concepts in a fundamentally new way, I got a great grade on the test. I realized that had I had access to tutors like my two friends—academically gifted, personable, exceptional communication skills—I would have had a better high school experience. I would have had better grades, enjoyed school more, and been less stressed. I asked my two friends if they would be willing to work as tutors, we haggled over a rate, and eventually came to an agreement. I borrowed a $1,000 from my parents to start the business and Varsity Tutors was born."

Case Scenario

Varsity Tutors participated in a $100 billion fragmented industry. As he said, "The top 10 companies control 8% market share; the other 92% is controlled by 5,000 mom & pops and one to two million independent tutors." Cohn saw Varsity Tutors applying its platform beyond school-related tutoring to other skills like do-it-yourself home projects, computer programming, chess, and yoga, which he saw as a $1 trillion market opportunity.

As Cohn devoted more attention to the company, after spending years working full time in investment banking and venture capital during the day while working on the company at night, he figured out how to make Varsity Tutors far more scalable. In 2011, he realized that he could build a large, profitable, fast-growing company. As he said, "The sales process was not standardized, there was no tracking of marketing spend, we were paying tutor interviewers to do nothing because the candidates did not show up, we had a weak website, and the e-mails we sent were no good. I was exposed to great operators and they told me how they would scale." So, he became its full-time CEO in 2012. He fixed the interaction between students and tutors and improved the overall customer experience, leading to rapid growth.

As a result, he was able to raise $107 million in capital for the company. By 2015, after turning it into a learning platform, Varsity Tutors switched from providing all its tutoring face-to-face to 70% online. The company had a relatively easy capital raising experience. As Cohn said, "I borrowed $1,000 from my parents and was basically profitable from the beginning. In 2014, we raised a $7 million Series A round of capital from two local entrepreneurs whom I asked for advice on how to scale the company. They asked me to pitch and they led the round." Things got easier from there because he realized that Varsity Tutors was scalable. "In 2015, we had improved our reporting and gotten our online business running. 40 firms contacted us, and we picked the five we respected most, raising a $50 million Series B round from Technology Crossover Ventures, a VC firm that has invested in Netflix, Spotify, Airbnb, and Facebook. They wanted in because we were profitable and growing and we had happy customers because we focused on getting more efficient at identifying great tutors as we scaled," said Cohn. Varsity Tutors raised more capital in 2018. "In January 2018, we raised another $50 million in a Series C round from Learn Capital, a global ed tech venture capital firm, and The Chan Zuckerberg Initiative. They shared our vision of the big opportunity from building a huge online business," he said.

Case Analysis

To raise capital during the second stage of scaling, founders must provide investors what they want -- a company that's growing fast and making a profit. While CEOs must spend time raising capital, such financial performance will attract interested investors. It is far easier to select the best investors from a set of interested candidates than to cold call hundreds of potential investors who do not know about the company.

More specifically, founders seeking outside funding at this stage should follow six principles:

- Target a huge market.
- Identify flaws in the business model that add cost and customer friction.
- Redesign operations to reduce the cost to acquire and service customers and boost customer's desire to buy more over time.
- Design, deliver, and service a product that customers love.
- Expand geographic scope through acquisitions and new sales offices.
- Select investors who share the CEO's vision for the startup.

Less Successful Case Study: Tipalti Raises $40 Million As It Ambles to Liquidity

Introduction

By 2018, Palo Alto, California-based Tipalti, founded in 2010 to help improve the way companies make global payments, had raised $60 million. Targeting the $1.9 billion (expected 2025) U.S. accounts payable software market, Tipalti saw itself scaling to liquidity after seven years. Tipalti was established to solve a problem for global online advertising or crowdsourcing networks. They faced a blizzard of complexity in getting funds to payees. Each country had different rules for different forms of payments and fees as well as myriad country-specific regulations to block money laundering and funding of terrorism.

Tipalti cofounder and CEO Chen Amit was a serial entrepreneur. He earned a BSc from the Technion, Israel Institute of Technology and an MBA from INSEAD and had an impressive track record. He founded ECI Telecom's ADSL business unit and led it to $100 million in sales. He was co-founder and CEO of a business intelligence software supplier and was CEO of Atrica, a Carrier Ethernet company that Nokia-Siemens acquired.

Amit and his co-founder started Tipalti in the summer of 2010 when the president of InfoLinks, an online advertising exchange, told them that mass payments were a pain that needed a solution. Amit wanted to be sure that the market opportunity for helping InfoLinks would be enough to warrant starting a company so they "conducted due diligence to make sure it was a generic need." The company launched its first version in September 2011 and a year later had signed up 25 customers and employed 15. Tipalti won new customers because of its financial and technical advantages, according to Amit. Tipalti "white labeled" its services, letting customers maintain their brands, but gave them access to its remittance capabilities with "a single line of code" so new customers could be "up and running in half a day." Tipalti charges customers various transaction fees and partners with leading banks and payment providers as "a layer on top of their payment methods."

Case Scenario

By 2018, Tipalti was growing rapidly, had 230 customers of which it retained nearly 100%, its revenues were growing at 100% a year, it employed over 100 people, and had raised $60 million in capital. Amit had built an organization of strong functional leaders. As he explained, "Our head of operations worked for a payments startup that was acquired by Fiserv; our head of marketing was previously a vice president of online marketing at NetSuite; our head of sales helped Coupa grow from $1 million to $100 million in revenue; and our head of engineering was hired out of the Technion and has grown into the CTO role. We are now looking for an internal CFO." Investor and cofounder Oren Zeev helped recruit these talented executives. As Zeev said, "When we were recruiting the head of marketing, he was not looking for a job. But he liked Tipalti's problem domain, was impressed that it had near-perfect customer retention, and he got a strong message about the value of its product. And Chen comes across as a grownup, not a jerk. It is rare that I sit down with someone who I believe is a good fit for the company and can't convince him. I have the credibility to convey the message."

Raising a $30 million Series C round in February 2018 was made easier because Tipalti had become more efficient at marketing. As Amit explained, "Our VP of marketing, hired about three years ago, helped us generate strong interest among potential customers, which we call inbound leads. We used to get 95% of our leads from direct sales calls, so-called outbound, and 5% from inbound. Now 70% are inbound and 30% are outbound." Zeev said, "At the seed round, I look for the size of the opportunity, the strength of the founder, and the value proposition of the product. When you get to later stages in a company's growth, you can get data on the customer churn rate, the lifetime value of the customer, and the cost of customer acquisition. We assume a Tipalti customer has an eight-year life and only 1% to 2% churn."

Zeev, who contributed $21 million of the $30 million round, and Amit saw Tipalti's potential for scaling thanks to three principles: Tipalti boosted its customers' productivity, its culture supported high customer retention, and Tipalti was able to sell more to its happy customers. As Amit said, "Tipalti's near-perfect record of customer satisfaction and retention rates [demonstrate how] much value our service generates for our clients. By modernizing the finance operation, we typically automate 80% of an organization's AP and cross-border payments workload, freeing the finance team to focus on scaling their business globally and [boosting their] profitability. This funding round enables us to continue [to innovate]." Tipalti's culture made it clear to employees that customers mattered. As Amit said, "We created a culture driven by our leaders. We hire people who will do a great job for customers. They in turn hire people who share those same values. And as the company has grown to 100 people, we have become more deliberate about articulating and communicating those values." Customers saw Tipalti as the best product in the industry. Zeev made his investment in part on his belief that Tipalti was delivering on this premise. As he said, "It was a relatively easy decision to continue investing in Tipalti since it's a category leader. When you talk to Tipalti's clients like Amazon, GoDaddy, Indeed, Roku, and Twitter, or read the company's five-star reviews, the consensus is that businesses around the globe love using Tipalti." Moreover, Tipalti was able to sell more to its current customers. According to Zeev, "The reasons our customers buy more from us is because they start in one division and the product works so well there that other divisions follow. At Twitter, we started in one business unit initially, expanded to three, and today we are being used in seven business units. Other companies made acquisitions and we're always on the winning side."

Case Analysis

Tipalti took about eight years for its business model to become scalable. To be fair, Tipalti decided to focus on providing customers with excellent service so they would renew their contracts with the company. In so doing, Tipalti was in no hurry to expand its customer base and it may have struggled to sell efficiently. To Tipalti's credit, it accelerated its growth in recent years, possibly due to an increase in inbound inquiries from customers that helped reduce its time to close new sales. Nevertheless, Tipalti's heavy dependence on Oren Zeev's capital to sustain itself raised questions about whether, perhaps due to the relatively small target market, he was one of the few investors to see high potential returns from Tipalti.

Principles

Founders seeking to raise capital to build a scalable business model should bear in mind the following dos and don'ts:

- **Do**
    - Target a market opportunity of at least $2 billion; a larger market is better.
    - Achieve rapid, profitable revenue growth; these results will attract many potential investors and make it easier to choose the best from among those interested.
    - Measure operations to identify opportunities to lower the cost of developing, marketing, and selling the product.
    - Monitor and take steps to assure high customer satisfaction to boost retention rate and increase revenue per customer.
- **Don't**
    - Target a market with less than $2 billion in revenue.
    - Spend much more money to build, market, and sell than you can collect from customers.
    - Operate a sales process that requires hiring expensive sales people who take too long to become productive and leave after they are unable to meet their quotas.

Stage 3: Sprinting to Liquidity

If a startup has succeeded in creating a scalable business model, it is ready to sprint to liquidity. For example, at this point it may have $40 million to $50 million in revenue and be enjoying revenue growth of 100% or more each year. At the beginning of Stage 3, the CEO should have raised enough capital from eager investors to "pour gasoline on the business" so it can reach $100 million in revenue and keep growing at 40% a year or more. If the company is also profitable or is trending towards profitability, then it should be able to go public. To raise enough capital to make the sprint to liquidity, investors will seek compelling evidence that your startup has the following attributes:

- **It is gaining share in a large market.** A market in the tens of billions of dollars growing at double digit rates is compelling to the venture capitalists, private equity firms, and institutional investors who may provide capital at this stage. Moreover, such investors are likely to be heartened if there are large, publicly-traded companies against which these startups are competing. Such public companies help investors estimate the price at which they may be able to sell shares in the startup in the hoped-for IPO.

- **It offers a product that customers love.** Investors will talk with your current customers to assess how enthusiastic they are about your startup's product, how likely they are to keep buying and using it, and whether they have unmet needs that they think your startup could satisfy.

- **Its executive team has prior success scaling to liquidity.** Potential investors will also evaluate the strength of the startup's executive team, specifically looking for each executive's previous success in scaling a startup to liquidity as well as the CEO's ability to motivate the executive team to collaborate in pursuit of rapid revenue growth.

- **Its business processes are sufficiently robust to enable the company to sustain high customer satisfaction as it grows.** Investors also will investigate whether the startup has robust business processes. This means they will examine whether it can develop new products that customers want without taking too much time or costing too much, whether it can market and sell the product quickly, and whether it can provide after-sale service that satisfies customers and does not require too much time or cost. Moreover, investors will want assurances that the startup can perform these activities effectively and efficiently as the startup grows rapidly.

The cases that follow highlight successful and less successful handling of these investor requirements.

Success Case Study: Anaplan Sprints to a 2018 IPO

Introduction

Founded in 2006, San Francisco, California-based Anaplan, a cloud-based business planning service, had raised about $300 million in capital by July 2018 and under a new CEO was able to go public in October 2018, months before its 2019 IPO goal. Anaplan was taking customers from IBM, Oracle, and SAP in the $20 billion market for enterprise performance management. CEO Frank Calderoni said Anaplan "helps companies to make better decisions in response to change through connected planning. For example, [our cloud-based planning service lets] Revlon connect information about customer retail purchases with its supply chain so that Revlon can stock the right product in the right place at the right time." Calderoni joined as CEO in January 2017. Before that he had spent 17 years as CFO, often paired with an operating role, at Cisco Systems and SanDisk. Most recently, he had been CFO and EVP of operations at Red Hat, an enterprise software company, where he spent less than two years.

Calderoni took over after its previous CEO, Frederic Laluyaux, who had previously been an executive at SAP, parted with the company in April 2016. Laluyaux spent over three years as CEO, having taken over in September 2012 from co-founder Guy Haddleton. Laluyaux raised $90 million in a Series E round of capital in January 2016, which valued Anaplan at $1.1 billion. But the board decided that the company would not be able to go public under Laluyaux's leadership, After Laluyaux left, then-Chairman Bob Calderoni (Frank's brother) said, "The board and Fred believe it's the right time to bring in a new set of talent to take us to a much higher level and become a much bigger company." Ravi Mohan, Anaplan board member and managing director at Shasta Ventures, said, "Unbridled growth [is no longer] the most valued characteristic. Now, it's profitable sustained growth, and we're building a company that reflects that."

Case Scenario

When he took over as CEO, Anaplan, which made money by selling monthly subscriptions, was large enough to go public and was still growing fast. As Calderoni pointed out, "In its fiscal year ending January 2017, Anaplan had $120 million in revenue, was growing at 75%, added 250 customers for a total of 700, employed over 700 people in 16 offices in 12 countries, had raised a total of $240 million in capital, and generated good cash flow." Anaplan believed that customers preferred its service to those from IBM (such as Cognos) or Oracle (Hyperion) because these products did not help companies respond as quickly to change. Calderoni said, "Customers are moving away from the spreadsheet model that compares actual results to plan. They want what we offer, which is to make it easy to connect large numbers of users to each other and to make decisions with the help of 'what if' analyses; for example, to help them set prices by estimating sales under different price scenarios."

By April 2018, the company had grown to over 1,000 employees and was getting ready for an IPO. As Calderoni explained, "In the early stage, you are in a trial customer situation where you hope to get 5 or 10 early adopter customers who see your product's benefits. In the middle stage, you are going to market, building on your proof points; you are setting revenue, growth, and customer acquisition objectives. In the late stage, you take your success, say, in three domestic vertical markets and expand globally. At this stage, where we are now, we want to sustain and repeat growth predictably so we can become a public company."

In December 2017, Calderoni raised a $60 million Series F round of funding which valued Anaplan at $1.3 billion. And in a July 2018 interview, he described how Anaplan's five rounds of capital raising fit within the three scaling stages. "Our January 2010 Series A and January 2012 Series B rounds raised $5 million and $11 million, respectively. The A round went to product development and the B round was to expand the sales force and win early adopter customers. At that point we had completed Stage 1 and were on to Stage 2. Our April 2013 Series C ($33 million) and May 2014 Series D ($100 million) rounds went to building out our expansion plan. With the Series C and D funds, we started out in the UK and California and expanded in Europe and the U.S. By 2016, we had 40% of our revenue outside the U.S. and were moving into Stage 3. Our 2016 Series E and 2017 Series F rounds helped us build disciplined processes and are helping us to scale to an IPO. At the Series F round, investors were asking whether we had customers with whom we could land and expand and whether we had a path to cash flow breakeven. We must achieve this while adding to our global sales and customer service operations tailored to each country's regulatory, language, and currency differences. We are also investing in developing partnerships with distribution channels and consultants to help us reach new customers. At the same time, we are becoming more efficient; we are articulating how we will lower our costs through better processes." And on October 12, 2018, Anaplan went public, valuing the company at about $3 billion.

Case Analysis

To succeed at raising capital during the third stage of scaling, investors look for a company that is on a clear path to $100 million or more in revenues and is growing at least 40% annually. Depending on market conditions, investors may also expect a company to be profitable. More specifically, if investors are feeling flush with cash, they may be willing to provide Stage 3 capital to a company that is unprofitable but growing quickly to $100 million; however, if they are afraid of a market reversal, they may only invest at this stage if they are convinced that the company is or can become profitable by the time it reaches $100 million in revenue.

More specifically, founders seeking outside funding at this stage should follow five principles:

- Set and achieve ambitious quarterly targets for revenue and customer growth.

- Build a team of top executives that has prior experience taking companies public and sustaining their growth.

- Assure that systems and processes for running a public company are in place and have been tested.

- Have a clear roadmap for sustaining rapid growth for at least three years into the future.

- Measure costs and customer satisfaction, and redesign the organization and key processes to assure that costs will drop and customer satisfaction will remain high as the company scales to an IPO.

Less Successful Case Study: SentinelOne Is Not IPO-Ready As It Grows to $100 Million

Introduction

In April 2018, Palo Alto, California-based anti-virus software provider SentinelOne expected to win $100 million in revenue from its rivals in 2019 but with $110 million in capital did not see itself as being ready for an IPO, probably due to the challenge of standing out from many competitors. SentinelOne, which was founded in 2013, said its endpoint security product was "a uniquely integrated platform that combined behavioral-based detection, advanced mitigation, and forensics to stop threats in real-time. Specializing in attacks that utilize sophisticated evasion techniques, SentinelOne was the only vendor who offered complete protection against malware, exploit, and insider-based attacks." SentinelOne's cofounder and CEO, Tomer Weingarten, was "responsible for the company's direction, products, and services strategy. Before SentinelOne, Weingarten led product development and strategy for the Toluna Group as a VP of Products. Prior to that he held several application security and consulting roles at various enterprises and was CTO at Carambola Media."

Case Scenario

At 300%, SentinelOne was growing faster than its industry—2018 endpoint security industry revenues of $11 billion were expected to grow at a 12.7% rate to $20 billion by 2023—and had raised $110 million to fund its growth, much of which came at the expense of incumbents. What's more, SentinelOne expected that in 2019 the revenue it would take from incumbents would total $100 million, which is typically sufficient for a fast-growing company to go public. The good news about SentinelOne was that its product received high marks for effectiveness and low price. According to an April 17, 2018 NSS Labs report, "Advanced Endpoint Protection Comparative Report," SentinelOne was recommended with a 97.7% security effectiveness score and a total cost of ownership per protected node of $148, which is 51% below the average TCO/node of $301 for the 11 recommended products covered in the report. Perhaps this strong relationship between effectiveness and price contributed to SentinelOne's growth. As Weingarten explained in an April 2018 interview, "We are growing bookings at 300%. 70% of them are complete rip and replace from McAfee and Symantec. Pandora replaced Symantec with SentinelOne. We win 70% of the time we compete in a proof of concept. We expect a displacement book of $100 million in 2019."

SentinelOne succeeded in raising $110 million over four rounds between 2013 and 2017, the largest of which was used to fuel aggressive marketing and sales expansion. SentinelOne was not preparing for an IPO. SentinelOne's seed rounds in March 2013 ($20,000) and August 2013 ($2.5 million led by Granite Hill Capital) were to be used to transition from beta to launch by September 2013 and to hire its initial workforce and sales force in the United States, according to Weingarten. It raised a $12 million Series A round in April 2014 led by Tiger Global Management and a $25 million Series B in October 2015 led by Third Point Ventures that valued the company at $98.2 million. The Series B was intended to scale sales and marketing and to add features to its platform, according to Weingarten, increasing the company's headcount from 50 to an estimated 120 by the middle of 2016. In January 2017, SentinelOne raised a $70 million Series C round in led by Redpoint to aggressively expand its sales and marketing efforts. At the time of the Series C closing, Redpoint partner Tom Dyal, who joined SentinelOne's board, was excited about the size of its market and its recent customer wins and distribution partnership, As he said, "Endpoint security [was] a $10 billion market opportunity as businesses migrate away from traditional anti-virus software. SentinelOne customers include Time and it [had] recently signed a North American distribution deal with Avnet."

Nevertheless, by April 2018 SentinelOne seemed to be growing rapidly but making organizational adjustments that suggested not all its operations were in shape for an IPO. According to Weingarten, "Between 2016 and 2017, we boosted new customer bookings 300%, increased our customer base 370% to 2,500, and added to our employee headcount by 175% to over 300." This growth was remarkable considering the organizational churn it suffered, which *hurt Sentinel One's execution and vision. According to the January 2018 Gartner "Magic Quadrant for Endpoint Protection" report, SentinelOne's biggest 2017 challenge was "churn in staff roles across product, sales, marketing, and other internal and client-facing groups. Gartner clients reported inconsistent interactions with SentinelOne throughout the year." SentinelOne viewed this turmoil as an investment with a positive return. "2017 was a year of significant change and development for SentinelOne. The company up-leveled its leadership team to take the product and go-to market to new heights. These leadership changes are exactly what has created the unprecedented results we're currently experiencing, and in record time! Key was the hire of Nicholas Warner, Chief Revenue Officer, who led Cylance's global sales growth," said Weingarten.*

Unfortunately for SentinelOne's investors, by January 2018 there appeared to be too many cybersecurity companies competing for a spot in a very small IPO window. Too many startups could not keep growing as technology changed. David Cowan, a partner at Bessemer Venture Partners, said "I have never seen such a fast-growing market with so many companies on the losing side." With so many vendors, investors were deciding to concentrate on just a few, which left the remaining companies stranded. Dave DeWalt, the former CEO of cyber security company FireEye, said, "Suddenly, we are in this situation where there are just too many vendors and too few can be sustained. You're starting to see companies go, 'Oh my gosh, what do I do? Can I get more capital? Do I have to merge?'" Meanwhile, unsuccessful IPOs in the sector seemed to have scared investors. A case was ForeScout Technologies, a provider of software that helped companies keep the devices of their employees secure, which raised $116 million in an IPO in October 2017 that valued the company at about $800 million, down from its $1 billion valuation in the private markets a year earlier. ForeScout's backers, including Intel Capital and Accel Partners, had to moderate their valuation expectations for the IPO to be successful. (By July 20, 2018, it was trading at a $1.5 billion market capitalization.) "Some have compared some cyber security companies to cockroaches," DeWalt said. "They can't die, but they aren't smoking hot either."

Case Analysis

SentinelOne's efforts to raise capital for the third stage of scaling appear less successful than Anaplan's. SentinelOne appears to be growing very rapidly, citing very high rates of growth in the number of customers and employees. Moreover, if the company indeed can gain $100 million in revenue by taking business from rivals, it should be able to go public with such high growth. On the other hand, the intensity of the rivalry in the industry, the rise in venture capital skepticism about being able to earn a high return on investment in the endpoint security market, and the organizational churn at SentinelOne seem to mitigate against hopes for a positive outcome for the company. In the absence of audited financial statements, it is impossible to discern whether the company needs a new round of funding to keep growing; however, unless the company is profitable, there is a good chance it will need to raise even more money to reach the level needed to go public.

Principles

Founders seeking to raise capital to sprint to liquidity should bear in mind the following dos and don'ts:

- **Do**
  - Aim at large markets.
  - Generate rapid revenue and customer growth that motivates venture capital firms to ask to invest in the company.
  - Have a clear path to reducing costs for designing, selling, and servicing products and boosting the value of the product to current and potential customers as the company grows.
  - Hire an executive team with prior experience taking a company public and continuing its growth after the IPO.

- **Don't**
  - Assume that capital providers will keep funding a growing company that has no plan to become profitable.
  - Shield your current executive team from pressures to adapt to the needs of Stage 3 scaling.
  - Target a small market and fail to shift focus in response to changing investor sentiment.

Stage 4: Running the Marathon

It is very rare that a founder can turn an idea into a public company and keep the company growing after the IPO to become a leader in a very large market. My conversations with hundreds of entrepreneurs suggest that virtually none of them will publicly acknowledge that the IPO is an important event in the company's development. Most often they refer to the IPO as a minor funding event that should not interrupt the company's inexorable march to becoming a company that grows so influential that it will change the world. Not surprisingly, given that only a handful of founders have achieved this, most founders who take their company public lack the skills needed to keep running their companies following their IPO until they surpass, say, $10 billion in annual revenues while growing at over 20% a year.

When it comes to raising capital for running the marathon, CEOs can consider three options:

- **Cash flow from operations:** Profits are always the lowest-cost source of capital. If a company is generating enormous amounts of cash flow from its operations, it can simply use that money to fund its investments in future growth.

- **Higher share price:** The key to success is taking actions that propel the company's stock price upward. That's because one of the easiest ways for a public company to raise more capital is to sell stock. And the higher the stock price, the more capital can be raised at minimum dilution to existing shareholders.

- **Borrow money:** If a company generates high cash flows, they will provide ample comfort for bankers or bond-holders should the company decide that borrowing money is a better way to raise funds for future growth because it does not require diluting existing shareholders.

To boost a public company's stock price, the CEO must in parallel do two things well:

- **Beat and raise:** Every quarter investors await the company's financial report and its forecast for the next quarter. If the reported results and forecasts for measures such as revenue growth, profit growth, and number of customers exceed investors' expectations, the stock price will rise. If investors are disappointed, the stock will fall. For a CEO to beat and raise each quarter, the company must be able to set ambitious goals, make sure that the right people oversee achieving those goals and have the resources they need, and monitor progress during the quarter to make any needed adjustments. Of course, even the best founder-led companies miss quarters occasionally. But if such CEOs can beat and raise in most quarters, investors are more likely to view such misses as a buying opportunity.

- **Invest in growth:** To keep beating and raising, CEOs must also take a longer-term view of their company's growth opportunities. Specifically, CEOs must try to make the most of the company's current sources of growth from among the five dimensions of growth I discussed in Chapter 2, but recognize that these sources of growth will become saturated. Such saturation means that unless the company invests in new and accelerating growth vectors, the company's overall growth will stagnate. Investing in the right growth opportunities, which could include selling current products into new geographies, acquiring new products, or building new products to sell to current and new customers, is an essential skill that few CEOs can master. Envisioning such opportunities requires creativity, vision, and a deep understanding of how customer needs, technology, and competitor strategies are evolving. But investing in the right growth opportunities hinges on affirmative answers to five questions:

  - Is the market opportunity large and growing rapidly?

  - Do we have the capabilities needed to build and sell a product that leads in that market?

  - If not, can we acquire those capabilities and integrate them effectively?

  - Do we, or can we obtain, the capital needed to fund the growth investment?

  - Can we communicate to investors our goals and progress in capturing the growth opportunity?

Success Case Study: Talend Goes Public and Its Stock Soars

Introduction

Redwood City, California-based data cleaning service Talend went public in 2016, 11 years after it was founded, and in the nearly two years thereafter its stock rose 146%. Talend provided open source software with a "wrapper" that cleaned data so companies could analyze it to make decisions. Its software platform, "Data Fabric, integrates data and applications in real time across modern big data and cloud environments as well as traditional systems," according to the company. Talend, which targeted the $2.7 billion (2016 revenue) data integration tools market, made money by selling subscriptions to software that cleaned up data errors. "We help companies get value from data used to make decisions. We work on the first mile in the data analysis process, which is to fix errors in the data before companies analyze it. Every customer's biggest problem is data quality. Our product is a combination of open source software and a wrapper that is sold by subscription," said CEO Mike Tuchen in a July 2018 interview. Talend was founded in 2005 but Tuchen signed on as CEO in January 2014 as the company was raising a round of funds. He came to the company with a strong background in the software industry but had never taken a company public or been CEO of one thereafter. He had previously been CEO from May 2008 to October 2012 of security data and analytics provider Rapid7; was General Manager of SQL Server Marketing at Microsoft; and had a nice string of degrees: a B.S. from Brown and M.S. from Stanford (both in Electrical Engineering) and an M.B.A. from Harvard.

Case Scenario

Talend enjoyed rapid revenue growth while reporting net losses and fluctuating free cash flow. Since 2013, its revenues had grown at a 29.5% compound annual rate to $148.6 million in 2017; its net loss increased from about -$20 million to -$31 million, and its free cash flow was negative in each of those years except 2016 when it was about +$2 million, according to Morningstar. Talend's 2018 unit economics looked good. According to a June 2018 investor presentation, in the first quarter of 2018, the company enjoyed over 100% cloud and big data growth; 121% net expansion, a measure of its ability to sell more to existing customers; 85% subscription revenue; and $5 million in positive free cash flow. Talend expected rapid growth in 2018. "When I joined the board in 2013, we had about 300 people and now we have 1,000. Our revenue was about $50 million in 2013 and we expect $203 million in 2018 revenue this year [which is 36.6% more than 2017 revenue]," Tuchen explained.

Under Tuchen's leadership, Talend prepared itself to be a public company, in part by changing who it sold to and how it sold. As he said, "In 2013, we sold to mid-market companies and lower enterprise customers. But the market was confused about the company. 72% of our customers stayed with us each year and we had no clear advantage in our position. We needed to be more efficient about how we sold. We changed the team, the strategy, and the way we set and hit goals." The changes Tuchen made worked, resulting in a 73% increase in sales productivity. "We changed our strategy from being a low-end disrupter to a next generation leader. Due to rapid changes such as the move to the cloud and the use of data lakes [a storage repository that holds raw data in its native format until it is needed] we had an opportunity to be a leader. We targeted early adopters in financial services, retail, high technology, and manufacturing (companies using sensor data). We improved the way we described our product benefits and the way we hired and trained our sales people. Since they were meeting their goals right away, our attrition rate dropped," according to Tuchen.

While Tuchen was figuring out how to fix these problems, he was also thrown into the middle of a major funding effort, raising $20 million in capital and retiring $20 million in debt, with hopes of going public thereafter. Investors ask different questions as a startup goes from Series A funding to later rounds, according to Tuchen. Before a Series A, they want to know what problem the company is trying to solve, the size of the market opportunity, why the company's solution will win, and whether the team can build a solution. In Series B, investors care about early customer traction, revenue, and repeatability. And in Series C, they want to see that you are getting the unit economics in line. When Tuchen was trying to close the pre-IPO round of funding, he was in a hurry. "We started in October 2013 and closed in December. Investors asked us how we would get our unit economics in line. We wanted to improve sales productivity but did not have all the details."

Tuchen also shed light on Talend's IPO process. As he said, "We started six months before the IPO with our pre-IPO road show, getting feedback on our presentation. Two weeks before the IPO, we went out on a corporate jet to visit with potential investors. Now that we are public, the marathon is just starting. I spend 20% of my time involved with externally-facing activities like investor meetings and earnings calls." Talend has not needed to raise money since the IPO. "With the exception of a $10 million acquisition, we have not touched the $109 million we raised in the IPO because we were cash flow positive when we did the IPO. We have done three follow-ons in which investors sold shares. I spent a couple of hours with lawyers; within two hours of the market close, two or three investors cashed out their stakes. One of our venture investors paid back its entire fund from those proceeds."

Tuchen was focused on the short- and long-term future of Talend. "You can't just beat-and-raise each quarter. We set a three-year goal and do detailed planning for the year ahead. If we are doing well each quarter, it is progress on a multi-year journey." In May 2018, Tuchen sounded optimistic after reporting its first quarter results. As he said, "Our solid financial results were driven by strong subscription revenue growth of 44% and continued success with large enterprise customers. We anticipate our cloud momentum will continue as we roll out our new cloud product roadmap in 2018 and collaborate more closely with leading cloud partners."

Case Analysis

As noted above, one of the best sources of capital after an IPO is cash flow from operations. Talend has been able to generate positive cash flow since it went public, and as a result, it does not need to sell more shares or borrow money. Tuchen's conduct as CEO, before and after the IPO, illustrates how leaders at the fourth stage of scaling can achieve such an outcome:

- Make the business model scalable before going public.

- Create structured processes that enable the company to set and achieve realistic yet ambitious goals for future growth.

- Plan three years into the future and make everyone accountable for achieving quarterly goals in the first year of the plan.

Less Successful Case Study: Domo Raises $690 Million and Loses 78% of Its Value in Its June 2018 IPO

Introduction

American Fork, Utah-based Domo designed and delivered an executive management platform as a service to help executives manage their business. It was founded in December 2011, went public in June 2018 at a 78% discount to its most recent private valuation, and a month later its shares had lost 32% of their value. Domo had 796 employees and 1,500 customers in industries such as financial services, professional services, technology, energy, consumer goods, manufacturing, healthcare, media, retail, and transportation. Its clients included small organizations to large enterprises, including 36% of the 2017 Fortune 50. IDC estimated that Domo's target market of business intelligence software would reach $24.4 billion in 2018. Founder and CEO Josh James, who controlled 86.1% of Domo's voting stock and owned 3,263,659 of its Class A shares, cofounded and was CEO of marketing services firm Omniture from 1996 to 2009, which went public in June 2006 and was acquired in September 2009 for $1.8 billion, a 24% premium to its pre-deal value, by Adobe Systems. James studied entrepreneurship at Brigham Young University for three years before dropping out.

Case Scenario

While Domo grew, its business model was unprofitable. For example, its 2018 revenue grew 32% to $108.5 million from the year before while it lost money in both years, but its 2018 loss of $176 million was 5% below its 2017 net loss. The basic version of its product was available for free for a year and allowed five users access to analyze up to five million rows of data. After a year, the users were required to choose from three pricing tiers "ranging from $83 per user per month to $190 per user per month. The highest tier subscription came with features such as the ability to analyze up to two billion rows of data, advanced governance and security, HIPAA compliance capability, consulting from certified partners, and premium support."

Domo failed to scale its business model before going public. Between January 2017 and April 2018, Domo went from no debt to $96.1 million as it burned through nearly $150 million in cash a year from its operations in both years. Indeed, without the proceeds of its IPO, Domo did not expect to be able to meet its expected cash needs. According to its June 2018 prospectus, as of April 2018, its roughly $72 million in cash coupled with a tapped-out line of credit would only be enough money to cover its operating obligations for the year ending April 2019 unless Domo was able to raise money in an IPO. Without the IPO, Domo said it would seek other forms of financing and absent "other equity or debt financing by August 2018, management [would slash] operating expenses, [including] significant reductions to marketing costs, including reducing the size and scope of our annual user conference, lowering hiring goals, and reducing or eliminating certain discretionary spending as necessary."

Domo raised 11 rounds of financing totaling nearly $690 million but compared to other venture-based startups generated relatively little annual recurring revenue. Indeed, Domo's valuation at the time of its $125 million Series C round was $825 million, a figure that soared to $2 billion when Domo raised its $200 million Series D round in 2015 and inched up to $2.3 billion at the time of its $100 million Series E round in 2017. Pre-IPO investors took a huge loss since Domo's June 28, 2018 IPO, which raised $193 million, valued Domo at $500 million, or 22% of its peak private market valuation. According to the so-called hype ratio, defined as the amount of venture capital invested in the company divided by its annual recurring revenue, Domo was a very highly hyped company. Other SaaS companies generated far lower hype ratios. Adaptive Insights, which raised $175 million and generated $106 million in revenue, had a ratio of 1.6 and Zuora, with $250 million in capital and $138 million in annual recurring revenue, had a ratio of 1.8. Domo, with a hype ratio of 6.4, topped them all. As technology executive Dave Kellogg wrote, "It's one of the most hyped companies I've ever seen."

James was optimistic about Domo's future, viewing the IPO as the best way to raise money to help achieve his vision. As he said on the day of the company's IPO, "We're hitting all the right metrics in terms of finally proving the enterprise. Now we have to go and execute." Domo went public to avoid getting "stuck on a bridge to nowhere, or in the middle of the desert, when something like that happens." Domo claimed to have 400 CEOs as users, thus making it different than rivals. He viewed Domo's high marketing and R&D costs as a positive investment in its future. He had no intention, for example, of stopping its Domopalooza conference, which had included celebrities such as Alec Baldwin, Nelly, and Kesha. James blamed Domo's change from targeting small businesses to big-company CEOs as the source of its afflictions in early years in the wake of the high turnover among smaller customers. Echoing Theranos ex-CEO Elizabeth Holmes's October 2015 CNBC interview, James said, "People have taken pot shots, people have questioned our product. When you're innovating and doing something that no one's done before, you are going to have a lot of doubters. That's why no one has done it."

Case Analysis

Domo cost its pre-IPO investors very large losses. The following factors may have caused those losses:

- James used his success with Omniture to insulate the company from scrutiny while raising capital.

- Domo spent too heavily on marketing and research, and assumed that investors would keep investing more to cover their losses.

- Domo raised too much capital before hurdling the second stage of scaling.

- Dome overconcentrated control in the CEO's hands.

Principles

Founders seeking to raise capital after the IPO should bear in mind the following dos and don'ts:

- **Do**
  - Try to generate sufficient operating cash flow to finance growth.
  - Beat expectations and raise guidance consistently each quarter.
  - Invest, after careful research, in new growth opportunities that can sustain rapid growth.

- **Don't**
  - Go public before building a scalable business model.
  - Demand total control of the board.
  - Expect investors to fund post-IPO operating losses.

Capital Raising Success and Failure Principles

To raise capital at each scaling stage, CEOs must satisfy investors' performance standards, which are summarized in Table 3-1.

Table 3-1. Summary of capital raising principles

Scaling Stage	Dos	Don'ts
1: Winning the first customer	If you are a first-time founder, try to raise capital from friends, family, crowdfunding, and business plan competitions. Use the funds to improve product so initial design partners will become enthusiastic customers.	If you are a first-time founder, don't try to raise capital from venture capitalists or angel investors, unless you have strong personal connections to them. Work on product in isolation from potential customers.
2: Scaling the business model	Look for venture capitalists who have industry expertise and knowledge of how to scale. Make sure you have at least 10 customers who are willing to recommend your company to others. Target a large market. Field an executive team of functional leaders who have enjoyed previous scaling success. Set and exceed growth targets. Redesign business processes to lower cost and boost customer retention	Try to raise capital for scaling before your business model is efficient. Focus on revenue growth at any cost. Field a team of executives who lack experience scaling. Attempt to raise capital without customers who are willing to serve as enthusiastic references. Focus on a market that is too small.
3: Sprinting to liquidity	Set and exceed aggressive quarterly revenue, customer count, and cash flow goals. Hire a team with experience taking a company public. Enhance sales, marketing, service, and product development processes to lower costs.	Raise capital for a business that consumes much more capital than it can generate.
4: Running the marathon	Beat revenue, profit, and customer count goals each quarter and raise guidance. Identify and invest in future growth opportunities with attractive markets in which the company can become a leading player. Plan for the long-term and make people accountable for the first year of the plan.	Grow revenues without controlling costs. Assume that investors will continue to finance operating losses.

Are You Doing Enough to Raise Capital at Each Scaling Stage?

Raising capital is essential to keep a company growing through the four stages of scaling until it can consistently generate positive cash flow from operations. Here are five questions that will help you know whether you are doing this properly:

- Do you have or are you creating customers who will happily refer you to others?

- Is your product targeting very large markets?

- Can your company offer so much value to customers that it will gain significant market share?

- Do you have a team of experienced executives with prior experience taking a company public?

- Does your company have the discipline to set and exceed ambitious quarterly goals for growth and profitability?

Conclusion

Raising the capital needed to fund growth is much easier if your company has or can build a reputation for creating value for customers and operating a business model that becomes more efficient as your company grows. If your company can set and exceed ambitious goals for revenue and customer growth paired with improving cash flow, investors will ask to invest in your company. When CEOs generate such inbound investor interest, they are more likely to be able to select investors who share their vision, can help the company achieve that vision through capital and advice, and are willing to accept a reasonable valuation of the company as they invest. A critical element of achieving and sustaining growth is creating culture, which we'll explore in Chapter 4.

Sustaining Culture

Culture is what people do when the CEO is not watching. When everyone is working together in a single room 80 to 100 hours a week, startups do not need to articulate culture explicitly. However, once a company adds new employees and begins to locate people away from headquarters, the CEO must define and communicate the culture and the company must use it to make key decisions and act. Culture is particularly crucial for a startup as it expands because, if done correctly, it guides people to take independent action in response to threats and opportunities. This idea of culture only makes sense if the company hires people with the potential to be successful entrepreneurs, turning their jobs into a real-world training ground for creating and building a new business. In such a company, the CEO does not want to make all the decisions; she wants people to feel that they have the right balance of freedom and guidelines to evaluate threats and opportunities, develop options, and pick the best course of action for the company. Culture is in the center of the seven scaling levers diagram because many of the other six levers flow naturally from culture. And if culture is managed properly, it is a major contributor to the startup's ability to grow rapidly because decisions are more likely to be made correctly, or if not, to be fixed right away—and far more quickly than they would if the CEO made all the decisions.

© Peter S. Cohan 2019
P. S. Cohan, *Scaling Your Startup*, https://doi.org/10.1007/978-1-4842-4312-1_4

Culture is a projection of the CEO's view of which of the company's stakeholders (e.g., its customers, employees, partners, and investors) are most important and how the company should conduct itself in its relationships with those stakeholders. Culture can be communicated in the form of values and stories that illustrate how people in the company turn those values into actions that benefits important stakeholders. A CEO should also use those values to hire, promote, and fire employees. While in theory there is a near-infinite combination of stakeholders and values that constitute a culture, in practice I've observed four common types in startups, which are listed from best to worst:

- **Customer-focused culture:** A customer-focused culture seeks to excel at providing customer benefits at a low price. Such cultures seek to attract and motivate employees with a passion for developing innovative products; delivering service that makes customers highly likely to keep buying from the company and to recommend the company to others; and a willingness to work with other departments in the company to get and keep customers. If the company can charge a high enough price for the value it creates for customers, its investors will also be better off. If the company grows while losing money, a customer-focused culture can be risky. Amazon's culture focuses on spending as little as possible while delivering value to customers (rather than extracting it). At its inception, founder and CEO Jeff Bezos wanted Amazon to achieve this by becoming a price and customer service leader. To signal that he did not want to waste money, he made it mandatory that all desks would be built from cheap Home Depot doors with legs nailed to them. Employees who do not like sitting at a door don't last long at Amazon.

- **Performance-driven culture:** A performance-oriented culture sets specific goals for everyone and expects people to exceed their performance targets consistently. Such a culture tends to focus on measuring what the CEO believes matters most to startup investors, which is revenue growth. People who meet the CEO's ambitious quarterly performance targets are rewarded and those who do not are quickly fired. Performance-oriented cultures often have negative side effects; for example, some may not care how results are achieved, so if those who get results do so by hurting other employees or short-changing customers, they are not punished for their under-handed behavior. Such cultures generally are difficult to sustain since the negative side-effects like high turnover of employees and customers overwhelm the ever-higher performance. Netflix sees itself as a sports team rather than a family. It seeks out the most talented person for each job and fires those who don't measure up. So far, Netflix seems to have benefited from the positive aspects of a performance-oriented culture and minimized the bad side effects. Netflix CEO Reed Hastings explained that Netflix wants to hire the most talented people and create an environment that motivates talent to work effectively and stay at the company if they are producing at the highest level. Hastings was eager to replace people who were not top performers as soon as their managers decided that they were not worth keeping. As Netflix grew, it opted out of the commonly used approach of adding formal processes to limit risk. Instead, Netflix promoted employee freedom. As Hastings said, "If you want to operate with very few rules, you need to set context. We added a chapter to our [100-page PowerPoint] culture deck called 'Context, not Control.'"

- **Employee-focused culture:** An employee-focused culture places primary emphasis on the development of employees' abilities. It hires people with entrepreneurial potential, encourages them to develop and test hypotheses about new product opportunities and uses the feedback to improve their business ideas and take on more significant challenges as they learn the skills needed to discharge greater responsibilities. If the company grows as employees' skills develop, the company will be better off. The risk of a learning culture is that the company develops the skills of its employees who then go to work for rivals who benefit from the company's investment in developing their talents. Agiloft, a Redwood City, California-based supplier of code-free development tools, enjoyed 45% 2017 revenue growth while encouraging employees to enjoy their personal lives without raising venture capital. As CEO Colin Earl, who founded Agiloft in 1992, told me in a June 2018 interview, "Employees are the core of our success. We are very selective and fewer than 5% leave every year. Our average employee tenure is seven years. We give our employees time to enjoy their personal lives, encouraging them to work no more than 45 hours per week, and pay everyone substantial bonuses from our revenues."

- **No articulated culture:** In such companies, the CEO has outstanding technical skills but less impressive leadership abilities. If such a CEO can attract and motivate a technical team that builds a product that sells itself, the company may not need to articulate a culture. But such companies generally do not scale unless a new CEO joins the company to provide the missing leadership skills. Such a case is Justin Moore, who between 2006 and July 2017, when it was acquired for an undisclosed amount, was CEO of Axcient, a supplier of computer disaster recovery services. By November 2011 when I interviewed him, Moore was known in Silicon Valley as a culture guru. As he explained, Axcient was his third startup and he was not always so interested in corporate culture. At one of his earlier companies, he neglected culture and that neglect caused unwanted turnover and low morale. This made him realize that culture must be created and managed and should be an important part of the CEO's job.

CEOs create a company's culture, and while it is common for a new CEO who takes over an existing company to change its culture, some new CEOs maintain the culture if they believe that it's working. Having said that, the process of changing an existing culture is far more challenging than creating a new one, especially for a startup with a handful of employees. To create a culture, the CEO should take the following six steps:

- **Look inside.** A company's founder has innate beliefs and values that shape its culture. If the founder has achieved success in previous endeavors, those values have probably contributed to the success and may therefore be the basis for the current startup's success.

- **Think about what matters to employees and customers.** While a list of the founder's values is a good place to start, such values should only be used in the startup if they also motivate employees to act in the company's best interests, which should be tied to what will help the company to create and keep customers. Simply put, the right values for a startup are at the intersection of three sets: the values and conduct that the founder believes will work, the values that will attract and motivate talented people, and the values that will motivate the employees to create superior value for customers over time.

- **Articulate values.** Once the company finds the four to six values at the intersection of those three sets, the founder should write them down, get feedback from others to improve them, and use the values to shape the way employees behave.

- **Create and tell stories that illustrate the values.** People tend to remember well-told stories. So, the founder should build a collection of stories to tell current employees and those that the company seeks to hire—stories that make it clear what kind of behavior embodies each of the values. The founder should tell these stories regularly, and as the company grows and adds new employees, the company should add more stories that reflect recent examples of how people have done things that embody the company's values.

- **Model the values.** The CEO can influence employee behavior through the way she behaves. If the CEO consistently and visibly takes actions that are consistent with the company's values, employees will realize that they ought to do the same. If the CEO behaves in ways that contradict those values, employees are more likely to be demoralized, lose respect for the CEO and the management team, and possibly seek employment elsewhere.

- **Use values to hire, promote, and let people go.** Another important way that a company can turn its values into action is to use the culture to hire, promote, and let people go. Simply put, the company should use cultural fit to screen people it wants to hire. And once hired, the company should reward individuals who embody its values and to let go those who act in ways that oppose those values.

- **Regularly celebrate and reward people who embody the corporate values.** As the company grows and adds new people, the company ought to have more formal ways to make sure that everyone understands the culture. For example, a company should hold regular meetings to publicly recognize individuals who have taken action that is consistent with the company's values. By holding regular meetings, the CEO can keep the culture alive by getting feedback on what aspects of the culture are working most effectively and which need to be changed. Such feedback enables the CEO to reshape the culture as needed to achieve better results.

Takeaways for Stakeholders

What should a startup's stakeholders do to create a culture that helps the company achieve its goals? The answers vary by stakeholder, as follows:

- **Startup CEO**

  - Choose and articulate values in which the CEO believes, and which will motivate employees to act in ways that will help the company to get and keep customers.

  - Create and tell compelling stories that engage employees emotionally with the values.

  - Model the values.

  - Use the values to hire, promote, and let go employees.

  - Periodically celebrate people who embody the values.

  - Assess whether the culture is helping the company achieve its goals and if not, find out why and change the culture.

- **Employees**

  - Give the executive leadership team feedback on how the values and culture affect their motivation and actions.

  - Make constructive suggestions on how to improve the culture and enhance the processes the company uses to communicate and use the culture in decision-making.

Culture Success and Failure Case Studies

Creating culture happens almost every time a new CEO steps in to lead a company. If the same CEO leads a company on the journey from idea to a large publicly-traded company, that culture is not likely to change much. However, if a new CEO steps into an existing company, it is likely that the new leader will assess the culture and decide whether to change it. The case studies presented below bring into focus the key questions that CEOs should use to assess how well a company's culture is working:

- Is the company's culture explicitly defined? For example, does the company have written values?

- Do people in the company know these values?

- Do the company's values guide the way people decide and act?

- Does the company tell frequent stories about people who decide and act in accordance with the culture?

- Is the culture reinforced by periodic public meetings in which people who embody the company's values are praised and rewarded?

- Is the culture used to hire, promote, and let people go?

- Does the company enjoy a low rate of unwanted turnover?

- Is the company meeting its goals?

- How clear is the connection between the culture and the company's achievement, or lack thereof, of its goals?

If the answer to most of these questions is "No" after an independent investigator interviews the company's people, partners, customers, and investors, then the culture needs to change. If most of the questions can be answered in the affirmative, the culture is effective and should be enhanced. While a company's culture can remain the same as it scales, the CEO must communicate and integrate the culture more systematically into the way people think and act. In general, when everyone in the company can fit comfortable in a lunch room, there may be less of a need to articulate the culture. However, as the number of employees increases, and their locations extend around the world, the CEO must create and lead processes that keep the culture vital to the many new employees.

Creating Culture Success and Failure Case Studies

In this section, I offer case studies of creating culture used by successful and less successful startups at each scaling stage, analyze the cases, and extract principles for helping founders to create culture at each stage.

Stage I: Winning the First Customers

When a company is struggling to win its first customers, it is also hiring its initial employees. To hire the right people and create an environment in which they excel, the CEO must, at a minimum, have an implicit idea about the right mindset for how the company will work with customers. However, the best CEOs communicate a clear understanding of the startup's culture so they can hire and motivate people to win its first customers.

Success Case Study: Twine Hires People to Do the Best Work of Their Life

Introduction

One of the reasons that startups grow more quickly than large companies is that they are more effective at attracting and motivating the most talented people. And culture, along with the company's mission, top management track record, and uniqueness of its product, is an important factor in attracting the best talent. So, it is quite surprising that an insurance company and a startup entrepreneur could create a blended culture that attracted highly talented people who built a product that customers were eager to use. The insurance company in question was Boston, Massachusetts-based John Hancock, a subsidiary of publicly-traded Toronto-based Manulife. The startup, San Francisco, California-based Twine, which made an app that helps people do financial planning, resided in a John Hancock startup incubator. Twine allowed users to link accounts with their spouse or partner to save money for the down payment on a house or a car, planning for a wedding, or taking a vacation. Once users agreed on a savings goal, they authorized the automated transfer of funds from their linked bank account into the Twine account. Algorithms generated advice and account management instructions, recommended changes in asset allocations and specific investment selections, and automatically rebalanced the account.

CEO Uri Pomerantz started Twine after a previous startup was acquired by John Hancock back in 2015. Pomerantz was born in Israel and moved to California during his childhood. He has an undergraduate degree from Stanford University in symbolic systems, a graduate degree from Harvard University in economic development, and an MBA from Stanford Business School. Before starting Twine, Pomerantz did finance and technology work at McKinsey & Co. and investment banking at Goldman Sachs. He worked as a program manager and business development manager at Microsoft Corp. He started Guide Financial in 2012, which John Hancock acquired in 2015, to use technology to scale and enable financial advisors to help clients increase their savings, make better financial decisions, and achieve retirement security.

Case Scenario

Twine, which was founded in 2015, was part of John Hancock's startup incubator.

Started in 2015, Manulife's Lab of Forward Thinking (LOFT) embraced "emerging technological trends in the face of impending disruption by smaller, nimbler startups. Through LOFT labs in Boston, Singapore and Toronto, (LOFT encouraged) ideas to be prototyped and launched without layers of approval. In addition to pursuing concepts internally, Manulife acquired startups and kept them operating in a manner consistent with the LOFT mission." One such startup was Twine. In 2015, Pomerantz and his cofounder began Twine to "positively impact the financial behaviors of couples and individuals, make quality financial advice available to all middle-class Americans, and use intuitive design and behavioral finance to make changes stick."

Twine launched its service in November 2017 and by July 2018 was "still early into testing product/market fit with (its) current target audience. As part of a digital innovation group within John Hancock, (Twine is) focused on scaling our technology to improve the financial lives of millions of customers in the U.S. and globally," Pomerantz said. Twine added staff and by July 2018 had 27 people in San Francisco and 19 in Boston. The staff included people with skills in engineering, design, product development, operations, legal, data science, and regulatory matters. Twine helped people "set goals such as retirement, a wedding or a vacation, lets them know how much they need to save each week to get there, and helps them save it in cash or a personalized portfolio," said Pomerantz.

Twine's culture appeared to be consistent with the LOFT mission and, surprisingly, was not set up to recommend John Hancock products to Twine customers. "We are a fiduciary and are not pushing John Hancock products," said Pomerantz. "We recommend what we think is best for the customer, whether it's products from Blackrock, Vanguard, or others." Twine also had its own culture. "We are building a new culture," according to Pomerantz. "Twine should be a place where you do the best work of your life. Our mission is to improve the lives of our customers. We want people to develop good relationships and to speak up. We want to stretch people and bring them a step up." He found that it was not easy to make corporate innovation work. "The vision and mandate have to start from the CEO; you have to allow the startups to be independent and walled off, so they can turn prototypes into products in a non-corporate manner; the startups need to have a clear vision for what success looks like over five years, and they need the right leadership," explained Pomerantz.

Case Analysis

Twine's ability to win its first customers reflects several factors, including culture:

- Talented CEO and cofounder
- Compelling mission, vision, and product
- Blend of big company backing and San Francisco location (near talent)
- Culture that attracts and motivates talented people to innovate

Less Successful Case Study: After Winning First Customers, First Republic Acquires Gradifi

Introduction

A Boston-based financial services startup raised initial capital, won its first customers, and sold itself to a publicly-traded San Francisco-based bank. The startup's initial success suggested that it had developed a service that people wanted, but its failure to raise more capital to remain independent raised questions about its business model, leadership, and culture.

The financial services startup was Boston-based Gradifi, which developed "a student loan paydown platform to solve the biggest problem millennials face: $1.3 trillion worth of student loan debt." Gradifi sold to companies (PwC (PricewaterhouseCoopers) is a big client) that help pay down employees' student loan debt in concert with employee contributions. Companies contributed directly through structured and secured channels towards their employees' student loan principal monthly. Companies paid Gradifi a monthly per-user fee. Gradifi charged companies $3 to $5 per employee, which was less than companies would pay to build and operate their own platform. But Gradifi's biggest benefit to companies was that it let them outsource to an expert the process of making payments directly to employees in a secure, efficient, and scalable manner, according to its founder and CEO, Tim DeMello. By 2016 DeMello, a former Babson College trustee, had been starting companies for the previous 30 years, before which he was a stockbroker. He founded and was CEO of Ziggs, Spotlight Media, and Replica Corporation. He also founded grocery delivery service Streamline.com in 1993 and was its CEO, selling it to Peapod for $12 million in cash in September 2000. DeMello got the idea for Gradifi in a Babson board meeting as he was listening to a discussion about student loans. He thought that students who typically borrow $35,000 could achieve a 25% reduction in their student loan payments if they could cut their monthly payment by $100.

Case Scenario

Since founding Gradifi in 2014, the company, with 28 employees and $7.5 million in capital as of October 2016, had been on an aggressive growth trajectory. Gradifi expected its service to be used by 10,000 employees by the end of 2016, 100,000 by the end of 2017, and 250,000 by the end of 2018. The key to Gradifi's growth was its "inbound marketing:" the ability to source new customers from its current ones, especially PwC. In October 2016, Gradifi had 600 customers and was adding 8 to 10 new ones each month. DeMello believed that culture was critically important, and Millennials made it harder for him to create the right culture. As he said, "The

Millennial workforce, that works to live, is different than the Gen X or Baby Boomer workforce, who live to work. To accommodate that, Gradifi focused people on outputs: weekly accomplishments, rather than inputs, such as the number of hours people spend in the office."

On December 9, 2016 DeMello sold Gradifi to San Francisco-based private bank First Republic for an undisclosed amount. He believed that Gradifi would be better off as part of First Republic. As DeMello said, "This is a great, sensational opportunity for the company to partner with a first-class organization." Since 2015, five companies had expressed interest in acquiring Gradifi. DeMello passed on two of them in 2015 and met with three "in the last three months." First Republic became a Gradifi customer in August 2016 and "saw value in our service immediately." Gradifi and First Republic took six weeks to negotiate the deal. DeMello was thrilled about this deal for three reasons: he expected to be able to maintain Gradifi's brand as one independent from First Republic's, he would make his investors happy, and First Republic would provide capital and a pay plan that would motivate his team to boost Gradifi's revenues.

Eight months later DeMello remained upbeat about the deal. In August 2017, he told me Gradifi had maintained its independent identity and was adding Fortune 500 clients at a rapid clip. As he said, "We have five or six companies sign up per week. It really has helped that we are still an independent entity called Gradifi. We have a five-person board and provide weekly reporting on our progress, as we did before the merger. We are doing an ad campaign for Gradifi on CNBC, Bloomberg, and CNN. And we had our stock options accelerated by 50%, plus a five-year incentive plan that's a function of the number of platform participants we sign up. The team really wanted the independent Gradifi brand, and First Republic has a good service culture."

Case Analysis

While Gradifi said that its acquisition by First Republic was successful, the terms were not disclosed so it is difficult to evaluate objectively. However, since the rewards are so great for CEOs who can go from an idea to a large public company, it would not surprise me if Gradifi was unable to develop a scalable business model and therefore was not able to raise private capital. Since DeMello did not shed much light on Gradifi's culture, beyond saying that he was struggling to figure out how to manage Millennial workers, it is hard to know whether Gradifi's failure to raise private capital was related to its culture. However, for talented people who want the chance to work for a company that goes public, being acquired by First Republic probably did not help the company to attract and retain top talent.

Principles

Founders seeking to create a culture that enables the company to win initial customers should bear in mind the following dos and don'ts:

- **Do**
  - Choose values that are consistent with the CEO's beliefs and that will attract and motivate talented employees to get and keep customers.
  - Articulate the values and tell stories that engage employees.
  - Act in ways the help employees see that they should embody the values.
- **Don't**
  - Assume all employees understand the culture.
  - Put primary emphasis on achieving quarterly sales goals, rather than articulating values.

Stage 2: Building a Scalable Business Model

As a startup seeks to build a scalable business model, it hires many new people to lead specific functions and make processes more efficient and predictable. Those functional leaders, and the people they hire, are unlikely to have a deep understanding of the company's culture. Therefore, the CEO should lead regular company meetings to articulate the culture and publicly recognize people who embody it. Moreover, at this stage, the CEO should oversee the creation of processes to ensure that the company's values are used in hiring, promoting, and letting people go. The cases that follow highlight successful and less successful handling of the challenges a CEO must overcome to create culture at the second stage of scaling.

Success Case Study: ezCater's Culture Helps Propel It to $700 Million Valuation

Introduction

Culture can help a startup to build a scalable business model. That's because the right culture can attract talented people who are close to the specific operational challenges that must be solved to make the company's processes more efficient. If the culture also encourages those people to think of solutions, try them, and make them better, then the company will become more efficient and effective as it grows. This comes to mind in considering ezCater "the only nationwide marketplace for the $21 billion business catering market. ezCater's online ordering, on-time ratings and reviews, and award-winning, 5-star customer service connect businesspeople to reliable catering for any meeting, anywhere in the United States." Started in 2007, ezCater raised $35 million in January 2017 from ICONIQ Capital, the family office and venture firm associated with Silicon Valley billionaires like Mark Zuckerberg, and Insight Venture Partners—bringing its total capital raised to $70 million. In June 2018, ezCater raised another $100 million, at a $700 million valuation, led by Wellington Management Company and its previous investors. At the time of that financing, ezCater had 60,000 restaurant partners and 470 employees, including 50 in its Denver, Colorado office. In July 2018, ezCater expanded internationally through the acquisition of Paris-based GoCater, which had an estimated 200 catering partners in France and Germany.

ezCater's CEO, Stefania Mallett, held a bachelor's and master's degrees in Electrical Engineering and Computer Science from MIT. Mallett cofounded ezCater after she and her partner, Briscoe Rodgers, who she referred to as "the idea guy," saw an opportunity to improve how business catering was done while running a previous company, PreferredTime, that helped get enterprise sales people in front of customers. "We noticed that the sales people needed to bring food into meetings and it was not enough to bring food in just for the individuals they were meeting with. Sales people needed to bring food for everybody," said Mallett. They built ezCater through systems that make life easier for its stakeholders. As she explained, "I learned about how to use technology to deliver great service to employees, vendors, and customers." They decided that they would build ezCater to make that process easier. Mallett credited MIT for giving her a can-do attitude, which she looked for in people that she hired. As she said, "My parents had four kids, all of whom went to hotshot schools. When my parents called MIT, they got a very different attitude than they did from the other schools. MIT exuded the feeling that you are a good person and there is probably something we can do here to work out whatever problem we may face."

Case Scenario

Culture was an important part of ezCater's success because it influenced how it treated customers, how its employees worked, and how it improved in response to feedback. In April 2018, Mallet sounded happy about ezCater's progress. As she said, "We're doing ridiculously well. We're doing another capital raise and just got our first term sheet; we're expecting a couple more on April 17. We have happy people, customers, and restaurants." She described the steps in ezCater's scaling process based on the number of management layers, "You start off with the founders doing everything; then you hire managers who are responsible for a process; then you hire managers of managers." EzCater differentiated and then integrated these functional teams. As she explained, "When we first got started, the people who signed up the restaurants on ezCater also entered information about their catering menus and delivery hours into our system. We realized that we should have a dedicated content team that would care about the accuracy and formatting of how the details were entered into our system and free up the sales people to bring in more new restaurants." ezCater then broke down the content task into smaller parts. As she said, "Then we found that our content people preferred to focus on specific types of restaurants such as Mexican or Thai and some people liked to enter text while others wanted to focus on photos. For a while, people wanted to split up data entry and quality control. Now everybody does some data entry and some quality control. The teams are always soliciting feedback from customers. The most important thing is that the team owns the process and decides how to make it better."

A culture that promotes growth values people who are passionate about inventing new products that customers are eager to buy and thereafter gives those customers excellent service so they keep buying over a long period of time. If the people love working for the company and the customers love its products and services, then the customers become its most compelling evangelists. ezCater's culture was based on the "growth mindset" idea that Mallet learned from Eve Grodnitzky. As Mallett said, "My cofounder and I are tinkerers. We ask, 'Can we make it go faster?' We come up with hypotheses, build a model, try it, track it, and learn from what works and what doesn't. We try to stay ahead of the curve rather than lag it. This growth mindset is at all levels of the company and it means that everyone shares responsibility for achieving growth." And ezCater's pursuit of growth was embedded in the way it set goals and held people accountable for achieving them. This was a complex challenge because it was far more difficult for an HR leader to identify what he could do to boost revenue growth than it was for an account executive with a specific sales quota. ezCater aspired to make everyone accountable for achieving the company's goals. As Mallett explained, "We have six company goals such as grow, uncover a new sales channel, and handle 500 employees by year end. Each department takes responsibility and breaks them down into smaller pieces. We push authority, responsibility, and reporting as far down as possible. We take a cue from the Japanese auto industry where anyone can stop the line if they see a problem."

Location also helped the company attract talent that fit within its culture. ezCater was located in Boston's Downtown Crossing, which offered startups a relatively low rent and proximity to public transportation, making the location a talent magnet. Indeed, changes in the economics of startups made ezCater's location very supportive of its growth. As Mallett explained, "It used to be that you needed to build your own server farms, which meant higher capital expenditures and more people. But thanks to the cloud, we don't need those costs. We are a software-enabled service and we need people who can talk to humans. There are a lot of good people here who are educated, either with or without degrees. And they bring their brains and their hearts to work."

Case Analysis

ezCater appeared to have taken its time to build a scalable business model and raised a significant amount of capital to boost its revenues to the point where it might be able to go public. While ezCater was in no hurry to get there, it appeared to have a clear idea of how it would be able to scale and was not being pushed by investor pressure to which other companies might succumb. In so doing, ezCater exemplifies five principles of creating a culture that supports a scalable business model:

- Adopt a clear mental model of how the company must operate to grow.

- Communicate that mental model to current and potential employees.

- Link that mental model to how operations will make partners, customers, and employees better off.

- Hire people with the traits needed to work effectively in such a culture.

- Empower teams closest to customers and partners to improve operations.

Less Successful Case Study: Threat Stack Grows but Leaves Unhappy Employees in Its Wake

Introduction

Startups with ineffective cultures may grow, but if their cultures contribute to high turnover and disaffected employees, they will struggle to create a scalable business model. And unless the company is growing so fast that investors are willing to fund its losses, the company will be in danger of bleeding out. This comes to mind in considering Boston-based Threat Stack, a cloud security service provider you first encountered in Chapter 2.

Case Scenario

CEO Brian Ahern said that Threat Stack's culture would support its growth ambitions, but by 2018, there were disquieting rumbles from its workforce. "We have four operating principles: no egos, no assholes (because teamwork matters), achievement vs. entitlement (everyone must earn their place in the company), raving vs. raging customers (make customers happy), and conviction for the mission (work hard)." Indeed, in June 2016, Threat Stack placed in the top five of Boston Business Journal's Best Places to Work in the extra small company category. Companies were selected by using employee engagement surveys that evaluated workplace satisfaction, peer relationships, and career opportunities. And Threat Stack was "recognized for its focus on fostering a fast-paced and rewarding work environment, its customer-centric approach, and commitment to giving back to the Boston tech community." Ahern said, "We're proud of our passionate, hardworking team committed to delivering the most reliable cloud security service to our customers and enabling quicker time to detection and resolution."

But there seemed to be some dissonance between the upbeat culture and the way employees felt. By 2018, anonymous employee comments on Glassdoor suggested that employees were not happy. Moreover, Threat Stack's responses on Glassdoor appeared to sidestep solutions to the problems raised by these employees. For example, one full-time employee who liked the office location and the catered lunches was disturbed by executives' lack of experience and widespread failure to fulfill compensation promises to employees. Another employee who also liked the location and the free lunches said, "[Threat Stack is] cheap, political, and on the decline. Customers and employees are both unhappy. Unfortunately, those great benefits are needed to compensate for the stress of working in this toxic environment. New upper leadership is needed. Until then, good luck!" A former employee wrote, "They keep changing direction, people are afraid for their jobs but [Threat Stack] can't seem to hire anyone without an eight-month process that goes nowhere. [Threat Stack seems] to lie to new employees and applicants. I had to leave for a company that doesn't demean you. Stop being so high in the cloud and listen to your employees." Threat Stack responded with what sounded to me like pablum: "Our employees are our greatest asset and we value and listen to their feedback." As we saw in Chapter 2, Threat Stack decided to lay off about 15 of its people in October 2018 with hopes of hiring more people in other areas to replace them.

Case Analysis

Threat Stack appeared to be less effective at integrating its culture with the other scaling levers. Its rapid growth rates suggested that it was taking market share from other companies and was selling aggressively. And the way Ahern articulated Threat Stack's values, with the emphasis on working hard and shunning a sense of employee entitlement, was somewhat consistent with the Glassdoor comments. However, other employee comments suggested that Threat Stack was having difficulty hiring the right people, both in executive and individual contributor roles. Perhaps Ahern's lack of prior experience building a scalable business model for a venture-backed company was reflected in employee comments about inexperienced executives, unkept promises to employees, and a lack of product innovation. If I were an investor in Threat Stack I would investigate those employee comments objectively and try to find out whether they reflect reality and if so, whether Ahern was the right person to repair the problems they described.

Principles

Founders seeking to create a culture that will help a company to build a scalable business model should bear in mind the following dos and don'ts:

- **Do**
    - Articulate the right values, ones that harness employee initiative to listen to customers and solve their problems quickly and effectively.
    - Model the company's values so employees will want to do the same.
    - Use the values to hire, promote, and let people go.
    - Communicate the values regularly and reward people who embody them.
    - Change the values if they make it more difficult for the company to achieve its goals.

- **Don't**
    - Assume everyone implicitly understands the culture.
    - Articulate values and act in ways that contradict the values.
    - Hire and promote people who get results regardless of whether they act according to the values.
    - Ignore the dissonance created in the minds of employees and customers caused by the difference between values and executive action.

Stage 3: Sprinting to Liquidity

In the sprint to liquidity, a company's culture should be harnessed to ease the company's rapid expansion. To that end, the CEO should be certain to do the following:

- **Hire executives who understand the culture.** Since the CEO will not be in direct contact with managers, top functional executives and newly-hired country general managers must embody the company's culture and use it to hire, promote, and let go the people who report to them.

- **Invest 20% of the CEO's time in bolstering the culture.** The CEO should devote considerable time through regular meetings with executives and employees to make the culture clear to everyone and to recognize and reward people who embody the company's values.

- **Respond effectively to mismatches between culture and action.** The CEO should speak with employees directly to identify mismatches between culture and the way people behave. The CEO must identify the reasons for the mismatch and make changes to people and/or processes to bring peoples' conduct back into alignment with the company's values.

The cases that follow highlight successful and less successful handling of the challenges such a CEO must overcome.

Success Case Study: $200 Million Capital Raise and Culture of Customer Loyalty Propels CrowdStrike to IPO

Introduction

The formula for reaching the sprinting to liquidity stage is simple to articulate: find customer pain, build a product that relieves that pain better than anyone else in the market, create a business model that lets you grow quickly and without spending too much money, and go public once you reach $100 million in revenue. The glue that holds together a company that does these things is a culture of customer loyalty—one that attracts and motivates people to win new customers and keep them buying from the company. Such loyalty enables the company to grow without spending too much on sales and marketing since customers are happy to recommend the company to other potential customers.

This comes to mind in considering Sunnyvale, California-based provider of a cloud-based service that used "AI- and (Indicator-of-Attack) IOA-based threat prevention to stop known and unknown threats in real time." CrowdStrike was started in 2011 with two cofounders and 12 members of the launch team. It started generating revenue in 2013; by July 2018, it had 1,200 people, the $100 million in revenue needed to go public, and triple digit growth. In the year ending June 2018, CrowdStrike enjoyed 167% growth in the number of subscription customers, 172% growth in new subscription bookings annual contract value, and 140% growth in annual recurring revenue. In June 2018, CrowdStrike raised a $200 million Series E round, led by General Atlantic, Accel, and IVP, with participation from March Capital and CapitalG, valuing the company at "over $3 billion."

CrowdStrike's CEO, George Kurtz, had an excellent background to prepare him to run this company and the success of the company was recognized by analysts. As he explained in a July 2018 interview, "I started as a CPA at Price Waterhouse and wrote a best-selling book about Internet security, *Hacking Exposed: Network Security Secrets & Solutions.* I started FoundStone in late 1999 and sold it to McAfee (for $86 million) in 2004. I was a general manager at McAfee for seven years and was asked three times to be Chief Technology Officer, which I ultimately accepted. In 2011, I assembled a team to start CrowdStrike, intending to provide endpoint security via the cloud."

Case Scenario

CrowdStrike pursued an effective approach to making its business model scalable. As Kurtz explained, "We are driving efficiency as we scale. We do inside sales, which is triggered by potential users downloading the software and trying the product out. We have the highest retention rate and for every dollar we sell, we have 130% upsell [meaning existing customers buy more]." And CrowdStrike changed its organization structure as it grew. "In phase one, we were in evangelical selling mode: everyone believed in the mission and did many jobs. In the second phase, we had the technology and we were growing. Not everyone from phase one was comfortable in phase two so we respectfully changed their roles. And in the third phase, where we are now, we are coin-operated: wash, rinse, repeat on the way to becoming a public company. We have functional leaders in marketing, sales, support, and others who have prior experience taking a company public. And the functions are matrixing with our regional general managers," Kurtz said.

Culture played a powerful role in helping CrowdStrike to grow. As Kurtz explained, "We've been recognized for our culture by Fortune. [In 2017, Fortune selected CrowdStrike as a Best Medium Company in Which to Work. Fortune quoted an employee as saying, "Everyone I speak to is so much more intelligent than I am. At my old company I was the smartest person in the room. Here I feel there is so much to learn because of the quality of the people. The work the company does is very interesting and feels important. I've never worked at a place that is part of the news in a positive and impactful way (following the Democratic National Committee breach), and that feels great when talking to friends and family about what you do."] We encourage people to believe in the mission: we help protect our customers from the bad guys. We're revolutionizing security and making a difference. We created a culture team of our spiritual leaders who know everyone in the company and talk about how we are operating according to our values. Customer success is important to us and we give them white glove treatment. Gartner rates us 4.85 out of 5 on customer satisfaction."

Case Analysis

CrowdStrike was prevailing in a highly competitive industry. Its growth, scale, and ability to raise capital were linked to the way the company managed its culture as it sprinted to liquidity. CrowdStrike's success helped highlight three principles of creating culture:

- Choose a mission that attracts talent and inspires people.

- Encourage employees to offer excellent service so customers are highly satisfied.

- Create formal processes, such as creating a team of culture carriers to link values to actions.

Less Successful Case Study: Copper Suffers Some Growing Pains As It Wins 60% of Its Bids Against Salesforce

Introduction

If a company offers a product that customers value, it can keep growing despite the growing pains that accompany the sprint to liquidity. One of the growing pains is the mismatch between people who have been at the company for a long time and the new executive team that the CEO hires to prepare the company for an initial public offering. While CEOs at this scaling stage often try to hire functional executives who have succeeded in other well-known companies, there is a danger that the CEO will weight their previous achievements more highly than their cultural fit. At the same time, these new executives are likely to hire people who have helped them succeed in the past, and that is likely to result in the departure of some of the people who worked there before. This comes to mind in considering Copper (known as ProsperWorks before a 2018 name change), a San Francisco-based customer relationship management (CRM) company founded in 2013 with five employees. Copper supplied "CRM solutions for companies that use Google applications." By August 2018, Copper had raised a total of $87 million, employed over 200 people, and served 10,000 customers as it aimed at generating $100 million in annual recurring revenues (ARR) by the end of 2018. Copper competed in the small (under 100 employees) and medium-sized (100 to 1,000 employees) business market segments (30% to 40% of the CRM market) and said it prevailed over Salesforce in competitive bids. As CEO Jon Lee explained in an August 2018 interview, "We beat Salesforce in 60% to 70% of the customer face-offs and 40% of our customers formerly used Salesforce. Salesforce is abandoning its SMB customers to focus on the large enterprise, so it can increase sales from $12 billion to $20 billion."

Lee was a banker and big company executive before starting three companies, two of which were acquired. Lee, who grew up in a Cupertino, Calif. family that fought about money, graduated from Berkeley. He had stints in banking at Merrill Lynch and running international business operations for Yahoo. Once he made some money (starting at 26, he founded three companies, selling the first to Epic Media Group and the second to Zynga), he realized that there ought to be more to life than that. After some "sprints in spiritual discovery" he realized that his purpose "was to serve others. I had talent and experience building software companies and I had a deep empathy to help other entrepreneurs like myself build game-changing companies and bring prosperity to their employees and the world at large." Copper changed its name from ProsperWorks because people could not remember it and Copper implies "a conductor of relationships," according to Lee.

Case Scenario

Copper believed that it offered customers a better deal than Salesforce. For starters, Lee argued that many CRM implementations fail. "Customer relationships are the lifeblood of their business. CRM naturally piqued my interest. As I did more research, I was shocked to read in a Forrester report that in this massive $42 billion market, nearly half of CRM implementations were considered failures." And the reason Lee found is that people don't use CRM. "As I dug deeper, the problem was very simple: users don't want to use CRM. It didn't help sales reps sell, it required too much data entry, and it wasn't integrated with the modern tools that sales reps use to communicate with and do work for customers. As a result, adoption was poor, leaving management without data-driven answers to key questions that drive a business," he said. Customers chose Copper because it took less time to install, cost less money, and delivered more value than Salesforce's product. As Lee said, "When you buy Salesforce, you have to pay a consultant three to four times the license value to implement it. That can take six to eight months. And users have to spend a day a week entering data, which few people do." Customers wanted faster time-to-value, which Copper provided. "Copper takes as little as 10 hours and at most a few weeks to install, and since our solution is integrated into email, chat, and other communication tools, users do not have to enter data to get value. We designed the product for self-service, so IT professionals do not need to get involved," he said.

Culture was important to Copper's growth and many employees were happy to work there, but some employees saw gaps between the culture and the conduct of the company's leaders. As Lee said, "We value scrappiness, hard work, and innovation. We encourage people to be ambitious, not to fear failure, to treat the customer like a friend and the team like a family. We want to be great at giving and receiving feedback. And at our biweekly meetings, in which we review the team's accomplishments, we celebrate and reward individuals who live our values." An anonymous full-time employee who had been working at the company for over a year in July 2018 said, "Tons of truly great people work here. The overall vision is sound, which makes its flawed execution even more frustrating. Disorganization abounds across all sectors of the company. A frenzied approach to setting goals and tackling initiatives leads to lots of motion but little tangible success. The loudest and most arrogant voices get the most attention and clumsily set the pace for the rest. Burnout has set in across the entire company. Both long-term employees and even some fresh faces are already departing or questioning their future with this company. The only people remaining are the toxic ones, the ones with some optimism left to spend, or the people who have been caught off guard by just how misaligned their perceptions were with the reality of the situation." To his credit, Lee responded to this comment, encouraging the employee to balance work and personal life and to participate with management in a process of addressing the problems cited in the comments.

Another employee cited a deeper problem, suggesting Copper's product was difficult to sell and that its CEO was not hiring the right people. According to the employee, "The product used to have an edge, which is gone now due to a lack of strategy. The CEO is incompetent. He doesn't know how to lead the company to the next stage and is in over his head hiring the wrong people. He hires people that want to bring in their own people, so the company becomes a revolving door for the new people of the new bad leaders the CEO hires. If you are joining in sales, know it's very difficult to meet your quota. It just doesn't sell." Lee responded to this comment by citing Copper's 15 months of consistently exceeding sales quotas, sympathy for the employee's challenges in meeting the quotas, and pride in the quality of Copper's newly hired team, which included, "Our CPO ran product for Service Cloud at Salesforce. Our CMO was CMO at Dialpad and SVP at Zuora and NetSuite. Our Emerging Small Business leader did the same at Zendesk. And our Partnerships lead ran Channel for Box. Each was attracted to the tremendous growth and potential of Copper, but most importantly, the opportunity to help accelerate the incredible team already in place. There is no revolving door. We have grown our headcount by more than 40% through June 2018 while our Regrettable Attrition Rate is less than 2%." Lee concluded by encouraging the employee to bring up these issues with their manager.

Copper was not living for an IPO but viewed funding rounds as ways to achieve its purpose of helping customers build their business through relationships. "If we get 1% of a $52 billion market, that's a $7.5 billion public company," said Lee.

Case Analysis

In July 2018, Copper was growing rapidly but also appeared to be suffering from some growing pains. It seemed possible that the employee dissatisfaction cited in the case would be temporary as newly hired functional executives got their footing and helped the company sprint to liquidity. It was also possible that the disruption of organizational and cultural change would knock Copper off its rapid growth trajectory.

Principles

Founders seeking to create a culture that helps a company sprint to liquidity should bear in mind the following dos and don'ts:

- **Do**
    - Articulate culture values clearly and often.
    - Use values to hire, promote, and let people go.
    - Hire executives with prior experience sprinting to liquidity who fit the culture.
    - Create formal processes to communicate culture and reward those who act in ways consistent with its values.

- **Don't**
    - Reward rapid sales growth that threatens the culture.
    - Hire executives with brand-name experience who do not fit the culture.
    - Give new executives unfettered power to replace people who report to them.

Stage 4: Running the Marathon

Once a company is publicly traded, its culture is likely to depend even more heavily on its CEO. If the CEO is the founder and the company continues to grow rapidly after going public, then the company's culture is likely to be deeply ingrained into its organization and processes. If the CEO is the founder but the company is struggling, then unless the CEO has voting control, the board may find a new leader who changes the culture. Moreover, since most public companies are not led by their founder, the CEO who steps in will need to assess the company's culture and decide whether and how to change it. To assess whether to change the culture, a new CEO should ask the following questions:

- **Why did the previous CEO depart?** If the previous CEO was forced out due to ethical or legal problems, then the incoming CEO will need to confront the culture left by the predecessor and invest considerable time to fix it. If the CEO left on good terms and the company was doing well, then the incoming CEO may investigate the strengths and weaknesses of the culture and perhaps move slowly to make any improvements discovered.

- **Is the company growing faster than its industry?** If the company is growing more slowly than the industry, a new CEO will want to investigate the causes of its lagging market position. If the investigation reveals that the culture does not focus sufficiently on delivering great products and excellent service, the CEO should change the company's culture to boost growth. If the company is already growing faster than the industry, the CEO should investigate whether the culture is supporting that growth in a sustainable manner and, if so, take steps to preserve the culture.

- **Is the company financially strong?** An incoming CEO should be concerned if the company is not generating positive cash flow or has borrowed too much money. If the company is financially vulnerable, an incoming CEO ought to move quickly to cut costs and reduce debt to shore up the company's finances. Moreover, the CEO should also investigate whether the company's culture has too lax an attitude towards spending extravagantly or borrowing to cover cash shortfalls. If so, the CEO should change the culture of profligacy and tighten up its spending and borrowing practices.

- **Do customers enjoy doing business with the company and keep buying?** If customers are leaving the company or not buying more, an incoming CEO must investigate the reasons and repair them. If the company's culture does not place sufficient emphasis on product innovation and excellent service, the incoming CEO must change the company's culture accordingly.

- **Is the company attracting and retaining top talent?** If the company is unable to attract top talent and is suffering high amounts of unwanted turnover, then the incoming CEO should determine the primary causes of these problems. If culture is the root cause, then the CEO should find out what aspects of the culture need to be changed. The CEO should also fix other sources of the problem, such as abusive executives, uncompetitive products, or employee compensation. If the company already excels at attracting and retaining top talent, the CEO should make sure to understand what aspects of the culture are supporting these positive trends and preserve these cultural strengths.

The cases that follow highlight successful and less successful cultures for running the marathon.

Success Case Study: Amazon's Culture Helps It Keep Its Lead in the $180 Billion Cloud

Introduction

For at least a decade after its 1994 founding, Amazon grew but was often chided for its lack of profitability. So, it came as a pleasant surprise to investors when Amazon first began to report the results of its AWS cloud services unit, which was growing rapidly and earning a substantial profit. Amazon's ability to create the cloud industry and maintain a dominant position reflects its culture, the people it hires, and their ability to innovate effectively and quickly to stay ahead of evolving customer needs. What does it take to create a new industry and keep the lead in the face of formidable competitors? The formula is easy to describe and hard to do:

1. **Visionary leadership:** Companies that create industries are led by CEOs with the right vision for how the future will evolve and what it would take to win there.

2. **Deep insight into customer needs:** Companies that turn the vision into a real business must have a deep understanding of what customers need and which of those needs is most important and widely shared.

3. **Superior technology and processes:** To take the lead and stay ahead, such companies must have better technology, talent, and business processes than their rivals, so they can build and service products that meet those customer needs more quickly than rivals.

One such case was the $180 billion cloud services industry which Amazon created and led as of 2018. According to Synergy Research, "The cloud incorporated six key cloud services and infrastructure market segments, which totaled $180 billion, growing at 24% in the year ending September 2017." Amazon created this market in 2006 and by August 2018 was still in the lead. AWS's 34% cloud infrastructure market share was way ahead of Microsoft Azure's 14% in the second quarter of 2018, according to Synergy, which found that Microsoft gained "3 percentage points of market share" in the year ending June 2018. Amazon painted a clearer picture of its cloud success than did Microsoft that quarter. Amazon reported a 49% pop in cloud revenue to $6.11 billion, which was a leading contributor to its $2.53 billion in total net income. While Microsoft did not disclose its Azure revenues, it said they grew 89%.

Case Scenario

Five competitive advantages kept AWS ahead in the cloud, and each of these advantages sprang from its culture of giving customers great value and excellent service. First, Amazon did what Silicon Valley investors call "eating your own dog food," which means Amazon used the product it was selling to customers. Their logic was that if a company is trying to build a new industry, it helps if the company is a successful pioneer who can create new opportunities and threats for everyone else. Leadership in that new industry forces such a company to solve a new set of problems just to keep its core business going. If a company can do that well, as Amazon did when it built and refined its systems for operating an e-commerce business at scale, it will be in a strong position to sell its solution to other companies. Since Amazon.com launched its online book selling service in 1994, it needed a way to take and fulfill customer orders. Over the ensuing years, companies came to Amazon to ask how they could use Amazon's back office systems to operate their online businesses, Jeff Barr, AWS chief evangelist, explained in July 2018 interview. By that point, Amazon believed that it excelled at "operating massive scale technology infrastructure and datacenters." In 2006, Amazon decided to "take it out to other businesses," he said, "supplying web services to a new customer segment: developers and businesses. We had relationships with developers and put some e-commerce APIs out there. We saw it as a business, so we supplied pricing and documentation. They would find use cases and email us, 'Look what I built.'" When Amazon started selling AWS, it knew that the service worked from its own experience.

Amazon also hired hundreds of people with potential to be entrepreneurs and put them in charge of slices of its AWS business. As I argued in my 1997 book, The Technology Leaders, a company's ability to hire and motivate entrepreneurial leaders confers a huge advantage over rivals who can't pull it off. After all, if all decisions must be made by the CEO, those decisions will take too long, and sometimes the CEO who makes those decisions will be wrong. With AWS growing a multi-billion-dollar business, it was a target for rivals like Microsoft, Google, and others. And Amazon CEO Jeff Bezos was too busy with other responsibilities to keep on top of the competitive dynamics in each of the specific service categories that made up AWS. Amazon solved this problem by hiring CEO-like people (Amazon called them builders) to take responsibility for creating and leading each of AWS's service categories. "On our development team we hire hundreds of builders. They each own their own destiny. We show them an opportunity and they pick it up, study it, and build a business around it," said Barr. The idea of attracting great talent and giving them a chance to build a business with fresh eyes springs directly from Jeff Bezos's Day One philosophy.

Inherent in Amazon's culture was the idea that innovation that springs from the mind of engineers is not what matters; instead, Amazon believed it was better to listen to customers and build what they needed quickly. Amazon did not want to pay for people in R&D to work on their favorite ideas and take a chance that customers might not buy the resulting products. Instead, Amazon sought out new product ideas by observing customers. To that end, Amazon spent time with customers, figured out which customer needs were worth turning into a product, launched prototypes of those quickly, and refined them based on customer feedback. Listening to customers and implementing products with the most business value were key to AWS's ability to stay in the lead. As Barr explained, "In the time I spend at our executive briefing center, I listen to customers quietly with a pad and pen and get the feedback to our service teams. We dive deep and try to understand their challenges. We don't implement every feature they ask for; we pick the ones with the most business value. We get something out there and iterate based on their feedback. As Jeff Bezos says, 'Our customers are delightfully dissatisfied; they always want something more.'" Amazon's culture of trying to satisfy customers helped AWS to keep customers happy. In July 2018, Al Smith, Chief Technology Officer of iCIMs, a recruiting software company that worked with AWS and Azure, said, "We work with Microsoft, which is making investments to improve, but Azure works with customers through channels. AWS does it better, faster, and more flexibly. Amazon's direct [go-to-market strategy] makes it easier for me to get direct access to its leaders and roadmaps, it introduces new products faster, it gives me support and training, and I know that what it provides has been tested based on global investments." When it comes to growth, Amazon believed that focusing on customers was more productive than on competitors. "We do have a competitive analysis group, but the resources we focus on customers are 10 times more than those allocated to competitors," said Barr.

Another key aspect of Amazon's culture was the idea that if you want people to produce results, you should measure how they're doing and ask them to explain what they will do if they come up short. To that end, Amazon kept close tabs on weekly results. As Barr explained, "We review thousands of metrics during our weekly business reviews. To keep our business growing [it was up 49% last quarter], we need our general managers to meet demanding weekly goals. If they do not meet a goal, the general managers must explain to [AWS head] Andy Jassy why and what they are doing to get back on track." And the value that Amazon placed on learning from experience boosted AWS's profitability even as it cut prices. "As we grow and get operational experience, we apply the lessons to get more cost-efficient. We speed up how we go from raw land to an operating data center and get better terms from suppliers," Barr said. AWS's attention to customers and costs seemed to be contributing to longer-term contracts and a larger backlog. AWS's second quarter backlog, the value of its signed contracts, was up 29% from the first quarter to $16 billion while the average length of those contracts rose from 3.2 years to 3.5 years, according to Amazon's June 2018 quarterly report.

Case Analysis

In 2018, Amazon was the most successful publicly-traded company that was still being run by its founder. To be sure, there was plenty of reporting on how difficult some found it to work there. Yet its ability to keep growing at over 20% a year as it surpassed $200 billion in revenue suggested strongly that Amazon's culture was extremely effective at turning its values into action. In so doing, it highlighted five important principles of creating a culture for running the marathon:

- Customer-focused values can be the basis for sustained growth at scale.

- Culture should replace complacency with a constant search for giving customers more value for their money.

- The CEO must model the culture and use powerful symbols to make core values unforgettable and easy to understand.

- The company must hire and promote individuals who embody the culture.

- Managers must use frequent quantitative measurement to identify and solve problems, boost customer satisfaction, and accelerate revenue growth.

Less Successful Case Study: Nutanix Grows Fast After IPO but the Path to Profitability Remains Elusive

Introduction

A company that grows rapidly, goes public, and enjoys a rapid increase in its stock price can't be considered unsuccessful. But if it suffers considerable turnover of its top talent and keeps losing money, what would happen to the company if investors suddenly decided that the company was overvalued because it had no path to profitability? This comes to mind in considering San Jose, California-based hyperconverged systems-provider Nutanix, which went public in 2016 and by August 2018 had enjoyed a 217% increase in its stock price to a stock market capitalization of $8.7 billion.

Hyperconverged systems, which combined the functions of as many as 12 different data storage and retrieval devices into one, represented a modest market that was growing rapidly. According to IDC, such systems grew 64.3% to $3.7 billion in 2017, accounting for 34% of the total converged systems market. Nutanix was founded in 2009 by a talented collection of entrepreneurs: Dheeraj Pandey (who was Nutanix's CEO), Ajeet Singh (who founded ThoughtSpot and in August 2018 hired Nutanix's president to join as CEO; Pandey congratulated Singh, saying he considered him a Nutanix founder), and Mohit Aron (who left to start Cohesity years before the IPO). Nutanix raised nearly $238 million in private capital before going public on September 30, 2016 at $16 a share. Nutanix enjoyed expectations-beating revenue growth but lost money. For its 2018 third quarter ending in April, Nutanix reported a 41% increase in revenues to almost $290 million—nearly $10 million more than analysts expected—while reporting a loss of nearly $86 million.

Case Scenario

Nutanix had many ideas about running its business, which sounded intriguing, but the company's failure to earn a profit raised questions about whether Pandey was ahead of the crowd in its thinking or attempting to mesmerize investors and others with a reality distortion field. To be fair, Nutanix was trying to become profitable. For example, its first quarter 2018 gross margin increased from 59.5% to 67% due to a shift to a software-based business and away from a hybrid of selling hardware and software. However, Nutanix believed that investors should not look at the company using traditional variables such as profitability. Instead, it wanted them to recognize that there is a tradeoff between growth and profitability. And as Pandey explained in an August 2018 interview, Nutanix had found the right balance between the two as evidenced by what he called, "the rule of 40: the revenue growth rate plus free cash flow as a percent of revenue should be at least 40." And Nutanix said it passed that test with flying colors by achieving a ratio well above 40. The problem was that Nutanix's ratio of 49 could only be achieved by assuming away the reality that it still obtained 22% of its revenue from less profitable hardware. In August 2018, Shane Xie, Manager, Investor Relations at Nutanix told me, "Nutanix looks at software and support (not all revenue) because we are removing hardware from the business as we transition to a software-centric model."

Pandey was quite a prolific management theorist. For example, he believed that it was better to pay attention to what he called "Main Street," Nutanix's customers and employees, than to focus exclusively on "Wall Street." He also said Nutanix had a strong culture. As Pandey explained, "We have 3,700 or 3,800 employees as of the second quarter. And we operate based on the 4Hs: Hungry, Humble, and Honest, with Heart." The culture was important for his relationship with Main Street. As he said, "When you must stay connected to Main Street, you must be humble, you have to be hungry, and you have to be paranoid and be very honest about things. Because Main Street doesn't give a hoot about what your stock price is. It is demanding more authenticity from itself; from CEO down, we are having to think about the consumer all the time. That is a great development for our industry."

The role of the CEO at Nutanix changed over the years, as did its culture. "In year one, I wrote 20,000 lines of code to get the product out the door. In year 2, I was acting as the VP of Engineering and writing code, and in year 3, I was acting more like a CEO—as a generalist. Even today part of my role is as a product manager and architect. But I have learned how to speak the language of marketers, sales, and finance. You have to speak their language [to lead them]," Pandey said. He was acutely conscious of the dangers of complacency that often accompany success. As he said, "Bain & Co. has an 18-minute video on the Founder's Mentality, which is amazingly instructive. When companies start acting like incumbents, they stop growing. The paradox of growth is that growth creates complexity which kills growth. We always think of it being Day 1; we keep our scrappiness. We are in 55 to 60 countries and we have 50 to 100 people in hubs, so we can be global and act local." And Pandey was working to make culture even more pervasive at Nutanix. "We are launching the 12 cultural principles to put the 4Hs into action. We will put them in the hallways and meeting rooms. Even though I cannot physically be in every room, with these principles I will be there mentally. These principles will help us fight cognitive biases, drive decisions, and resolve conflicts," he said.

Nutanix also tried to balance what Pandey called its "heart" and "brain." As he said, "Engineering and the product are the heart of the company. All the other functions, such as customer success, are the brain. Our goal is to earn a high net promoter score from our customers [a measure of how eager customers are to recommend the company to others]. We don't sell and run; we sell and stay." Pandey believed such a balance was particularly important when innovating. As he said, "People love new things (they're neophilic) and they don't love new things (neophobic). For example, Google Glass failed because it was not socially acceptable to record a video of the person you were talking to. To find the right balance, we build products that are Most Advanced Yet Acceptable (MAYA). We also apply this principle to customer experience, organizational design, and business design."

Nutanix's organization pushed responsibility for individual services down to general managers. "Our products support 10,000 customers and products get very complicated. So, we break the products down into smaller pieces; we call them micro-services. We have general managers who oversee service level agreements, product design, and go-to-market [functions such as marketing and sales]. Otherwise it becomes a hairball. We believe in scale out; we have these general managers all over—in Bangalore, Durham, and Seattle. Eventually it all comes together again, with the customer being our true North," Pandey said.

Case Analysis

Nutanix's value increased after it went public yet it lost money consistently, targeted a modestly-sized market, and suffered considerable turnover among members of its founding team. To be sure, those departing executives were mostly leaders of their own companies, which was a gain for them, although possibly a loss for Nutanix. Moreover, its management processes and organization were a hodgepodge of intriguing-sounding ideas, such as MAYA, heart and brain, Main Street and Wall Street, Rule of 40, and micro-service general managers. As of August 2018, questions remained: Would Pandey's ideas help were investors to decide they cared about growth *and* profitability? Was Nutanix on a path to rapid, profitable growth? If so, could it sustain its stock market momentum and become a large company that changed the world?

Principles

Founders seeking to raise capital to fuel the process of winning initial customers should bear in mind the following dos and don'ts:

- **Do**
    - Choose values that focus attention on creating ever-higher levels of customer value.
    - Build into the culture the assumption that the company must fight complacency to retain ever-dissatisfied customers.
    - Use powerful symbols to make core values unforgettable and easy to understand.
    - Hire and promote individuals who embody the culture.
    - Use frequent quantitative measurement to embed the culture in daily activities.
- **Don't**
    - Base values solely on investor-developed performance measures.
    - Hire functional executives with strong track records who do not fit with the company's values.
    - Behave in ways that undermine the values in the eyes of employees.
    - Assume that posting values in conference rooms and hallways will communicate the culture.

Creating Culture Success and Failure Principles

To create and sustain culture at each scaling stage, CEOs must follow the principles summarized in Table 4-1.

Table 4-1. Summary of Culture Creating Principles

Scaling Stage	Dos	Don'ts
1: Winning the first customer	Choose values that are consistent with the CEO's beliefs and that will attract and motivate talented employees to get and keep customers. Articulate the values and tell stories that engage employees. Act in ways that help employees see that they should embody the values.	Assume all employees understand the culture. Put primary emphasis on achieving quarterly sales goals, rather than articulating values.
2: Scaling the business model	*Same as Stage 1, plus* Use the values to hire, promote, and let people go. Communicate the values regularly and reward people who embody them. Change the values if they make it more difficult for the company to achieve its goals.	*Same as Stage 1, plus* Articulate values yet act in ways that contradict the values. Hire and promote people who get results regardless of whether they act according to the values. Ignore the dissonance created in the minds of employees and customers caused by the difference between values and executive action.
3: Sprinting to liquidity	*Same as Stage 2, plus* Hire executives with prior experience sprinting to liquidity who fit the culture.	*Same as Stage 2, plus* Give new executives unfettered power to replace people who report to them.
4: Running the marathon	*Same as Stage 3, plus* Build into the culture the assumption that the company must fight complacency to retain ever-dissatisfied customers. Use powerful symbols to make core values unforgettable and easy to understand. Use frequent quantitative measurement to embed the culture in daily activities.	*Same as Stage 3, plus* Base values solely on investor-developed performance measures. Behave in ways that undermine the values in the eyes of employees. Assume that posting values in conference rooms and hallways will communicate the culture.

Are You Doing Enough to Create Culture?

Creating culture is essential to extending the CEO's way of thinking and acting to sustain a startup's journey from idea to large company. If your culture enables the startup to attract and keep happy customers and hire and motivate top talent, with minimal unwanted turnover, then you are excelling at creating culture. Here are four questions that will help you know whether you are doing this properly:

- Have you articulated your startup's values?

- Are your startup's values consistent with your beliefs and what will attract and motivate employees to create products that customers love?

- Do you consistently behave in ways that embody your startup's culture?

- Do you use the startup's culture to hire, promote, and let people go?

Conclusion

Creating culture is an essential element of overcoming the hurdles needed to turn an idea into a large company. As we saw in this chapter, culture is at the core of many of the other scaling levers. For example, values shape the way a startup organizes its work; decides whom to hire, promote, and let go; measures performance; and creates processes for communicating as the company hires new people to support its growth. If your company can create a culture and keep enhancing and applying it effectively as the company grows, then it has a greater chance of realizing its mission. As a startup scales, it must pass a critical test of the effectiveness of its culture: the ability to redefine its job functions while reinforcing its core values, which we will examine in Chapter 5.

Redefining Job Functions

Imagine if a CEO could turn an idea into a large company without hiring anyone else. That lonely but economically tantalizing idea remains utterly out of reach, yet some startups have gotten close. For example, Instagram had 13 employees when Facebook acquired it for $1 billion in April 2012, a few weeks before its initial public offering. Instagram built an app that attracted 30 million users and a private market valuation of $500 million. Instagram's ability to create $77 million worth of value for each employee at the time of its acquisition—4.7 times more than Facebook's $16.6 million for each of its 30,275 employees— highlights a question of great interest to startup investors and the people in whom they invest: What is the purpose of hiring people and how can a founder manage those people in a way that maximizes the value of the firm? In the case of Instagram, its 13-person staff zoomed from the first to the third stage of scaling by building an app that sold itself to 30 million people without extensive sales or marketing. Most companies, especially ones that sell to businesses, can't skip directly from Stage 1 to Stage 3.

Why do most startups hire and how do they define jobs as they scale? Founders hire people because turning their idea into a large company means that work must be done and founders can't do all the work themselves. So, founders define jobs—their own and the ones that they want to fill. As we'll see in this chapter, the nature of those jobs changes as a startup advances through the four stages of scaling. In the first stage, a founder defines jobs more broadly,

© Peter S. Cohan 2019
P. S. Cohan, *Scaling Your Startup*, https://doi.org/10.1007/978-1-4842-4312-1_5

giving each employee the freedom within certain limits to do whatever they believe is needed to meet the goals set by the founder. For example, before a startup makes its first sale, a founder with outstanding product development skills may hire a sales cofounder who is charged with winning the first customers. To do that, the sales cofounder may do everything, such as helping the first customers get financing to buy the product, installing the product, and getting feedback on what is working well and what needs to be changed. However, as a startup enters scaling Stages 2 and 3, the CEO will split that sales cofounder's job into smaller pieces: the jobs of speaking with the media, creating advertisements, ranking sales leads, and working with partners will be assigned to a Chief Marketing Officer, who will in turn hire Vice Presidents to lead each of these more specific functions. The CEO will divide up the sales parts of the sales cofounder's job into parts (North American Sales, European Sales, Customer Success), each being done by Vice Presidents who report to a Chief Sales Officer.

This section of the book transitions from the mission and strategy layer, which I addressed in Chapters 2, 3, and 4, to the execution layer covered in the next four chapters. In the mission and strategy layer, founders describe the enduring purpose of their startup and create a culture to help achieve that purpose. In addition founders chart the strategy and raise the capital needed to finance it. The execution layer guides the CEO's actions to achieve the startup's growth goals. More specifically, as illustrated in Figure 5-1, it is the interaction between four scaling levers (holding people accountable; redefining jobs; hiring, promoting, and letting people go; and coordinating processes) that enables a company to master the four stages of scaling.

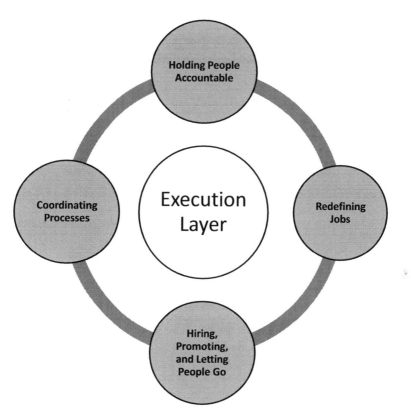

Figure 5-1. Execution layer: interaction of four scaling levers

Here's how CEOs should use these four levers to build a scalable business model:

- **Holding people accountable:** To build a scalable business model, CEOs must hold people accountable for keeping the cost of acquiring a customer well below the amount of revenue that customer generates during its relationship with the company (I will cover this topic in Chapter 7). Doing so means that companies must lower their sales, marketing, and other expenses as a percent of revenue as the company grows. It also means that the company must add new customers, make them enthusiastic about the company's products and service so they will keep buying, and encourage them to buy more.

- **Redefining jobs:** To meet these goals, the CEO must redefine jobs, specifically creating executive positions that will be responsible for key functions such as R&D, product management, sales, marketing, and service (addressed in this chapter). Reporting to each of these executives will be Vice Presidents or managers who run key parts of those functions. For example, the Chief Marketing Officer might oversee Vice Presidents for Public Relations, Sales Training, Event Management, and Distribution Partner Management. Defining more specialized roles facilitates greater efficiency.

- **Hiring, promoting, and letting people go:** To fill these roles, CEOs must decide whether they should hire people who have already scaled these functions successfully or promote current employees into those roles (this topic is discussed in Chapter 6). Moreover, the CEO must decide whether to let go people who have been in those roles before to make way for more qualified individuals.

- **Coordinating processes:** Finally, building a scalable business model depends on coordinating processes that enable specialized functions to work together as needed to achieve the goals the CEO sets (covered in Chapter 8). For example, to get new customers, marketing must work with sales to generate sales leads that help sales people to close deals. And to create loyal customers, sales and product management must listen to evolving customer needs to create new products and customer service must assure that customers perceive that they are benefiting significantly from using the ones that they've already purchased.

When it comes to redefining job functions, CEOs should the follow the steps outlined in Figure 5-2 as the company grows.

- **Identify the most basic jobs to be done.** When a company is started, its CEO must consider whether to hire cofounders. Cofounders create an executive team to do the jobs that the founder believes must be done to win its first customers. While the most basic jobs vary by startup, in general the other members of the founding team should excel at important tasks which the CEO does not do well. For example, a CEO who is great at selling and managing people should bring in a technical cofounder who manages engineers and listens to customers as the company cycles through building prototypes and improving them based on customer feedback. Conversely, a technical CEO should bring in cofounders with great sales and possibly management skills (if the CEO lacks them).

- **Fill those basic jobs with the best people available.** Having defined the key jobs needed to win the first customers, the CEO must find people to fill those roles. Ideally, a CEO should hire people who've excelled in those roles and worked well with the CEO in the past. First-time CEOs may have trouble hiring excellent people to do these jobs—and may have to bring in the best people willing to take them. At the first scaling stage, individuals may do many different jobs because the company lacks the resources to hire new people to do each of them. As the company scales, CEOs will need to weigh the tradeoffs between appointing proven performers who fit with the startup's culture and hiring an outsider who has previously done the job well at the startup's next scaling stage.

- **Assess how well the structure is working.** As a company starts trying to win its first customers, the CEO must assess some basic questions: Is the product prototype getting built quickly and well? Is the company developing relationships with customers who can help develop the product? If not, how should the company reorganize its work to complete the first stage? Often the CEO must wait until after raising capital before hiring better people to do the company's jobs, which should be easier to do once the company begins the second stage of scaling.

- **Redefine jobs that are not working well.** In the second stage of scaling, the CEO must rethink roles so the company does everything more efficiently and effectively. Jobs that were previously done in an ad hoc manner must be split into smaller pieces and filled by people with specialized expertise. For example, a Chief Sales Officer would oversee teams of sales people responsible for meeting revenue growth targets in specific geographic regions. A Chief Marketing Officer would be measured by growth in the number of high quality sales leads generated, improvements in the startup's net promoter score (NPS), and the strength of its brand. The CMO might supervise public relations, advertising, and partner relationships. The aim of the job redefinition is to make the startup's business model more scalable so it is ready for the third stage of scaling.

- **Boost functional specialization and limit span of control.** As a company sprints to liquidity, the CEO must monitor whether the organization is adding new customers, selling more to current customers, and boosting operating cash flow. If the organization is becoming less effective and/or efficient, the CEO must consider whether redefining specific jobs might solve the problem. For example, if a manager's span of control is growing beyond six or seven direct reports, the CEO should shift some of that manager's responsibilities to a new manager. Consider the case of a manager in charge of European sales whose country sales reps are responsible for meeting revenue targets in Spain, France, Italy, Germany, England, Norway, and Portugal. Were that European sales manager to fall short of his sales goals, the CEO might assign Germany, England, and Norway to a Northern Europe Sales Manager and create a Southern Europe Sales Manager position charged with meeting sales goals in Spain, Italy, and Portugal.

- **Subtract functions that no longer add value.** Finally, the CEO should eliminate functions that were important in the past but now slow down decision-making without adding enough value to justify their existence.

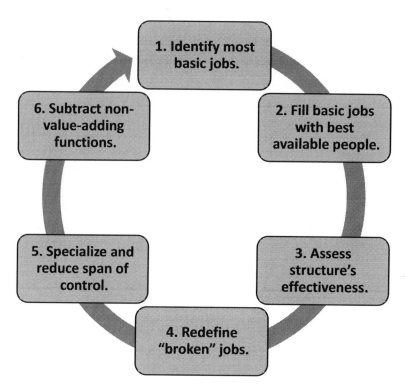

Figure 5-2. Steps to redefine jobs

Takeaways for Stakeholders

While redefining jobs affects a startup's various stakeholders, including customers, partners, employees, and investors, the startup's CEO has sole responsibility for redefining jobs. And the CEO's imperatives for redefining jobs vary by scaling stage, as follows:

- **Winning the first customers**

    - Envision the most essential capabilities the startup will need to win its first customers.

    - Identify the CEO's greatest strengths and weaknesses.

    - List the most important skills for the startup's success that the CEO can't provide.

    - Hire skilled cofounders who can provide the missing skills.

    - Set goals and collaborate to achieve them.

    - If startup does not achieve goals, consider redefining jobs to strengthen the team.

- **Building scalable business model**
  - Identify key business functions, such as engineering, sales, marketing, and customer service, that must become more efficient.
  - Define specific job categories within each of the key functions.
  - Agree on corporate and functional goals for growth in the number of customers, revenue per customer, operating efficiency, NPS, and brand recognition.
  - Assess progress in meeting all goals as frequently as every week.
  - If goals are not being achieved, consider redefining jobs to boost performance.

- **Sprinting to liquidity**
  - Create general manager jobs responsible for adding revenue in new geographic markets, new product lines, and new channels of distribution.
  - Split general management jobs into smaller parts to boost entrepreneurial opportunities and limit span of control.
  - Assess performance relative to quarterly goals and adjust job functions to boost performance.
  - Tap into the experience of newly-hired vice presidents and C-level executives to improve the startup's organization structure.

- **Running the marathon**
  - Add job functions responsible for growth through acquiring new companies, forming partnerships, and strengthening relationships with sales channels and original equipment manufacturers (OEMs).
  - Identify and eliminate job functions that cost more than the value they generate.
  - Assess performance relative to quarterly goals and adjust job functions to boost performance.

Redefining Job Functions Success and Failure Case Studies

In this section, I offer case studies of redefining job functions used by successful and less successful startups at each scaling stage, analyze the cases, and extract principles for helping founders to redefine job functions at each stage.

Stage I: Winning the First Customers

To win the first customers, a startup requires two basic functions: product development and sales. Like stem cells that become specialized, differentiating to become heart muscle cells, blood cells, or nerve cells, a startup's organization becomes increasingly focused as it grows. Before a company has revenue or capital, a small number of cofounders must do many jobs that later become specialized as the need for more focused functions becomes more critical and the startup's success attracts the capital needed to hire people to perform those functions. For instance, before a startup gets its initial customers, the cofounder in charge of sales will perform many jobs, such as identifying sales leads, closing sales, getting customer feedback on product prototypes, forming distribution partnerships, hiring, and raising capital, most of which are later assigned to individual executives and managers. And the product development cofounder will architect and build product prototypes as well as hire and direct engineers.

A CEO who is strong in sales should recruit a cofounder who excels at product development and vice versa. The CEO's role in defining jobs is not as simple if the startup can raise capital before it gets off the ground. In that case, the CEO will have the capital needed to define new roles such as engineering, customer service, and marketing and hire people to fill them. Moreover, CEOs must decide how to evaluate tradeoffs when they allocate capital between hiring new people and marketing and promotion. First-time CEOs will likely need to learn how to define the right jobs at the right time and ought to seek advice from others, possibly board members or mentors who have done so successfully.

Success Case Study: Ethos Wins Customers and Boosts Staff to 20 Three Months After Launch

Introduction

San Francisco-based Ethos, a life insurance startup founded by a pair of former Stanford Business School (SBS) roommates, got off to a rapid start in turning an idea born of one of its cofounder's unfortunate decisions into a company that raised a big round of seed capital and grew to 20 people within three months of its launch. Given SBS's stringent admissions standards, the cofounders were skilled at doing what was required to raise capital and win Ethos' first customers rapidly. Their initial success was due to a combination of factors: their abilities as leaders, their focus on a large market, their service that provided consumers with a far better experience, and how the company defined its jobs as it grew.

Lingke Wang's unfortunate decision was to buy so-called permanent life insurance, which only paid a death benefit if a policyholder never missed a premium payment, as a 20-year-old college student. Such permanent policies generated huge agent commissions. But 85% of those policies lapsed or were surrendered because the insured stopped paying. In June 2018, Wang and his SBS roommate, CEO and co-founder Peter Colis, launched Ethos to solve Wang's problem with the mission of "helping individuals and families feel safe and protected, not bought and sold by commissioned sales agents," according to my August 2018 interview with Colis. Ethos took 10 minutes to provide consumers with life insurance policies, compared to 15 weeks for insurers like MetLife and New York Life, which sold through agents who were motivated to sell the most expensive policies to maximize their commissions, according to Colis. Ethos used predictive analytics to provide a life insurance policy without a medical exam or a lengthy approval process, it did not employ commissioned sales agents, and at the time was available in 49 states through partnerships with insurance companies Munich Re and Nebraska's Assurity Life. Ethos raised an $11.5 million Series A investment from Sequoia through partner Roelof Botha, who was previously CFO of PayPal, two famous actors, and a basketball star (Robert Downey Jr., Will Smith, and Kevin Durant).

Case Scenario

Wang, who earned a degree from Brown in applied mathematics, did not define his role as strictly a coder. Indeed, he used a design thinking approach to product development and spent time hiring staff. In 2015, Wang and Colis first started a platform for cashing in life insurance policies. Ovid Life operated a platform to enable holders of permanent life insurance policies to sell them to institutional investors. At Ovid, Wang considered himself responsible for software development, growth, and hiring. He prioritized tasks based on how much they directly affected revenue, cash flow, product, or employees. To develop products, he used design thinking, encouraging Ovid's team to generate many ideas that might seem "outlandish or impractical" while withholding "all judgement and cynicism." When developing its product, Ovid spent a considerable amount of time focusing on customers, "figuring out their problems and building stuff to solve them." Wang believed that without "a crystal-clear idea of what problem" it was solving, Ovid would fail. He also used Heap Analytics, which tracked behavioral metrics and pinpointed which parts of the product were not working, to measure the effectiveness of its product.

Colis, a philosophy graduate of the University of Colorado, Boulder whose grandfather was a successful life insurance salesman, liaised with investors, partners, and the media. He gave a 60-minute presentation to a large team from Downey Ventures and talent agency Creative Artist Agency. As Colis said, "We didn't have enough chairs in the office for everyone. So I gave the 60-minute investment pitch while sitting on a hot radiator, while trying to act cool. One of our first uses of their investment capital was purchasing more chairs." Sequoia's Roelof Botha, who led the Series A funding round and joined the board, was confident that Ethos had room to grow. "This is a team that's gotten a lot done with very little. That shows a creativity and resourcefulness that is attractive as an investor." Colis was also optimistic about Ethos's future. "We are going after a $20 trillion market, the legacy players are broken, the market is ripe for disruption, it's an execution-heavy business, and our team really cares about solving the problem. We're processing thousands of customers and growing rapidly with a team of 20 in engineering, design, and customer success. Our customers are coming from advertising on Facebook, partnerships, and word of mouth from customers. Ethos will be the next great life insurance company because our product is so good that it is bought, not sold," concluded Colis.

Case Analysis

Ethos won its first customers quickly and raised a large Series A round early in its development. This funding enabled Ethos to hire people who could perform the activities that its CEO thought were most essential at this stage for assuring that its customers were happy with their experience: engineering, design, and customer success. Ethos hoped to create highly satisfied customers who would recommend the company to others in their networks, helping the company grow quickly without spending too much money.

Less Successful Case Study: After 12 Years and $484 Million, Fuze Lacks A Scalable Business Model

Introduction

Can a company that claims over $100 million in revenue and $484 million in capital be less than successful? Possibly, if it took 12 years to get there, it still lacked a scalable business model, and its most recent capital raising slashed 48% from its valuation. This is what happened to Fuze, a Boston-based office communications platform founded in 2006, which by August 2018 employed 700 people (about the same as at the end of 2015) and had raised a total of $484.4 million. Sadly for Fuze's previous investors, the company's valuation was slashed 48% from $765 million in February 2017 when Fuze raised $134 million to $400 million in May 2018 when investors provided it $150 million. In 2006, Fuze, cofounded by former CEO Steve Kokinos, was called Thinking Phones. The company initially focused on voice communications.

ThinkingPhones later expanded to operate on mobile devices and to integrate with outside applications like Salesforce and LinkedIn. Between 2014 and 2017, ThinkingPhones acquired three companies: Whaleback Managed Services, a cloud-based communication service for medium-sized businesses; Contactive, a caller ID and data analytics company; and Fuze, which provided cloud-based video conferencing, voice calling, and document sharing services. In 2016, ThinkingPhones changed its name to Fuze and opened offices in Australia, Germany, Switzerland, and Spain and three new data centers in Hong Kong, Singapore, and Australia. These offices were added to Fuze's operations in the U.K., the Netherlands, Denmark, Portugal, and France.

But Kokinos was moved out as CEO eight days after Fuze raised its $134 million. Why? As Colin Doherty (who took over as CEO from Kokinos in February 2017) said "We'd like to get more predictable revenue and execute as a public company. That's a little bit about process, execution, market growth, being a little more predictable in terms of balance sheets and financial metrics." Of his being deposed from the CEO role, Kokinos said that Fuze brought on Doherty because of the "operational horsepower" necessary to reach the company's next stage of growth. In August 2018, Doherty told me, "Steve is a serial entrepreneur and I am a serial operator. Steve had the idea that people who were using iPhones in their personal lives wanted to do the same thing at work. He wanted to replace plastic phones with cords. And the product evolved from cloud-based telephony to include video, messaging, and collaboration. I was brought in to establish systems, processes, marketing, sales force, and growth."

Case Scenario

Fuze was competing in what it deemed to be the $100 billion market for office communications. However, that market attracted significant competitors, including business messaging service Slack and videoconferencing service Zoom, which were doing far better than Fuze. After all, in August 2018, Slack announced a $427 million round valuing the company at more than $7.1 billion. With three million paying users, Slack had been able to generate "hundreds of millions of dollars in annual revenue." And Zoom, which Doherty did not view as a competitor since it did not supply telephony and messaging, was valued at $1 billion in January 2017, when it raised $100 million. But Doherty was unflappably optimistic about Fuze's prospects, he said, "There has always been speculation on private company valuations and we have never commented on any of them. Our revenue is over $100 million, and we are growing at 40% a year. There is a huge market opportunity and we win most times we compete with Microsoft's Skype, Cisco's WebEx, and Avaya."

By August 2018, Fuze believed it was entering the second stage of scaling. As Doherty said, "We have 1,700 customers and we are modifying our go-to-market from a direct sales model to a blend of direct sales and partnering with the channel, which we think will welcome the opportunity to replace high cost hardware with a variable cost service. We are going after a more than $100 billion opportunity: 400 million knowledge workers who could potentially pay $35/seat/month. We are competing with products that cost companies $75 per seat per month and we combine six to 12 enterprise applications into one." Trying to bring in revenue from the channel had the potential to help Fuze grow without spending as much on its sales force. Moreover, by adding a focus on the channel, Fuze hoped to improve its execution. Indeed in Gartner's "2017 Magic Quadrant Unified Communications as a Service Report," Fuze was among the leaders on Completeness of Vision but fell below the center line on Ability to Execute, according to industry analyst Michael Finneran who said, "To fuel their international aspirations, it looks like they're stepping up to the plate with regard to bolstering their channel program, so the key now will be execution." Chief Sales Officer Chris Doggett said in February 2018 that Fuze's expanded program would enable value-added resellers, solution providers, and IT/communications solution consultants to offer Fuze's products.

Doherty hired people who had considerable experience and who fit with Fuze's culture. "I look for people with the ability to recognize patterns. When they see a familiar problem that can suggest the right solution. I emphasize EQ over IQ; it's how you use your intelligence and how you collaborate. I want people with a fantastic attitude, high energy, the ability to collaborate to solve problems, and a will to win." Fuze was organized by function. As Doherty explained, "I hired Doggett, who is doing an excellent job. He oversees sales, sales engineering, customer success, customer deployment, and account cultivation. Our Chief Marketing Officer directs media and public relations, lead generation, partnering, and market outreach. We also have heads of engineering and R&D, product management, and G&A functions like IT, finance, HR, and legal." Fuze's investors had placed a huge wager on Doherty's ability to get them a return. He said, "We have done a lot of work and are looking at the possibility of an IPO in 18 months."

Case Analysis

Fuze took a very long time to win its first customers and its founder, who did succeed in raising an unusually large amount of capital in the 11 years he led the company, was unable to create a scalable business model. Interestingly, Kokinos raised another $150 million in capital a bit over a week before he was replaced by Doherty. It appears to me that Kokinos was given a face-saving exit; he was seen as having raised $134 million and choosing his successor. However, it would not surprise me if investors gave as a condition of providing the capital that Kokinos would need to step aside for Doherty. To be fair, Doherty seemed to have put in place a functional organization and culture that appeared logical. Yet roughly 15 months later, Fuze raised another $150 million but at a 48% lower valuation. If Fuze had more than $100 million in revenue and was growing at 40% a year, as Doherty said, it should have been able to go public, even if it was unprofitable. Doherty's August 2018 statement that Fuze had not built a scalable business model signaled that its operations needed to become more efficient. But it did not disclose the sources of the problem; perhaps its direct sales model was too expensive.

Principles

Founders seeking to define jobs to win initial customers should bear in mind the following dos and don'ts:

- **Do**
    - Hire the best cofounders possible to perform most critical jobs needed to win first customers, such as product development and sales.
    - Make listening to customers and building prototypes key parts of the cofounders' jobs.

- **Don't**
    - Add new job functions without considering cash flow or profitability.
    - Assume that investors will keep funding organizational expansion without a path to profitability.

Stage 2: Building a Scalable Business Model

Most startups do not follow Instagram's easy path of going from finding its first customers with 13 employees to being acquired. Instead, once they succeed in the first stage of scaling, they try to replicate that success while adding far more customers. While startups can achieve rapid revenue growth by targeting new growth vectors, as we explored in Chapter 2, many startups choose to do so without regard to profitability, deferring Stage 2 and skipping directly to Stage 3. The reason is that these startups believe that investors want startups to reach at least $100 million in revenues, regardless of profitability, while growing over 40% a year so they can go public sooner. But that is a risky strategy for a CEO who wants to build a large company that will change the world. That's because investors can change their attitudes abruptly. It happened in 2015 when a handful of venture-backed IPOs did not do well as public companies and spooked investors, who told portfolio companies they would not invest until they became profitable. That change of heart caused big trouble for money-losing companies that were rapidly burning through their dwindling pile of cash. Simply put, while few companies build scalable business models before they take on huge capital investments to grow quickly, all of them should. And a key scaling lever for accomplishing that is how the CEO redefines jobs.

Success Case Study: Growing at 300% a Year, Hired Raises $132 Million with a Quick Path to Profitability

Introduction

One formula for successful startups is to find a big market and deliver a much better solution to the problem that people are spending so much money to solve. If customers like the startup's product more than the incumbent's, the startup grows fast and the incumbent slows down. This simple formula does not work unless the startup overcomes some big challenges.

- How does the startup get people to try its product if they know the startup has a good chance of running out of money?

- If the startup gets initial customers, will it be able to raise enough capital to keep going?

- If it gets big enough to go public, will its CEO be able to keep beating investor expectations each quarter so its stock rises?

This comes to mind in considering the battle for a piece of the market for talent recruiting. For example, LinkedIn was a huge player—in 2018, LinkedIn was doing well: Microsoft (which bought the company in 2016 for $26.2 billion) reported that LinkedIn revenue grew 37% to almost $1.1 billion. San Francisco-based Hired, founded in 2012, was a LinkedIn challenger that raised $132.7 million and was growing at 300%, most likely from a much smaller base. Hired flipped the traditional model of online recruiting on its side. Instead of wasting candidates' time sending out applications and never hearing back, Hired put technology talent in the driver's seat. As CEO (since 2013) Mehul Patel explained in a July 2018 interview, "We allow companies to apply to tech talent. Through Hired, job candidates and companies have transparency into salary offers, competing opportunities, and job details. On June 20, we announced a subscription service that enables companies to meet more predictably their employment requirements with higher quality people." Hired reduced the pain of talent recruiting for candidates and employers. As Patel, previously a marketing and business development executive with a law degree from University of Virginia, said, "We remove the painful job application process for candidates who can spend more time interviewing instead of sending out resumes and employers [can cut the time they spend screening candidates who don't fit], reducing time to hire by 33%."

Case Scenario

By August 2018, Hired was adding employees and customers at a rapid clip, but close to profitability. "In 2017, we saw 300% growth in bookings. We have grown from five employees in 2013 to over 200 employees across the globe, with

140 of those employees sitting in our San Francisco headquarters. We have over 10,000 companies using our platform to hire including Dropbox, Zuora, WeWork, Nordstrom, and Booking.com," said Patel. Hired believed it was targeting a large market opportunity. "The total addressable market for hiring knowledge workers is $400 billion and our segment of that—paying agencies to hire engineers, project managers, and data scientists—is $80 billion to $100 billion," he explained. And Hired was working on building a scalable business model, expecting to reach profitability by the end of 2018 and then sprinting to liquidity.

Hired's culture was set up to keep it from falling into the many pitfalls that can cause startups to fail. "I was in venture capital for a while where's it's all about pattern recognition. Most startups fail. Why? The market is not big enough, there is no product/market fit, they can't raise money, they can't scale their people and culture. I believe it's crucial to get culture right," Patel said. Culture is the operating systems that keeps Hired's level of bureaucracy low. "I talk about values every week and interview people for values. Since the company is now too big for me to look at everyone, I am relying on everyone having the same understanding to make decisions consistently that benefit the customer. We revisit this every six months because I want constructive conflict, for example, if we go to a new category, but after the debate everyone commits to the joint decision," he said.

Hired's organization became more specialized as it grew. According to Patel, "Early on we hired generalists before we had product/market fit. As we grew up, we added functions and looked for specialists and the generalists left. When our [contracts] got to six or seven figures, we added an enterprise sales team. Our departments include engineering; marketing (to candidates and companies along with brand and PR), and sales (to get new clients, to help grow the client relationship, and to solve problems for existing clients)."

Case Analysis

Hired's rapid growth and ability to raise capital resulted from its creative business strategy. By focusing on scarce high-tech workers and the companies that seek to employ them, Hired diminished the pain of its platform participants; high tech workers were able to reduce the time they wasted pursuing opportunities that did not fit, and employers were able to plan for and fill positions more efficiently. In short, Hired followed one of the most basic principles for startup success: find customer pain left unrelieved by rivals and provide a product that sharply reduces that pain. Hired defined and filled the jobs needed to bring in new customers, keep them buying over time, and expanding revenues for each customer. In addition, Hired had a clear path to profitability, suggesting that Patel was redefining jobs to make its business model more scalable.

Less Successful Case Study: Growing at 300% with $56 Million in Capital, Pendo Trades Off Profitability for Growth

Introduction

A startup that competes with large companies in a newly developing market faces significant challenges. For example, if those large rivals are established, respected companies for which the startup's sole focus is a small product line, potential customers may wonder why they should risk buying from a startup that might not be around in six months. Moreover, even if that startup is growing rapidly because it offers a superior product, investors may hesitate to provide capital because that newly developing market does not feature any publicly-traded companies that focus solely on the startup's product line. In short, investors in such a company must believe that the emerging product category will become a large market and that the startup in question will be a successful pioneering IPO. This comes to mind in considering the emerging market for product engagement software which helps companies learn whether customers are using a product after the purchase and, if so, which parts of the product get the most use and which do not. Such software is valuable because if the product is not used, customers won't buy more, and if a company knows this early, it can improve the product. Product engagement software is a new $20 billion in revenue category, according to one the startups. Raleigh, NC-based Pendo, populated by startups and products from large companies like Google Analytics and Adobe Analytics.

Pendo, which was founded in 2013, was growing fast. It enjoyed a 170% increase in bookings in the second quarter ending July 2018 (adding 90 new customers). The new customers included "Instacart, Digital River, Inc., RingCentral, ADP, Lithium Technologies, Mimecast, First American Financial, and MetLife." As cofounder and CEO Todd Olson said in an August 2018 interview, "Pendo has raised $56 million in venture capital from Bay Area investors like Battery Ventures. As of July 1, 2018, we've landed more than 600 customers and employ 200 people across offices in Raleigh, San Francisco, New York, and Yakum, Israel. Annual recurring revenue has grown between 300% and 400% each year since our inception in late 2013." Olson's background prepared him for Pendo. He was previously CEO of 6th Sense Analytics, which he ran for four years before selling it to Rally Software in 2009. Rally went public in 2013; in 2015, CA Technologies acquired the company for $480 million. His Rally experience inspired Pendo. As he said, "I came up with the idea for Pendo when I was leading the product team at Rally. Each week I'd receive dozens of requests for new features, but I had no product usage data to help me decide which were worth the investment of time and capital. When I started Pendo, I wanted to solve this problem for product managers."

Case Scenario

Since it provided a channel through which companies could receive and respond to feedback from their customers, Pendo's product helped its customers grow faster and more profitably. And in so doing Pendo's customers could boost the likelihood that customers would recommend their product to others through a higher net promoter score (NPS). Indeed, some early customers, like Cisco Cloud, saw a 20% increase in their NPS after installing Pendo's platform. With data, Pendo was able to help companies determine the best ways to engage with users to get feedback.

Pendo was not profitable but it believed it could become less unprofitable if it spent less on sales and marketing, but that would apply the brakes to its growth rate. As Olson said, "We are not cash flow breakeven. But I can invest $1 in sales and marketing to get $3 to $5 in revenue. I can control my cash burn, but I grow faster by spending. We can keep growing between 100% and 200% without killing the company." Pendo started off without a formal culture but in 2014 Olson started writing down the company's values. As he said, "We have a maniacal focus on the customer, which fuels many aspects of our business and we are transparent, sharing almost everything. We believe that if we eliminate the information asymmetry between executives and individual contributors, they will make better decisions. We use culture to decide whether to hire and promote people." As it grew from a few people to 200, Pendo formalized its organization in response to problems. "We started out with people who were jacks of all trades. Later we carved things out based on pain. Sales was a problem and we hired a head of sales. Our head of customer success lacked enough experience; we needed a new marketing head. We bring in people ahead of the need. We don't want to wait until it breaks. I have 5 or 6 direct reports; 10 to 15 is too many."

Case Analysis

Pendo was growing rapidly, had raised considerable capital, and its product could improve its customers' NPS. Moreover, Olson had a clear idea of how changing Pendo's organization would affect key goals such as bringing in new customers, boosting the odds that customers would renew, and selling more to each customer. He also redefined jobs to make them more effective and hired people to fill those new jobs who would be able to keep up with evolving demands. Yet a nagging problem with Pendo was its inability to build a scalable business model, which would become a significant problem were Pendo to lose access to new capital. This left open questions about its business model and how its organization might change to accommodate growth. Could Pendo grow without adding so many expensive sales people? If not, could Pendo pay for these sales people by raising its price? Was there another way for Pendo to grow and become profitable?

Principles

Founders seeking to define jobs to build a scalable business model should bear in mind the following dos and don'ts:

- **Do**
    - Redefine jobs to make the business profitable based on specific customer metrics such as renewal rates, revenue per customer, and cost of acquiring customers.
    - Add new jobs that boost the company's performance on these metrics.

- **Don't**
    - Assume that it is better to trade off profitability for growth.
    - Keep adding new job functions—for example, to manage operations in new geographies—without regard to their effect on profitability.
    - Assume that investors will keep financing losses if revenue keeps growing.

Stage 3: Sprinting to Liquidity

As mentioned earlier, it's risky for startups to sprint to liquidity without a scalable business model. After all, if investors decide to stop funding the losses of such a company, it will almost certainly lose its independence unless it can quickly become profitable or survive a few years until investors change their minds and decide that being unprofitable is fine if the company is growing fast enough. However, it's much better for a startup's long-term prospects if its business model is scalable before it takes on significant capital to sprint to liquidity. A startup will be far better off if its CEO designs the organization to add new customers efficiently and keep them happy so they renew and buy more. Such as scalable business model puts a startup in a better negotiating position with investors, whether it is raising capital in Stage 3 or seeking to boost its share price in Stage 4.

Success Case Study: Growing at 60% a Year, Redis Sprints Towards a 2021 IPO

Introduction

A startup boosts its odds of success if it targets a very large market, for example, larger than $10 billion or $20 billion. That's because investors expect a company to have at least $100 million in revenue before it goes public and consider it unlikely that a startup will be able to get more than 10% market share. Sadly for founders, such large markets are often dominated by a handful of large competitors who have locked customers into long-term contracts. For a startup to grow quickly, it must offer a product that solves a customer's problem far more effectively and at a much lower price; otherwise, the cost of switching from the incumbent is so high that it's not worth the trouble. Hurdling that challenge will not gain the startup enough market share unless it can grow its organization in ways that boost its customer count. And to build a scalable business model, that growth must come at low enough cost to make the company profitable as it sprints towards liquidity.

This comes to mind in considering Mountain View, California-based Redis Labs, which said in August 2018 that it was on its way to disrupting Oracle in the $60 billion market for databases. Redis had 8,300 customers of its Redis Cloud service, which it introduced in 2013, and 250 customers for the same functionality as downloadable software, which it launched in 2015. As CEO Ofer Bengal told me in August 2018, "Our customers include six of the Fortune 10, 40% of the Fortune 100, three of the top five communications companies, three of the top four credit card companies, and three of the top five health care companies."

Redis, which was founded in 2011, raised $86 million in capital, employed 225 people, and had a technology edge. It was based on an open source database developed by Sicily native Salvatore Sanfilippo (Antirez), who went to work for Redis. Redis believed that its so-called NoSQL technology was much faster and cheaper to own and operate than Oracle's SQL database. "Companies were demanding much faster response time to operate their wireless apps on much larger databases. Traditional database response times were too slow. Specifically, customers wanted response times of under one millisecond to process 10 million transactions per second. We are the fastest database in the world: 100 times faster than Oracle and much cheaper to own and operate," Bengal said.

Case Scenario

Redis believed that part of its success was the choice of which segment of the database market to target. As Bengal said, "10% of the market is for new applications and that segment is growing much faster than the overall market. Our revenues are in the tens of millions, we are growing at 60% a year and can maintain that rate for the next several years." Customers explained why they liked Redis's product. Gartner verified 68 favorable customer reviews of Redis, a total of 4.7 out of five stars. One manufacturing customer said, "Redislabs has been the most stable, secure, and highest performing vendor we have ever worked with. We have thrown increasingly ridiculous workloads at our cluster and it has never faltered." Identity verification service Whitepages said, "Our Identity Graph product handles [a huge amount of data which makes] our applications extremely latency-sensitive. Redis Enterprise provided the single-digit latency we required."

Redis, which operated R&D in Tel Aviv, was adapting its organization to keep up with the growth in demand. "When we first started, everyone did everything. Before you have a product it's hard to attract top talent in Tel Aviv and Silicon Valley, so you take what you can get. Today it's easy to attract talent. We have 110 people in sales, which is run by Jason Forget, the former Chief Operating Officer of Imperva; Manish Gupta, our CMO, was CMO at many Silicon Valley companies; our cofounder, Yiftach Shoolman, is Chief Technology Officer," explained Bengal. Redis had several Vice Presidents within its major functional departments. As he said, "Under our Chief Operating Officer we have VPs of Sales for North America, EMEA, and Customer Success (who runs our database as a service), and Solutions Architecture (who provides proofs of concept for potential customers). Under marketing we have Vice Presidents of Product Marketing, Demand Generation, and User Community. And our CTO oversees Vice Presidents of R&D and the CTO team that develops cutting edge services like Redis Search."

Case Analysis

While Redis appeared to be years away from reaching the scale needed to go public, it seemed to have overcome the hurdle of building a scalable business model, as suggested by its low customer churn and ability to double revenues per customers within 18 months of closing its first deal with each one. The way Redis designed its jobs suggested that it had experimented extensively with how best to break down key business functions to achieve its goals. Moreover, Bengal's success in attracting and motivating executives with previous experience managing these functions in public companies reinforced the likelihood that Redis was sprinting towards liquidity.

Less Successful Case Study: After 21 Years Will Click Software Be Acquired Again?

Introduction

It's unusual for a tech startup to go public, get acquired by a private equity firm, and then aspire to go public again. It's particularly difficult to pull this off when the company competes in a relatively small market and faces rivals with far more capital behind them. The one advantage that this private-equity owned company might have is that its sole focus is on that one industry which could give it a competitive advantage over rivals that participate in many different industries.

This comes to mind in considering the market for software that helps companies to schedule customer service visits; consider Comcast dispatching vans to newly signed up customers' homes and offices to install service. This global field service management industry is not particularly large; it reached $2 billion in 2017 and was expected to grow at a 16.5% compound annual rate to $4.45 billion by 2022. Despite its small size, the industry featured many large rivals. For example, GE, which Gartner dubbed a leader in this industry, owned ServiceMax, which raised $200 million in capital before GE bought it in November 2016 for $915 million (in December 2018, GE announced plans to sell a majority stake in ServiceMax).[1] Oracle acquired another player, TOA Software, for $550 million in 2014 after it raised $120 million and employed 500 people. Microsoft bought FieldOne in 2015 and in June 2018 SAP acquired Coresystems, which uses AI to help companies find available field service technicians.

The biggest standalone player in this industry was ClickSoftware Technologies, based in Petach Tikva, Israel and Burlington, Massachusetts. The company was founded by an Israeli professor, Moshe BenBassat, in 1997, went public in January 2000, and in July 2015 was acquired for $438 million in cash by Francisco Partners. Prior to the deal, ClickSoftware expected to report a loss for the quarter ending March 31, 2015 and revenue in the range of $26 million to $27 million. ClickSoftware's CEO, Mark Cattini, joined in February 2018. He had a track record of taking over companies that stalled and selling them. Before ClickSoftware, he was CEO of Autotask, maker of a business management platform for IT service providers, which Vista Equity Partners acquired in June 2014, and publicly-traded MapInfo, which Pitney Bowes acquired in 2007 for $480 million. As Cattini said in a July 2018 interview, "We have 700 employees and when I joined I benefited because my predecessor had done good things. We see a much bigger opportunity to expand beyond field service to customer service more broadly, offering solutions to empower our customers to retain and create better experiences for their customers. Thanks to Francisco, we can expand organically or by acquisition."

---

[1] "GE's digital unit to sell majority stake in ServiceMax," Reuters, December 13, 2018, https://www.reuters.com/article/us-ge-servicemax/ges-digital-unit-to-sell-majority-stake-in-servicemax-idUSKBN1OC1MS.

Case Scenario

ClickSoftware did not reveal its revenues but claimed to have many customers. "We have 400 enterprise customers, including some of the largest utilities and telecommunications service providers in the world. We also have 9,000 SMB customers, and nearly a million field service professionals are scheduled every day by our software. We have very healthy growth on the bottom and top lines," said Cattini. Companies bought from ClickSoftware because the money it saved them exceeded the price they paid for the product. As Cattini said, "We demonstrate ROI. If a company has 200 to 500 technicians, we can cut 15 miles per technician for 250 working days from their routes. An energy company in Australia told us we saved them tens of millions of dollars. We charge from $200,000 to $3 million per year." ClickSoftware's culture and organization contributed to its growth. "Our culture is the most important thing. We value people who are team-oriented and passionate about customer satisfaction. We also want people to act with a sense of urgency and accountability. We're organized functionally, with sales and marketing, product development, and customer service. Because of our great software and excellent customer service, we have a strong recurring revenue base."

Case Analysis

ClickSoftware had a long and somewhat rocky interaction with capital markets. It went public during the dot-com boom but was not profitable and was taken private. Its CEO had a track record of fixing up less-than-stellar companies and selling them to private equity or corporate buyers. Indeed, Cattini seemed to think that ClickSoftware's growth might come through acquisition thanks to capital from its private equity owner. To be sure, ClickSoftware's product created measurable value to customers and it was able to raise its revenue per customer over time. Moreover, its culture and organization seemed to support these outcomes. Nevertheless, by August 2018, it was unclear whether ClickSoftware was growing rapidly enough to have hopes for an IPO, whether it was profitable or could become so, and exactly how Francisco Partners intended to generate a return on its then three-year-old $438 million investment.

Principles

Founders seeking to define jobs to build a sprint to liquidity should bear in mind the following dos and don'ts:

- **Do**
  - Include executive roles to run key departments such as marketing and sales, and fill them with people who have performed these roles in companies that went public.

- Define vice president jobs to run key functions within the departments.

- Evaluate effectiveness of organizational roles by assessing how well each contributes to the company's growth and profitability.

- **Don't**

  - Depend too heavily on acquisitions to expand the scope of the organization.

  - Design the organization and run it without monitoring its effectiveness.

  - Delay making changes to the organization if it is not functioning well.

Stage 4: Running the Marathon

Once a company goes public, its organization structure should change as it pursues new growth opportunities. Depending on the growth vector, a public company may change the organization structure in different ways. Here are some examples:

- **Geographic expansion:** If the company decides to expand into new countries, it may hire general managers and put them in charge of achieving revenue and profit goals there.

- **Developing new products internally:** If the company develops a new product, it may assign a very entrepreneurial team to explore the market opportunity, and then create a more formal organization structure should it be successful.

- **Growth through acquisition:** If it acquires a company, the target's CEO may stay on and be charged with meeting ambitious growth goals or the acquirer may assign an internal executive to that task.

As we'll discuss more in Chapter 6, public companies more frequently replace the people who perform existing organizational roles. For public companies, the spotlight puts additional pressure on the board to use these scaling levers in ways that can withstand scrutiny as they run the marathon.

Success Case Study: Netflix Disrupts Itself with Help from Chief Content Officer Ted Sarandos

Introduction

Founded in 1997, Netflix invented the business of DVD-by-mail, which contributed to the demise of video rental store chain Blockbuster. Then Netflix created online streaming, which founder and CEO Reed Hastings knew would cannibalize its DVD-by-mail business so he focused most of his effort on building the online streaming business and planned for the decline of its DVD-by-mail business and in so doing created a new role called Chief Content Officer (CCO), which Netflix filled by hiring college dropout and video store operator Ted Sarandos. The CCO role was particularly important to Netflix's online streaming business because the studios that create movies and TV programs had no financial incentive to let Netflix stream their content on its platform, or at least would not do so without charging Netflix a prohibitively high price. Creating a CCO was also a new idea for Netflix since its DVD-by-mail business did not require it to create content; it simply bought DVDs in bulk from wholesalers. To keep content costs under control, Hastings realized that Netflix would need to backward integrate by making its own content.

Case Scenario

The CCO role changed dramatically during Sarandos's tenure. Although Netflix did not launch its online streaming service until 2007, Sarandos first met Hastings in 1999 and became the company's CCO in 2000. At their first meeting, Hastings described his vision for the company as providing streaming video delivered to subscribers via the Internet. Hastings's vision impressed Sarandos even though there was no content to be created at the time because all of Netflix's revenues came from DVD-by-mail, which contributed $53 million to company profits in the second quarter of 2018 from its three million subscribers. Sarandos was thinking about how to create online programs for Netflix while Hastings waited to launch until broadband speeds and streaming technology in consumer devices were strong enough to support instant online streaming. As Hastings said, it would be time to launch online streaming when the cost of mailing DVDs exceeded the cost of streaming video, which happened in January 2007. The service, dubbed Watch Now, started out small with around 1,000 titles—about 1% of Netflix's 70,000-video physical library.

After launching online streaming via licensed movies and a few TV shows, Netflix's CCO role began to evolve as Sarandos tried to anticipate the kind of content that Netflix subscribers would want to watch online. As consumers subscribed to online streaming, Sarandos tracked how they watched TV and discovered two important insights: first, consumers liked to binge watch shows and second, algorithm-driven recommendations could keep subscribers engaged for hours at a time. The CCO *role ultimately became what it is today: a supplier of original content for Netflix subscribers. That began with the February 2013 launch of House of Cards. Sarandos ended up paying $100 million to license this UK series because his analysis revealed a significant market opportunity for people who rented House of Cards DVDs, watched political dramas, and preferred David Fincher and Kevin Spacey films. Sarandos concluded that the network effects of publicity for the show would boost viewing figures and enable Netflix to earn a return on its investment. This sort of data-driven insight into customer preferences helped Netflix to lower the risk of its in-house content gambles by setting appropriate budget limits for such projects.*

Sarandos's role evolved into a recruiter of programming talent. Unlike ratings-obsessed TV networks, Netflix was more eager to give talented people a chance to experiment. Netflix's culture appealed to well-known show-runners who had succeeded on network TV. Examples include Netflix's deals with Ryan Murphy, who produced American Crime Story, American Horror Story, and Nip/Tuck, and Shonda Rhimes, who created Grey's Anatomy and Scandal. One of the most appealing things about Netflix for such creative executives was that it gave them the freedom to explore a wide range of different projects, regardless of ratings, according to Sarandos.

Case Analysis

Netflix founder and CEO maintained a clear vision for the company since he cofounded it. He understood that evolving technological, industry, and consumer trends created new opportunities and threats for the company after it went public. By reinventing Netflix's strategy, organization structure, and top executives, Hastings created opportunities for the company's highly talented team to change their job definitions to keep up with changing market opportunities.

Less Successful Case Study: Okta Grows Rapidly, Goes Public, Yet Remains Far From Profitable

Introduction

A company that goes public, grows quickly, enjoys a rise in its stock price, and has no track record of profitability or a path to becoming profitable raises a simple question: What happens if investors decide that they won't buy the stock unless it makes a profit? That's what comes to mind in considering San Francisco-based Okta, a 1,300-employee provider of a cloud-based service that verified the identities of people (employees, customers, and partners) who sought to access a company's IT systems. Okta, founded in 2009, charged subscription, support, and professional services fees to the 4,700 companies that used its product.

Okta's 2018 revenue of $259 million had increased at a four-year compound annual growth rate of 58.7%. In 2018, Okta posted a net loss of $114 million and negative free cash flow of $37 million. By August 30, 2018, its stock had risen 153% in the previous 12 months, valuing its shares at $6.6 billion. Okta's cofounder and CEO Todd McKinnon previously held executive positions at Salesforce and Peoplesoft.

Case Scenario

Okta believed it had a large market opportunity and pursued a multi-pronged strategy to grow rapidly within the market. Based on its average calculated billings, share of each customer's budget, and the number of worldwide business and educational institutions, Okta estimated that its total addressable market was $18 billion. To gain a bigger share of that opportunity, Okta pursued a multi-pronged growth strategy: adding new customers, boosting its share of existing customers' budgets, expanding internationally (it opened offices in the United Kingdom, the Netherlands, Canada, and Australia), expanding relationships with systems integrators, adding new services, and providing analytics.

Okta's growth was straining its organization, including functions such as management, customer operations, research and development, marketing and sales, administration, and finance. To keep up with demand, Okta expanded its functional departments. Its sales organization was structured to meet the specific needs of its various customer groups and was divided by geography, customer size, use case, and industry. Its direct sales force was supported by sales engineers, security team, cloud architects, and professional services staff. Its marketing function generated and communicated customer success stories from the Chief Information Officers of its client. Its marketing function also ran Oktane, a conference with over 1,000 registrants that included customer success stories and new product announcements. Okta's R&D department designed, architected, created, and maintained the quality of Okta's Identity Cloud. Its customer support and professional services organization helped maintain customer service and satisfaction.

Sadly, Okta did not have a scalable business model and as it added to its organization to meet growing demand from customers, it continued to lose money with limited hope for becoming profitable. Okta expected "to continue to incur net losses for the foreseeable future." Moreover, the company expected its operating expenses to significantly increase "over the next several years" as it hired more people in sales and marketing to "expand and improve the effectiveness of [its] distribution channels, expand [its] operations and infrastructure, both domestically and internationally, and continue to develop [its] platform. Okta also expected a rise in legal and accounting expenses. Moreover, Okta was uncertain whether revenues would increase enough to cover future operating expenses.

Case Analysis

Okta enjoyed rapid revenue growth and a successful IPO. Its culture focused on getting new customers, serving them well so they renewed their subscriptions and added to their product line. Yet Okta faced considerable competition from established companies and upstarts which sustained a high level of price competition. As Okta grew, it hired more people to keep up with the needs of its customers and the imperative to sustain high levels of revenue growth. Okta's expenses continued to rise above the level of the revenue it generated from these efforts and despite a well-designed functional organization, Okta had yet to enhance its efficiency enough to have confidence in its ability to generate a profit or positive cash flow.

Principles

Founders seeking to define jobs to run the marathon should bear in mind the following dos and don'ts:

- **Do**
    - Create new organizational roles to lead changing elements of strategy.
    - Empower talented people to determine how to implement new strategies.
    - Monitor the effectiveness of the strategy and adapt key roles to sustain growth.

- **Don't**
    - Get locked into a high cost organization that only grows by raising costs above revenues.
    - Maintain the current organization structure despite changes in strategy.

Redefining Job Functions Success and Failure Principles

To redefine job functions at each scaling stage, CEOs must follow the principles summarized in Table 5-1.

Table 5-1. Summary of the principles of redefining job functions

Scaling Stage	Dos	Don'ts
1: Winning the first customer	Hire the best cofounders possible to perform most critical jobs needed to win first customers, such as product development and sales. Make listening to customers and building prototypes key parts of the cofounders' jobs.	Add new job functions without considering cash flow or profitability. Assume that investors will keep funding organizational expansion without a path to profitability.
2: Scaling the business model	Redefine jobs to make the business profitable based on specific customer metrics such as renewal rates, revenue per customer, and cost of acquiring customers. Add new jobs that boost the company's performance on these metrics.	Assume that it is better to trade off profitability for growth. Keep adding new job functions—for example, to manage operations in new geographies—without regard of their effect on profitability. Assume that investors will keep financing losses as long as revenue keeps growing.
3: Sprinting to liquidity	Include executive roles to run key departments such as marketing and sales, and fill them with people who have performed these roles in companies that went public. Define vice president jobs to run key functions within the departments. Evaluate effectiveness of organizational roles by assessing how well each contributes to the company's growth and profitability.	Depend too heavily on acquisitions to expand the scope of the organization. Design the organization and run it without monitoring its effectiveness. Delay making changes to the organization if it is not functioning well.
4. Running the marathon	Create new organizational roles to lead changing elements of strategy. Empower talented people to determine how to implement new strategies. Monitor the effectiveness of the strategy and adapt key roles to sustain growth.	Get locked into a high cost organization that only grows by raising costs above revenues. Maintain the current organization structure despite changes in strategy.

Are You Doing Enough to Redefine Job Functions?

Redefining job functions assures that a startup has the right roles to achieve its growth goals. As the company grows, the job functions tend to become more specialized, with the executive taking charge of operating key activities that must be done well to win new customers, keep them buying from the company, and filling their need for new products. To test whether your company is doing enough to redefine jobs functions, ask these four questions:

- Are you adapting your organizational structure to your evolving business strategy?

- Are you splitting organizational responsibilities to limit managers' span of control to six or seven direct reports?

- Are you holding key executives accountable for results and giving them freedom to redefine their roles as the company grows?

- Are you eliminating roles that cost more than the value they create?

Conclusion

Redefining jobs is an element in a cluster of scaling levers that enable a company to implement its growth strategy for turning an idea into a large company. Underlying the process of redefining jobs is the notion that once a company wins its first customers, it must go from hiring entrepreneurial leaders, setting a goal, and letting them improvise solutions to increased specialization and formal process. Such formalization is essential to achieving growth without spending too much money. As a company sprints to liquidity and runs the marathon, the CEO must create new roles that will be held accountable for capturing new growth opportunities. And once the new roles have been designed, the CEO must decide whether to promote current employees into the new roles or part ways with them and fill the position from outside the company. Such decisions are a test of the CEO's ability to hire, promote, and let people go, which we examine in Chapter 6.

Hiring, Promoting, and Letting People Go

When a venture is getting off the ground, one of the CEO's most important jobs is to recruit, motivate, promote and let people go. As I discussed in Chapter 5, the jobs those people do become more specialized as the company scales. In this chapter, I'll examine who CEOs hire, promote, and let go and how they make and implement these choices. The case studies I offer in this chapter reveal four general principles for hiring, promoting, and letting people go as a company grows:

- **A startup's ability to attract the best people increases as it becomes more successful.** However, if a company's founding team has enjoyed previous startup success or helped build a new business within a respected company, the quality of the founding team may be perceived as excellent. And that high quality will make it easier to recruit other high-quality team members.

© Peter S. Cohan 2019
P. S. Cohan, *Scaling Your Startup*, https://doi.org/10.1007/978-1-4842-4312-1_6

- **The skills that a startup needs to hire for become more specialized as a company grows, and some individuals can adapt while others can't.** Many founders prefer to promote original team members who have excelled as the startup has grown because these individuals have demonstrated that they can learn new skills and they fit with the culture. But those who can't go further may leave the firm or find a position where they can contribute effectively.

- **As a company seeks to build a scalable business model, the CEO must hire from the outside.** If people who have been with the firm since the beginning can't take on bigger jobs, the startup will usually try to hire people who have done the jobs at a company in the industry that enjoyed a successful IPO. Hiring such experienced leaders can have considerable advantages, but can also cause significant problems if the new leaders do not fit the startup's culture.

- **As companies specialize by function, they often adopt more specific performance measures.** We will examine how startups hold people accountable in Chapter 7. However, as a company scales, it adopts specific goals and systems to measure performance. CEOs can use these systems to identify whom to promote and whom to let go.

CEOs must lead the process of deciding whom to hire, promote, and let go. The CEO's role changes as the company progresses through the four stages of scaling. In the first stage, the CEO often establishes the interview process and meets with the best candidates, decides how much to pay them, chooses whom to promote and let go, and tells them the news. However, as the company gets larger, the CEO delegates many of these activities to members of the executive team who direct specific functions, and the CEO may only get personally involved in decisions about strategically important individuals.

Later in the chapter, I will discuss in greater depth how the CEO's role in hiring, promoting, and letting people go changes as the company scales, as depicted in Figure 6-1.

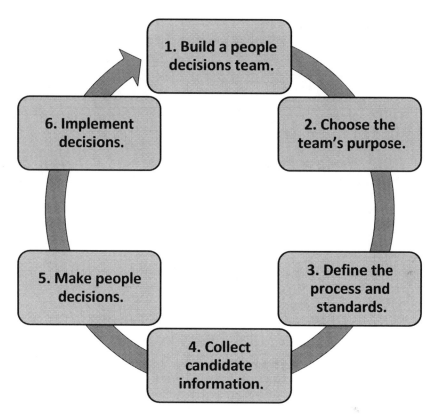

Figure 6-1. Six steps to hiring, promoting, and letting people go

Here is a description of each step:

1. **Build a people decisions team.** In the first stage of scaling, the CEO will assemble a team of people to interview candidates. Team members usually include leaders of key functions such as product development, sales, marketing, and administration. As the company scales, the hiring teams for lower level positions will be decided on by department heads and may be coordinated by human resources. Decisions about promotions and firing may be made by teams chosen by those department heads. In cases of strategic promotions and firings, the board, CEO, and top executive team may also be involved.

2. **Choose the team's purpose.** The CEO will lead the process of gaining consensus on the mission of the people decisions team. To that end, the CEO should articulate the company's values and vision and incorporate them into the team's statement of purpose.

3. **Define the process and standards.** The CEO could ask the people decisions team to propose a process and standards for deciding whom to hire, promote, and let go. The CEO would review the proposal, make suggestions, and modify it based on feedback after the company has used the process to make people decisions.

4. **Collect candidate information.** The company will gather information about candidates for hiring, promotion, and letting people go. To hire people, the company will seek candidates from internal referrals and job postings, and outside recruiters will interview the best candidates, check references, and offer positions to the ones with the best cultural fit and qualifications. For promotions, the company will speak with people who have worked with the candidate, both inside and outside the company, as appropriate, and make decisions based on the individual's performance and potential to excel in the new position. In letting people go, the company will also speak with people who have worked with the individual, gathering different information depending on the reason.

5. **Make people decisions.** Once all the information has been gathered, the people decisions team will meet, discuss what to do, make some decisions, and possibly seek out more information for other decisions.

6. **Implement decisions.** Ultimately, the company must carry out its people decisions. It will communicate job offers and sign contracts with them; share promotion news including job responsibilities, office location, and compensation; and prepare termination contracts and communicate with employees let go.

Takeaways For Stakeholders

Hiring, promoting, and letting people go is a shared responsibility of the board, the CEO, and a company's employees. Here are the imperatives for each of these stakeholders:

- **Board**
  - Identify key roles that must be filled to meet goals.
  - Refer strong candidates to the CEO.
  - Offer feedback on most strategic people decisions.

- **CEO**
  - Create a people decisions team.
  - Define vision and values, and incorporate them into the process of hiring, promoting, and letting people go.
  - Delegate people decisions where appropriate and step in where needed.
- **Employees**
  - Refer candidates for new positions.
  - Apply for promotions and help create new positions that will boost the company's growth.

Hiring, Promoting, and Letting People Go Success and Failure Case Studies

In this section, I offer case studies of hiring, promoting, and letting people go by successful and less successful startups at each scaling stage, analyze the cases, and extract principles for helping founders to hire, promote, and let people go at each stage.

Stage I: Winning the First Customer

Before a startup can win its first customers, it must win the battle for the most outstandingly qualified cofounders. The best cofounders are essential to winning a startup's first customers because such leaders have a better chance of finding customers who are willing to help the company design its product and possess the technical skills needed to build a series of ever-better prototypes to make those early customers willing to use and serve as references for the startup's product.

What makes outstanding cofounders varies for each startup. Yet the cases examined below reveal that such cofounders are

- Passionate about the problem they are trying to solve by starting a company
- The most talented product developers or company builders from the most successful companies and the best schools
- Well-networked in their industries

At the first stage of scaling, cofounders must attract the best talent they can to solve the many problems required of a company seeking to win its first customers. And cofounders who satisfy these tests have a much better chance of hiring the best talent for achieving the startup's mission.

Success Case Study: With $173 Million in Capital, Cloudian's Experienced Team Builds a Scalable Business Model

Introduction

If a startup targets a large market with a product that gives customers more bang for the buck, it has a shot at winning its first customers. Moreover, if the startup wins enough customers under the leadership of its founding team, it may be able to attract considerable private capital to fuel that growth. Indeed, that success should make it easier to attract a team of functional leaders who can help the company build a scalable business model. Once that team is in place, the startup may be able to sprint to liquidity. This comes to mind in considering Cloudian, a San Mateo, California-based distributed file systems purveyor supplying so-called object storage to the $52 billion enterprise storage market, which was growing at a more than 34% annual rate. But Cloudian was growing much faster than the industry, always winning against incumbents like NetApp and EMC when potential customers did a technical evaluation of its product.

Case Scenario

While Cloudian's business model was not yet scalable, it won customers for three reasons: it spent years building an excellent product for one of the world's most demanding customers, it started with an excellent technical team, and it was able to hire experienced functional leaders. Cloudian built a product that made a large company very happy and willing to recommend the company to others. "We spent three years making sure that our first customer, [Tokyo-based telecommunications giant] NTT, would be so happy with our product that it would be willing to tell the public about it. We will end 2018 with about 220 people, and to build a scalable business model we are increasing the proportion of revenues through value-added resellers (from 25% in 2016 to 90% in 2017)," said CEO Michael Tso. Cloudian was founded by technically outstanding leaders. For example, one of its cofounders, Hiroshi Ohta, is known in Japan for his engineering prowess. And Tso is an exceptionally talented engineer. He moved from mainland China to Hong Kong and then to Australia for high school. He was accepted at the only school he applied to, MIT, where he earned two BS degrees in Electrical Engineering and Computer Science and an MS in Electrical Engineering—all in 1993. He is a prolific inventor. According to Pitchbook, "Tso holds 36 patents and has been a technology trailblazer for over 20 years. At Inktomi, Tso led engineering for an e-commerce search engine, and designed a network congestion control system for KDDI which later became an industry standard. At Intel, he [led the development of] NarrowBand Sockets, commonly known as SmartMessaging, which enabled the world's first SMS ring-tone download service."

Such experience and excellence made it easier for Cloudian to attract talented functional leaders, particularly as it grew. "Our heads of sales, marketing, customer success, engineering, and finance have all been in the industry for a long time. The team can take us to an IPO, though our investors are very patient," Tso said. For example, consider Jon Ash, Cloudian's Vice President of Worldwide Sales. Ash, who was hired into the position in September 2014, was put in charge of Cloudian's direct and channel sales teams and its systems engineering organization. He had previously been Vice President of Sales at storage software vendor Nexenta. Ash said he was drawn to Cloudian by its "unbeatable value proposition, battle-hardened software platform, compelling appliances, and expanded sales team. Cloudian will introduce enterprises to entirely new levels of scalability, flexibility, and business value from their storage infrastructure." By August 2018, Ash was still leading Cloudian's sales, which helped the company to grow to 160 employees and 240 enterprise customers.

Case Analysis

Cloudian did all the right things to win its first customers. It made sure that its product would create value for an influential customer who would be a good reference for potential customers; its cofounders had outstanding technical credentials, which made it easier to attract top talent; it raised a substantial amount of capital; and its initial success made it easier to hire and motivate experienced functional executives who helped propel the company's growth.

Less Successful Case Study: Sapho Enjoys 320% Growth in a Small Market but Can It Get Large Enough to Go Public?

Introduction

One of the most important decisions a founder makes is which problem the startup will try to solve. The right choice is for the startup to deliver a product that offers customers in a huge market much more value at a lower price than rivals do. The wrong choice is to solve a problem that seems compelling to the founder but not to potential customers. A founder who does that may struggle to build a company large enough to change the world and in so doing may encounter challenges in hiring the people it needs to grow. While such a company may make gradual progress and do its best to overcome the limitations of its relatively small market, long sales cycles, humdrum mission, and less than stellar executive team, it is likely to struggle when it comes to attracting the world's best talent. That's what came to mind when I learned about San Bruno, California-based Sapho, which offers a company's employees "a modern portal experience that surfaces personalized and relevant tasks and data using micro apps," according to CrunchBase.

Founded in 2014, by September 2018 Sapho had raised nearly $28 million and said it was growing fast as it offered what it claimed was an easier way for employees to engage than did Microsoft SharePoint. Sapho was enjoying rapid percentage growth. As Fouad ElNaggar, cofounder and CEO, explained in a July 2018 interview, "We tripled revenues in 2016, experienced 320% revenue growth in 2017, and are on track to almost quadruple our revenues again in 2018. We have dozens of customers." Sapho was seeking to operate in a scalable manner. As ElNaggar, who earned an undergraduate degree in economics from Dartmouth and an MBA from UCLA, said, "We are much more focused on building a scalable, profitable business, which means we grow employees at a lower rate than revenues. We have grown our employee base by 50% to 75% per year every year since we started."

Case Scenario

Sapho's growth strategy hinged on investing heavily to build its product, delivering measurable economic benefits to customers, managing long sales cycles, and hiring people whom it believed would support its long-term growth. As ElNaggar said, "We've invested $30 million over four years to build the patented technology that powers Sapho. Solving the integration, workflow, tooling, deployment, and security challenges in a way that enables our customers to roll out our solution in a compliant way to their entire employee base in a matter of weeks instead of eating up a year took a lot of thought in architecting our solution."

Sapho made money by charging subscription fees. And given companies' security and compliance concerns, Sapho took a considerable amount of time to close sales transactions. "It takes us three to six months before we can meet with the Chief Information Officer or high-level IT executive who is in a position to make a purchase decision. We seed the organization by explaining how we can help companies engage more effectively with their employees. And once we sign up a company, we deploy quickly, with no systems integrators, and customers get value within a month."

ElNaggar wanted to make sure that employees were doing the right thing for customers. As he said, "We are building a rational business. We don't want to starve our growth. And we measure employee engagement and productivity. We sign three-year deals with customers, and unlike competitors, we stay with them to make sure they are getting high usage and return on investment from our product. We want to change how people work and make our customers happy enough to be willing to give us references."

Despite ElNaggar's interesting background, he lacked outstanding technical skills or previous success leading startups to profitable exits for investors. For example, he had extensive business development experience and served as a venture capitalist on the boards of several startups, none of which had successful exits. Sapho's other cofounder, Peter Yaro, started five enterprise infrastructure startups that were acquired by VMware and Sun Microsystems, among others. Marque Teegardin, Sapho's Chief Revenue Officer since May 2017, previously held senior sales positions in various software companies, including NICE Systems, StoredIQ (acquired in 2013 by IBM), and Mirantis, an open cloud infrastructure provider that had raised $220 million by September 2018.

Case Analysis

Sapho had won "dozens of customers" after four years in business. While it claimed to be growing rapidly, the high growth rate was likely attributable to its low revenues, although in the absence of disclosing revenues, there was no way to know how successful the company was. One possible flaw in Sapho's strategy was its decision to focus on solving a relatively unimportant problem, the solution to which would not have a dramatic economic benefit for customers. Another challenge was that the previous accomplishments of its top executives were insufficient for Sapho to attract world-class talent.

Principles

Founders seeking to hire, promote, and let people go to win initial customers should bear in mind the following dos and don'ts:

- **Do**
    - Hire the best cofounders possible to attract the best talent.
    - Use initial customer traction to raise capital so that the startup can afford to hire more talent.
    - Promote from within if the candidate can learn to excel in the next job.

- **Don't**
    - Assemble a founding team that lacks the skills needed to be successful.
    - Fill a position with a mediocre candidate because of pressure to achieve growth goals.

- Hold on to initial team members who can't contribute enough to the company's future.

- Hire an executive who has a strong track record but does not fit with the culture.

Stage 2: Building a Scalable Business Model

Building a scalable business model is a difficult challenge—made even more difficult if the company's CEO and board are not committed to doing so. As we've seen throughout this book, many rapidly-growing companies seek to sustain very high revenue growth and they fear that worrying about how to do so profitably is a distraction. However, if a company can go public while burning through capital, it will eventually have to forge a path to profitability. A handful of charismatic CEOs, such as Tesla's Elon Musk or Elizabeth Holmes, former CEO of Theranos, can defer that day of reckoning by galvanizing investors' emotions. However, the better path at this stage is for a company to stop growing quickly until it can make its business model self-sustaining. If that does not happen, the company will have trouble holding on to its talent.

Simply put, to build a scalable business model, a company must start with a clear understanding of why it's important to have one. And from there, the company should take the following steps to hire and promote the right people:

- Design an organization with the key functions that must be managed efficiently to build a scalable business model.

- Promote or hire executives to lead the functions who fit the culture and have or can learn the skills needed to make their function far more efficient so the startup's business model is scalable.

- Let people go or move aside executives who can't contribute to this effort or try to slow it down.

Success Case Study: Confluent's Scalable Business Model Is Built on World Class Talent

Introduction

If the talented inventors of a key product built for a respected company decide to start their own company, good things can happen. The good things are particularly pronounced if the company targets a large market that needs the product they invented. If the company builds a product that delivers better value to customers at a lower price, growth is likely to follow. And that should ease the recruitment of talented executives and others. This comes to mind in considering Palo Alto-based Confluent, a player in the $27 billion market for middleware, software that tracks the flow of data from its source to its destination. Confluent was founded in September 2014 by a team of techies from LinkedIn and by September 2018 had raised nearly $81 million. With over 300 employees (up from three in 2014), Confluent boosted its subscription revenue four-fold in 2017 and said it expected to do the same in 2018, according to my August 2018 interview with CEO Jay Kreps. Kreps was the lead architect for data infrastructure at LinkedIn and developed the open source Apache Kafka distributed streaming platform the business social network used, before cofounding Confluent. He helped develop Kafka to manage the growing complexity of distributed systems brought on by new applications and larger data sets. His unit was spun out and won business from Netflix, Uber, Airbnb, Goldman Sachs, and Target. Audi said that Kafka was powering its connected cars.

Case Scenario

Confluent's business model was scalable, meaning it grew revenues far faster than its costs so it had a path to profitability. As Kreps said, "We offer a subscription product and as companies get more value, they pay more. This means that we don't need to grow headcount as fast as we grow revenue. We can't mess it up. Despite the surplus of private capital, we have to focus on efficiency and make sure that the cost to acquire a customer is less than the amount of recurring revenue that customer generates." Confluent was organized by function and said it made money on its customers, although it spent money to grow. "We have sales (by region), marketing (public relations, lead generation, advertising, and conferences), customer success (training and service), engineering (architecture and implementation), and product management (developing and tracking the roadmap). Growth requires investment, which is not bad if the core economics are sound," he said. Confluent tried to promote from within but was doing quite a bit of hiring from the outside. "This organization structure works well. But we often hire functional leaders and executives who have done it before from the outside. We usually know the person we hire and are confident that they can be successful at Confluent. We need people for execution and give them a runway," said Kreps.

Confluent's founding team helped it to attract excellent talent. In addition to Kreps, cofounder and Chief Technology Officer Neha Narkhede was one of the initial engineers who created Apache Kafka and was responsible for LinkedIn's petabyte-scale streams infrastructure. Confluent also hired and promoted Todd Barnett, an experienced sales executive who had previously led the America's sales force for Acquia, that helped organizations use Drupal (another open source platform) for web engagement management. Barnett joined Confluent as Vice President of Worldwide Sales in April 2016 and in August 2018 was promoted to Chief Revenue Officer. Confluent believed that Barnett would help accelerate its growth when he was hired. According to the company, Barnett had previously worked at "Aperture (acquired by Emerson), Systinet (acquired by Mercury Interactive) and others. With a strong track record for creating momentum-driven sales models that expand both the mid-market and enterprise customer base, Barnett is responsible for expanding the Confluent sales team and driving global sales."

Case Analysis

Confluent grew much faster than the middleware market while creating a scalable business model by offering a groundbreaking product that was used by LinkedIn. The outstanding technical accomplishments of its founding team made it possible for Confluent to raised considerable capital to fund its rapid growth and to attract outstanding talent such as Barnett, who had previous experience scaling organizations like Confluent.

Less Successful Case Study: BigID Targets a Large Opportunity but Can It Build a Scalable Business Model?

Introduction

When a company says it's growing at over 100% and won't disclose its revenues, you can be confident that it's not quite ready for an IPO. But it's unusual for me to talk with a CEO who reports 800% revenue growth in a $19 billion market and claims his company is winning business from IBM, Oracle, and a raft of smaller companies like Varonis, Talend, and Symantec.

But that's what Dimitri Sirota, CEO of Manhattan-based data protection provider BigID, told me in an August 2018 interview. Sirota, who studied physics at McGill and University of British Columbia, was head of strategy for CA Technologies after it acquired cloud security provider Layer7 Technologies, which he cofounded. As he commuted to work from New York City, he was reading and hearing about the abuse of personal information and realized that there was no purpose-built solution for protecting it. This gave him an idea for BigID, "A lightbulb went off in my head: what if you could secure personal information and help companies comply with GDPR and privacy legislation that's likely to go into effect in Japan, Korea, Australia, Brazil, Chile, and India? There was a gap in the market."

Case Scenario

Sirota believed that the opportunity for BigID was large and he raised considerable capital to support its growth. As he said, "Access governance is a $1 billion market, data governance is $3 billion, data loss protection is a $1.5 billion market. And the market for data governance is growing at a breakneck pace to $19 billion." BigID was growing. "Between February 2016 and August 2018, we've grown from six people to about 60 and expect to end the year with 80 people and we've raised $46.1 million. We were growing so fast that we did Series A and Series B rounds in quick succession. That's because we were able to get product market fit and repeatedly bring in customers quickly. We are using the money to build a salesforce, putting people in new territories as we generate sizeable revenues from our accounts." By August 2018, BigID was targeting its next round of financing by growing from about $10 million to $40 million. "We are training people to sell and build a support organization that can provide 24x7 coverage. We are also showing partners interested in the market what we are doing. When we get our Series C, we will go into new territories, expanding into Asia and Europe," he said.

BigID's top executive team was missing people with a track record of tremendous success. For example, it lacked a head of sales and was trying to hire one by the end of September 2018. As Sirota said, "We want somebody who has had experience growing from $30 million to $60 million and is a good cultural fit. We should laugh at each other's jokes. The person should have worked in more places than one and know the challenges and how to solve them." Nimrod Vax, BigID's head of R&D, formalized the product development processes as the company grew. According to Sirota, "At the beginning, it's important to have clarity about what you want to build. You must make sure your minimum viable product solves a problem. After you get product/market fit, you must build a product that can handle commercial realities such as security, scaling, and performance. Then you must support a variety of use cases, introduce quality assurance, and build add-on products." Prior to BigID, Vax had worked as a development manager at identity management software provider Netegrity, which CA acquired in 2005 for $430 million, and he rose to VP of Product Management before leaving to start BigID. And BigID employed Scott Casey as COO/CFO, yet his previous experience as CFO of previous startups did not include any successful exits and he had not previously served as Chief Operating Officer.

Case Analysis

BigID grew rapidly from a small base as it took advantage of a major push in the spring of 2018 for companies to comply with European privacy regulations. It raised considerable capital, yet it was missing key strengths in its management team and was struggling to hire the talent needed to expand the company, build a scalable business model, and find new markets that would enable it to sustain its growth. It was unclear whether its founding team had the skill to recruit the talent it would need to reach its growth goals.

Principles

Founders seeking to hire, promote, and let people go to build a scalable business model should bear in mind the following dos and don'ts:

- **Do**
    - Hire the best functional leaders possible to make key processes such as landing new customers, generating high quality sales leads, and assuring high customer satisfaction more efficient and effective.

    - Seek candidates for these roles from people in the founders' professional networks who fit the startup's culture and have demonstrated their ability to lead a company to an IPO within the startup's industry.

    - Once hired, give the executives the freedom to identify and solve business problems.

- **Don't**
    - Hire quickly to fill a key slot without assuring cultural fit and relevant experience.

    - Attempt to control the key decisions of the newly hired executive.

Stage 3: Sprinting to Liquidity

Sprinting to liquidity works best when the company has made its business processes scalable. If the company has achieved this, it will have hired or promoted key executives into the leadership roles needed to build a scalable business model and sprint to liquidity. Having achieved this goal, the company should be able to raise enough capital to hire sales teams, boost marketing efforts, build or acquire new products, and provide excellent service to bring in new customers at a rapid rate and keep them happy enough for them to boost their spending on the company's products. If the company has world-class executives, they should be able to attract and promote talented people who can manage the teams of individual contributors in roles such as sales, marketing, product management, engineering, and service who will do the work needed to sprint to liquidity. By setting clear goals and holding everyone accountable for achieving them, such a company should be well positioned to go public.

Success Case Study: With Leadership from Two Nutanix Executives and $296 Million in Capital, ThoughtSpot Sprints to IPO

Introduction

When a startup achieves unicorn status, a private market valuation of at least $1 billion, it marks a considerable leap forward on the path to an initial public offering. The chances for such a liquidity event are increased if the company has excellent top leaders, targets a huge market, is boosting revenues rapidly, and has a scalable business model in place. What's more, the prospect that such a company could soon go public would ease the recruitment of talented executives who had previously led a private company to an IPO. This comes to mind in considering Palo Alto-based data analysis service provider ThoughtSpot (which raised nearly $296 million in venture capital). ThoughtSpot, which raised $145 million in May 2018 at a pre-money valuation of $855 million, was founded in June 2012 by Ajeet Singh, a Nutanix cofounder. In August 2018, he stepped aside from the CEO position and up to Executive Chairman to bring on Nutanix's President, Sudheesh Nair, as CEO. ThoughtSpot was growing rapidly. As Nair told me in a September 2018 interview, "We are growing at triple digits [fourth quarter fiscal year 2018 revenues were up 180%, according to Barron's], winning at the tip of the pyramid, and revenue from our largest customer is eight figures."

Case Scenario

ThoughtSpot was doing so well because it offered customers what they perceived as a better product in a huge market. By bringing in a new CEO who was well-acquainted with its founder, it was positioning itself well for an IPO. ThoughtSpot viewed an IPO as a funding milestone, a step in its long-term mission. As Nair said, "It's a tremendous market worth over $100 billion, according to IDC. The value will only increase, and the market will get bigger at a rapid clip. We are solving a difficult problem with the right team. We are investing in a search/artificial intelligence platform. We have three of the five Fortune 5 companies. They choose us due to our platform's performance, usability, scale, security, and ability to integrate with their systems." ThoughtSpot was growing—and taking business from publicly traded rival Tableau— because it took advantage of three key trends better than rivals. As Nair said, "First, data is created everywhere at a much more rapid pace from the cloud and IoT—coming from Salesforce, AWS, Azure, and Oracle databases. Second, businesses are in a race with the competition to see who can turn data into actionable insights most quickly. Finally, in looking at one and two, people are the bottleneck; there are not enough database administrators, data analysts, and data scientists to satisfy the demand. A Tableau report takes seven to 10 days to produce. That's too long. ThoughtSpot shortcuts it all."

Between Singh and Nair, Nutanix's pain from losing top talent was ThoughtSpot's gain. Nair explained that he enjoyed the building stage of a startup when it's "us against the world." And he clearly felt he was getting back to that feeling when he joined ThoughtSpot. In September 2018, Singh told me that the combination of his long-standing relationship with Nair from Nutanix and his interest in focusing on product development made him comfortable with the idea of ceding the CEO job and giving Nair the responsibility for achieving ThoughtSpot's ambitious growth goals. Nair was happy to have someone to talk with about the challenges of being CEO. As he said, "I knew Ajeet and the people he assembled. Being CEO is a lonely job and Ajeet is not pulling out. He will be as involved, and we will work side by side focusing on different decisions." Nair saw joining ThoughtSpot to change the kinds of conversations he had with customers. As he said, "Nutanix and cloud players were sucking the oxygen out of the industry by cutting prices 40%. I wanted to go from having conversations about saving money to talking about how to help customers make money." Singh wanted help scale ThoughtSpot after raising the latest round of funding. As he said, "We raised $145 million and I needed help scaling the business. Sudheesh was an angel investor in ThoughtSpot. My passion is product; I was Chief Product Officer at Nutanix. I am like a kid in the candy store and ThoughtSpot was my most ambitious undertaking. I was hoping to have him along for the journey."

In September 2018, ThoughtSpot had 300 people and wanted to preserve its culture based on the values of selfless excellence, team, and doing the right thing as it grew to 1,000 people. As Singh said, "40% of the team works on product, 40% on sales, and 20% on marketing, general, and administration. We are expanding into Australia, Japan, and Europe and are operating offices in Palo Alto, Seattle, Dallas, and Bangalore." Filling new roles as the company grew was a challenge. As he explained, "The talent we have developed since the beginning of the company is some of the most valuable. But we need different scaling skills to build new product and business streams. We have a sales person who built a team and became a chief evangelist who landed customers in Japan, Singapore, and Australia." Before hiring Nair, ThoughtSpot had already succeeded in hiring excellent executive talent. Consider the example of its Chief Revenue Officer, Brian Blond. He joined the company in 2016 having previously led strategic business development and sales, resulting in rapid global growth at enterprise software companies. He had previously been at Vitrue, a social marketing platform provider acquired in 2012 for $300 million by Oracle. Prior to that, he was a sales executive at Moxie Software and BladeLogic, contributing to its 2007 IPO.

Case Analysis

ThoughtSpot reached unicorn status six years after it was founded—and a few months after raising $145 million was able to hire a CEO to supplement the founder's product development skills. The company's outstanding executive team was able to develop a product that customers found compelling, which propelled its growth. It seems likely that ThoughtSpot will be successful at continuing to build the company and ultimately go public.

Less Successful Case Study: After Five Years, Exabeam Raises $115 Million to Accelerate Its March to 10% Market Share

Introduction

A company that takes its time to build a scalable business model is better off than one that can't get more efficient as it expands. If this company is targeting a relatively small market filled with rivals, the challenge is made even greater. For such ventures, the question is whether the company's cofounders can hire the kind of top-notch talent it will need to sprint to liquidity. Through patience, determination, and disciplined execution, such a company might eventually reach the point where it could go public. By August 2018, these questions loomed large for Exabeam, a San Mateo, California-based security information and event management (SIEM) company founded in 2013. SIEM providers searched through billions of pieces of data in a company's computer infrastructure to try to figure out which PCs and laptops had been hacked. In an August 2018 interview, Exabeam CEO Nir Polak explained that he saw combat in the Israeli army and served as a top executive at Imperva, a Redwood Shores, California-based $322 million (2017 revenue) cybersecurity firm, and its application delivery platform-subsidiary Incapsula. He came up with the idea for Exabeam because he thought that companies could find the hacker's path more quickly if an AI-backed algorithm did the searching instead of a person.

Case Scenario

Exabeam had grown rapidly by taking market share from the leading publicly-traded SIEM provider, Splunk. And Exabeam's success was due to several factors including the perceived value of its product, its ability to raise enough capital, the way it orga-nized its people, and its culture. However, it remained to be seen whether its people could take the company to an IPO.

Exabeam had added staff quickly and organized by function. "We had four people in 2013, we launched in February 2015 and began hiring. Now we have 250. To make sure we are scaling efficiently, we track top line growth and the ratio of cost of goods sold to revenue. We look at how we compare on sales and marketing, general and administrative, and research and development expenses and margins to publicly traded companies when they were at our stage. Every year we need to be much more efficient," he said. Exabeam had a strong culture and, with its five-star rating on Glassdoor, did not suffer much turnover. "We hire raw talent and let them grow; we have little attrition. I share information from board meetings with everyone. We work together and win together; hold cross-departmental events so people can connect socially; have a no-ego executive staff; engage in open communi-cation. We trust and share, and we do what's right for the customer." Exabeam hired people who were seasoned in private and public companies like FireEye and EMC. As Polak explained, "We have heads of marketing, field operations, customer success, engineering, general and administration, and IT who report to me. We are all trying to meet our revenue goals within budget. And we have a strong board with a fiduciary responsibility that will push you."

Exabeam hired executives with prior experience helping startups to go public. For example, Executive Vice President of Field Operations Ralph Pisani previously led the Imperva worldwide sales organization from an early stage through its successful IPO. Prior to Imperva, he was Vice President of Worldwide OEM Sales at Secure Computing, which was acquired by McAfee. In July 2014, when Exabeam hired Pisani, Polak said, "Ralph brings his vast experience in cybersecurity and sales to play a key role on our team as we continue to grow and develop our technology. [Given the number of competitors in the SIEM market,] having an influential player like Ralph will elevate Exabeam above the noise," Pisani said he joined Exabeam because of its "impressive founding team that's applying big data security analytics to arm IT with the tools it needs." By November 2018, Exabeam had added two more senior executives to its team: Manish Sarin, who since 2012 had been Executive Vice President of Corporate Planning and Development at Proofpoint, as its new CFO and Rajiv Taneja, who had previously been Vice President of Engineering at Cisco, as Executive Vice President of Engineering. As for Exabeam's future, in August 2018, Polak said, "In three years we will be much bigger, a leader in our industry."

Case Analysis

Exabeam achieved considerable success, although compared to ThoughtSpot, it had chosen a smaller market opportunity and after almost the same amount of time in business had yet to reach unicorn status as of August 2018. Nevertheless, Exabeam was able to grow rapidly, claimed to be displacing the incumbent in competitive bids, and had attracted a talented executive team from a previous publicly traded company where the CEO and the head of field operations had both worked. It seems that Exabeam will be able to go public by 2021; however, many challenges need to be met to reach that goal.

Principles

Founders seeking to hire, promote, and let people go while sprinting to liquidity should bear in mind the following dos and don'ts:

- **Do**
  - Promote or hire executives to key leadership roles who have previous experience taking companies public.

- Let people go or move aside executives who cannot fulfill the responsibilities as the company goes towards an IPO.

- Set specific quarterly goals for the company and key functions, reward executives who meet the goals, and hire replacements for those who, after a chance to improve, cannot.

- Share information with all employees.

- **Don't**

  - Promote people into executive roles who lack the skill and attitude to fulfill them effectively.

  - Hire executives from outside who do not fit with the company's culture.

  - Hide information from all but favored executives.

Stage 4: Running the Marathon

Success Case Study: SendGrid's CEO Takes the Company Public in 2017 and Sells Out to Twilio in 2018

Introduction

What happens when you put a talented turnaround executive in charge of a flailing medium-sized, money-losing, stagnant tech company? In the case of Denver-based SendGrid, a firm founded in 2009 that supplied cloud-based email service, you get a publicly traded company that was growing fast and generating positive cash flow and in the 10 months following its IPO had roughly doubled its stock price. SendGrid described itself as a leader in the $11 billion "digital communication" market that provided links to ads, password changes, and other sites at the bottom of emails. In September 2018, SendGrid said it "had 74,000 paying customers, including Spotify, Airbnb, and Uber, and sent 1.5 billion messages on an average day, touching more than three billion unique email recipients every quarter."

SendGrid's CEO took on the job in September 2014. According to SendGrid's 2018 proxy statement, Sameer Dholakia, who had a BA and MA from Stanford and a Harvard MBA, was previously Group Vice President and General Manager of the Cloud Platforms group from 2011 to 2014 and Vice President of Marketing from 2010 to 2011 at Citrix Systems after Citrix's 2010 acquisition of VMLogix, a provider of virtualization management software, of which he was CEO. These experiences helped prepare him to be CEO of a public company. As he told me in a September 2018 interview, "VMLogix was a pre-revenue, pre-cash flow company when I joined with seven employees. I built it out and in 2008 we had a term sheet to be acquired by Citrix and then the financial crisis hit. We kept the company going and in 2010, Citrix bought the company. I stayed at Citrix and soaked up insights from its CEO about how to manage a company with 5,000 or 6,000 employees." SendGrid gave Dholakia a chance to go back to being CEO. "I met with a partner at Bessemer Ventures and he told me the SendGrid opportunity was all the things I cared about. SendGrid placed a strong cultural value on humility. It had $30 million in trailing revenue, nearly 200 people, a decelerating growth rate, and a negative 30% margin. I saw the potential for it to be a great company and I joined in 2014," he said. By October 15, 2018, SendGrid lost its independence after Twilio announced that would acquire the company for $2 billion.

Case Scenario

After its IPO, SendGrid continued to grow quickly and generate positive cash flow although it was unprofitable. In the process of turning around SendGrid, Dholakia replaced most of the executives who were there when he joined, added a new product line, and made the business more focused and productive with a clearly-articulated culture. In the second quarter of 2018, SendGrid, which went public in November 2017, reported faster revenue growth (32%) and $3.9 million worth of free cash flow while reporting a $300,000 net loss. Dholakia, who lived in Silicon Valley, faced a challenge in boosting growth and reducing cash bleed of a company that had most of its people in Denver and in Irvine, California. As he said, "I saw that we could be a leader in push notifications (delivering messages and conversations with end users). We stopped hiring so many people who we couldn't ingest and make productive. We created alignment around a mission and vision in 2014 and 2015." SendGrid also launched a second product for marketing, which nearly doubled the company. As he said, "The new product was instrumental; we had a $25 million run rate. And we became laser-focused on improving weaknesses in our product relative to the competition from the perspective of customers. This gave us a tailwind in 2016 and 2017 leading up to our November 2017 IPO."

Getting the company to IPO-readiness was not without pain. "Getting the right people is a difficult topic. When I stepped in we changed executive leadership. Only one (the general counsel) out of the eight original members of the executive team are still with the company. We had people who were important to getting the company from $0 to $30 million in revenue, but the skill set for a public company is different. If they didn't have the right skills, we helped them with love and grace in an honest and clear conversation," he said. For example, in August 2016 Dholakia replaced SendGrid's head of sales and customers success with Leandra Fishman, who had previously been VP Global Corporate Sales at Jive Software, VP Worldwide Inside Sales at EMC, and VP Sales at VMLogix (where Dholakia had been CEO). Another big change was in culture and organization design. "We have a 4H culture: Happy,

Hungry, Humble, Honest. As a public company we have made changes in our go to market, opening new ways to get to customers. We are making long-term investments in product and engineering that will take three to five years to pay off. We are also extending the planning cycle from quarterly before we were public to three to five-year views," said Dholakia. He was in no hurry to move elsewhere. As he said, "I have so much fun every day. You must love what you're doing, believe in the mission and vision, and love building the business. We created the category and we are the leader amongst 6 to 12 players (which include AWS's simple email service). I also love the people and you need a great culture to keep people wanting to be there." Would Dholakia continue to love the culture after the deal closed in 2019? Twilio said that SendGrid would become a wholly owned subsidiary of Twilio but Dholakia would not be taking over the CEO slot at Twilio.

Case Analysis

SendGrid faced an existential crisis when it brought in Dholakia as CEO in 2014. He took the company public about three years later and by September 2018 had overseen rapid growth, positive cash flow generation, and a more than doubling of its stock price. A key part of that success was its ability to broaden its product line, expand its geographic scope, and replace almost every member of its executive team with skilled outsiders. As of September 2018, Dholakia appeared to be enthusiastic about the company, his job, and the people he worked with. However, the next month SendGrid was acquired. I'd give Dholakia high marks for turning around the company when he joined and finding a good exit for the company.

Less Successful Case Study: Anaplan Files for IPO with Inexperienced Executive Team

Introduction

Companies can go public despite imperfections. For example, as we saw in Chapter 3, planning software provider Anaplan had raised substantial amounts of capital with help from a new CEO who had brought in many new executives. And in September 2018, Anaplan filed for an initial public offering despite losing substantial amounts of money and fielding a team of executives with little experience working together, including a then-recently departed accounting officer who the week before had quit Tesla after working there for less than a month.

Anaplan, which was founded in 2006 and valued at $1.4 billion in November 2017, had undergone considerable turmoil at the top. Anaplan's CEO since January 2017, Frank Calderoni spent 17 years as CFO, often paired with an operating role, at Cisco Systems and SanDisk. Most recently, he had been CFO and EVP of operations at Red Hat, an enterprise software company, where he spent less than two years. Calderoni took over after its previous CEO, Frederic Laluyaux, who had previously been an executive at SAP, parted ways with the company in April 2016. Laluyaux spent over three years as CEO, having taken over in September 2012 from cofounder Guy Haddleton. Laluyaux raised $90 million in a Series E round of capital in January 2016, which valued Anaplan at $1.1 billion. But the board decided that the company would not be able to go public under Laluyaux's leadership. After Laluyaux left, then-Anaplan Chair Bob Calderoni (Frank's brother) said, "The board and Fred believe it's the right time to bring in a new set of talent to take us to a much higher level and become a much bigger company." Ravi Mohan, Anaplan board member and managing director at Shasta Ventures, said, "Unbridled growth [is no longer] the most valued characteristic. Now, it's profitable sustained growth, and we're building a company that reflects that." When he took over as CEO, Anaplan, which makes money by selling monthly subscriptions, was large enough to go public and was still growing fast. As Calderoni pointed out, "In its fiscal year ending January 2017, Anaplan had $120 million in revenue, was growing at 75%, added 250 customers for a total of 700, employed over 700 people in 16 offices in 12 countries, had raised a total of $240 million in capital, and generated good cash flow."

Case Scenario

In September 2018, Anaplan filed for an IPO. It reported 40% revenue growth along with considerable losses and a management team with very limited experience working together. Anaplan's prospectus indicated that its revenues had risen about 40% to $168 million in fiscal 2018, its user count had soared 126% from 434 in January 2016 to 979 in July 2018, and its net loss increased 19% to $47.5 million in 2018. Along with the losses came a management team with strong prior experience, little of which occurred at Anaplan. For example, its CFO, David Morton, was hired in early September 2018 after he had toiled for less than a month as Tesla's Chief Accounting Officer. From 2015 to August 2018, Morton had been Seagate Technology's CFO. Anaplan's Chief Revenue Officer, Steven Birdsall, had been onboard since February 2018; previously he held brief executive positions at Radial, an e-commerce startup, and Hearst Business Media. Prior to that Birdsall was a top executive at SAP, including Chief Operating Officer. What's more, Anaplan's Chief People Officer, Chief Marketing Officer, and Chief Account Officer had also joined within the year before its IPO filing. As Anaplan's prospectus warned, "These members of management are critical to our vision, strategic direction, culture, and overall business success. Because of these recent changes, our senior management team, including members of our financial and accounting staff, has not worked at the company for an extended period and may not be able to work together effectively to execute our business objectives." As we saw in Chapter 3, by November 2, 2018, it was clear that Anaplan's IPO had been successful, valuing the company at $4 billion—way above its $1.4 billion valuation in its last pre-IPO financing round.

Case Analysis

Anaplan endured considerable turmoil at the top but its most recent CEO was able to file for an IPO in September 2018. While one of Anaplan's lead investors was eager for the company to grow profitably when the board appointed Calderoni as CEO in January 2017, its financial filings presented a mixed picture: rapid growth with growing losses. Moreover, Calderoni scrambled to appoint executives responsible for revenue, marketing, people, and finances after his appointment. In so doing, he assembled a team of people with strong prior work experience who had not worked together effectively. By November 2018, it was unclear whether its executive team would be able to lead Anaplan to profitable growth after its successful IPO.

Principles

Founders seeking to hire, promote, and let people go while running the marathon should bear in mind the following dos and don'ts:

- **Do**
    - Articulate the company's vision and values clearly and embed them in the process for hiring and promoting people.
    - Hire a top executive team that is motivated by the company's vision, shares its values, and has prior experience running key functions in a rapidly growing public company.
    - Replace top executives who are unable to achieve the company's short- and longer-term goals.
- **Don't**
    - Neglect the formulation and communication of vision and values.
    - Hire executives with strong functional expertise but limited experience in the industry and unclear commitment to the company's vision and values.

Hiring, Promoting, and Firing Success And Failure Principles

To hire, promote, and let people go at each scaling stage, CEOs must follow the principles summarized in Table 6-1.

Table 6-1. Summary of principals for hiring, promoting, and letting people go

Scaling Stage	Dos	Don'ts
1: Winning the first customer	Hire the best cofounders possible to attract the best talent. Use initial customer traction to raise capital so that the startup can afford to hire more talent. Promote from within if the candidate can learn to excel in the next job.	Assemble a founding team that lacks the skills needed to be successful. Fill a position with a mediocre candidate because of pressure to achieve growth goals. Hold on to initial team members who can't contribute enough to the company's future. Hire an executive who has a strong track record but does not fit with the culture.
2: Scaling the business model	Hire the best functional leaders possible to make key processes, such as landing new customers, generating high quality sales leads, and assuring high customer satisfaction, more efficient and effective. Seek candidates for these roles from people in the founders' professional networks who fit the startup's culture and have demonstrated their ability to lead a company to an IPO within the startup's industry. Once hired, give the executives the freedom to identify and solve business problems.	Hire quickly to fill a key slot without assuring cultural fit and relevant experience. Attempt to control the key decisions of the newly hired executive.
3: Sprinting to liquidity	Promote or hire executives to key leadership roles who have previous experience taking companies public. Let people go or move aside executives who cannot fulfill the responsibilities as the company goes towards an IPO. Set specific quarterly goals for the company and key functions, reward executives who meet the goals, and hire replacements for those who, after a chance to improve, cannot. Share information with all employees.	Promote people into executive roles who lack the skill and attitude to fulfill them effectively. Hire executives from outside who do not fit with the company's culture. Hide information from all but favored executives.

(continued)

Table 6-1. (*continued*)

Scaling Stage	Dos	Don'ts
4: Running the marathon	Articulate the company's vision and values clearly and embed them in the process for hiring and promoting people. Hire and motivate a top executive team that is motivated by the company's vision, shares its values, and has prior experience running key functions in a rapidly-growing public company. Replace top executives who are unable to achieve the company's short- and longer-term goals.	Neglect the formulation and communication of vision and values. Hire executives with strong functional expertise but limited experience in the industry and unclear commitment to the company's vision and values.

Are You Doing Enough to Hire, Promote, and Let People Go Effectively?

Hiring, promoting, and letting people go effectively assures that a startup has the right people to achieve its growth goals. As the company grows, the people in the roles tend to change along with the organization structure. The best CEOs realize that there are advantages and disadvantages to promoting from within and from hiring from the outside. To test whether your company is doing enough to hire, promote, and let people go people, ask these four questions:

- Have you articulated a clear vision and values that inform the process of hiring, promoting, and letting people go?

- Are you weighing the advantages and disadvantages of promoting from within to fill a new executive or management role?

- If a strong contributor does not fit the requirements of a new role, do you help the person find a new job or manage them respectfully out of the company?

- If you hire from the outside for a new role, do you evaluate whether the candidate embraces the company's vision and values, has the skills needed to do the job as it evolves, and will take responsibility for achieving the company's goals?

Conclusion

Hiring, promoting, and letting people go effectively is an element in a cluster of scaling levers that enable a company to implement its growth strategy for turning an idea into a large company. Underlying the process of hiring, promoting, and letting people go effectively is the notion that a leader must be hard-headed and warm-hearted when it comes to deciding which person should perform a key role in the organization as it progresses from winning its first customers to running the marathon. The right person for each role should embrace the company's vision and values and can meet the goals the company expects of the role as it changes to help the company sustain its growth. Chapter 7 will focus on how companies hold people accountable for achieving the company's short- and longer-term goals.

Holding People Accountable

In Chapters 5 and 6, we explored how CEOs define organizational roles and fill those roles as the company scales. And while CEOs generally hire talented people and let them choose how best to do their jobs, they hold people accountable for specific outcomes. CEOs hold people accountable for specific outcomes because the board does the same to the CEO, usually expecting the company to meet quarterly revenue growth targets. The CEO must overcome three challenges to hold people accountable for achieving the startup's goals:

- **Impact and control:** Not all functions can directly affect revenue growth. For example, sales people are usually accountable for quarterly revenue goals, but how should the CEO measure the activities of marketing, engineering, and other functions? Can these metrics encourage functions to contribute to corporate goals in ways that are meaningful and that they can control?

- **Buy in:** Each function should be confident that it can meet specific targets, and doing so requires agreement between the CEO and the functions about the variables to be tracked as well as the value of those variables that the functions will be expected to meet.

© Peter S. Cohan 2019
P. S. Cohan, *Scaling Your Startup*, https://doi.org/10.1007/978-1-4842-4312-1_7

- **Assess and improve:** These first two challenges must be overcome without really knowing which metrics will drive the right behavior and the desired outcomes. In holding people accountable, there is a danger of creating too many measures that drive people in different directions. The best hope for CEOs is that over time they will learn what works and what distracts people.

To overcome these challenges to holding people accountable, the CEO must take the seven steps detailed in Figure 7-1.

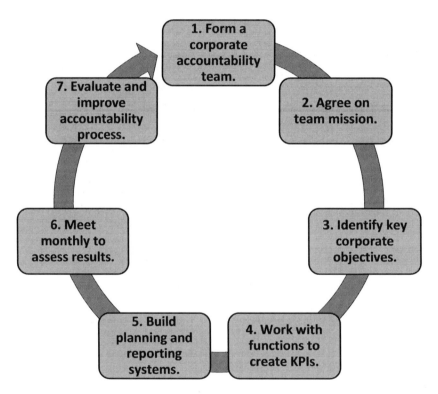

Figure 7-1. Seven steps to holding people accountable

These steps are the following:

1. **Form a corporate accountability team.** The CEO must first assemble a team of key functional executives. The team should consist of the heads of sales, engineering, marketing, service, finance, and human resources.

2. **Agree on team mission.** The team should meet to agree on its purpose. A good mission for the team might be to create and improve processes to hold people accountable for achieving the company's goals.

3. **Identify key corporate objectives.** After the team has agreed on its mission, the CEO should suggest a set of three to five corporate objectives, such as specific revenue growth goals, new product initiatives, and plans to expand into new countries. Such corporate objectives would evolve in response to changing customer needs, new technologies, and other factors.

4. **Work with functions to create key performance indicators.** The heads of the functions should propose key performance indicators that are linked to the corporate objectives. For example, sales might be measured on the number of new customers it brings in; marketing could strive to generate new opportunities for sales; customer service could be assessed based on net promoter score, customer renewal, and revenue per customer targets; and engineering could be assessed based on achievement of product roadmap objectives and revenue from new products. These key performance indicators should be debated within the functions and in meetings of the corporate accountability team to make sure that they are internally consistent, align with the corporate objectives, and are controllable by the functions.

5. **Build planning and reporting systems.** While the company is building consensus around accountability measures, it should be thinking about how to build a system that will provide a reliable and timely plan with actual data. Absent such a planning and reporting system, the company will not be able to hold people accountable.

6. **Meet monthly to assess results.** The CEO should meet with the corporate accountability team periodically—monthly. The purpose of the meeting should be to compare the actual performance to the plan, to assess gaps between results and expectations, and agree on tactics to close these performance gaps.

7. **Evaluate and improve accountability process.** The CEO should reevaluate the accountability process each quarter or each year, depending on how well the company is meeting its goals. If the company can set and achieve ambitious goals consistently, then the process does not need to be updated as urgently. However, if the company falls short of its goals and struggles to get back on track, the CEO must consider whether the process should be analyzed and fixed, or whether the people in charge of specific functions are the source of the problems.

Takeaways for Stakeholders

Holding people accountable is a shared responsibility of the board, the CEO, and a company's employees. Here are the imperatives for each of these stakeholders:

- **Board**

  - Hire a CEO with experience holding people accountable.

  - Review and advise the CEO on corporate objectives.

  - Help the CEO learn best practices to hold people accountable.

- **CEO**

  - Work with the executive team to set corporate objectives.

  - Collaborate with functional executives to develop key performance indicators that are controllable and linked to corporate objectives.

- Every week or month, compare actual performance to plan, analyze variances, and act to get back on track.

- Evaluate and improve the effectiveness of the performance management process.

- **Employees**

  - Help identify key performance indicators that are controllable and consistent with corporate objectives.

  - Take responsibility for achieving performance milestones.

  - Help analyze variances between goals and actual performance, and propose corrective action.

Holding People Accountable Success and Failure Case Studies

In this section, I offer case studies of holding people accountable in successful and less successful startups at each scaling stage, analyze the cases, and extract principles for helping founders to hold people accountable at each stage.

Stage 1: Winning the First Customer

Success Case Study: With $27 Million in Capital, Arcadia Data Holds Its 65 People Accountable for 500% Growth

Introduction

As a startup wins its first customers, investors might wonder whether the CEO has the skills required to build a scalable business model. As we saw in previous chapters, the skills required for Stage 1 are different than the ones for Stage 2. And if a CEO can't adapt, the board will probably need to replace the CEO. There are many ways to tell whether a CEO will be able to make it to the second stage, one of which is how the CEO holds people accountable. This comes to mind in considering San Mateo, California-based business intelligence software supplier Arcadia Data, which grew revenues 500% in 2018 and in October 2018 raised $15 million, bringing its total to $27 million. With over 2,500 customers and eight-fold growth between September 2016 and September 2018, Arcadia, founded in 2012, had achieved success in attracting its first customers.

Behind Acadia Data's growth was a quantum value leap, meaning its product delivered more bang for the customer's buck than what rivals were offering. As CEO Sushil Thomas said in a September 2018 interview, "We compete for the biggest use cases with 40 petabytes of data and 1,500 business users a day. We win 90% of the proofs of concept against Tableau, Tibco Spotfire, IBM Cognos, and SAP BusinessObjects. The hardware required to run these systems can cost between $50 million and $100 million; then companies must spend $2 million to $3 million to buy an Oracle data warehouse and Tableau software and to hire a database administrator and data analysts for each project. And after all that, companies still can't get the kind of access to data we provide. It can take them five hours to produce a report we can do in 15 minutes via a Google-search-bar-like user interface."

Case Scenario

Arcadia Data was growing its staff, but not as quickly as its revenues. "We started with four people in 2012, had 35 people in 2016, and 65 in 2018. 40% of our people are in sales, 40% in R&D, and 20% in marketing," he said. Arcadia Data had a rigorous process for planning and evaluating its business. As Thomas explained, "We want to be a data-driven company. For the last few years, at the beginning of every year we do an annual revenue and headcount plan. Over the next 12 months, we plan revenue and headcount in sales, marketing, and engineering in our four channels: inbound, outbound, partners, and upselling to existing customers." The plans were based on benchmarks from previous years. "We know the average deal size and the number of deals we need to close to make our revenue forecast. From there, we can estimate the number of leads in the pipeline we need to close the number of customers we need. All the numbers go in a spreadsheet and become part of each department's objectives. We track all the data on dashboards, analyze it compared to our budget, and know if things are going according to plan," he said. It is more difficult to give specific metrics to engineering. As Thomas said, "We are in a competitive market, so engineering must build visionary, next-generation products. Our engineers talk to customers and customer success lets engineers know what changes customers need and what bugs to fix. We track our bug-fix rate, the customer churn rate, and the upsell rate. And we introduce a new version every six to eight weeks."

Case Analysis

Arcadia Data achieved very rapid growth by offering customers a product that better met their needs at a much lower price than incumbents. With a functional organization and a rigorous annual planning process, Arcadia stated its corporate goals and held each function accountable for meeting key performance indicators under its control. Its sustained rapid growth suggested that Arcadia's process of planning and tracking results was effective.

Less Successful Case Study: After Eight Years, PowerInbox Struggles to Scale

Introduction

When a company is trying to compete with the biggest giants in online media, it must grow fast and be efficient. After all, there's a good chance that investors will be skeptical of the startup's ability to build a large company, so it might have to rely on self-generated cash to fund its operation. This comes to mind in considering New York City and Tel Aviv-based PowerInbox, an audience engagement and digital monetization partner for publishers and marketers, that saw itself competing with Google and Facebook in the $50 billion online media industry. Founded in 2010, PowerInbox monetized email for publishers by charging advertisers 40 cents or more for each push notification at the bottom of an email message. PowerInbox received a portion of the revenue, most of which went to publishers who received a recurring revenue stream.

PowerInbox, which generated 2017 revenue of $18.9 million, claimed that its clients got "30% higher engagement rates and four-fold return on investment" supporting "over 2.5 billion emails a month from leading marketers, publishers, and agencies including Bonnier, Crains, HarperCollins, Hearst, *New York Magazine*, *Palm Beach Gazette*, ReachMobi and *The Seattle Times*." The company seemed to be growing from a small base. Its CEO since December 2011, Jeff Kupietzky, was a Harvard Business School graduate who was previously CEO of domain name owner Oversee.net. In a September 2018 interview, Kupietzky said PowerInbox saw "more than 7,500% growth over the last three years—a direct result of our focus on lean operations and heavy investment in R&D, product innovation, and customer needs. We raised an $18.4 million Series A capital round in 2014 and maintained our headcount at about 40 employees between 2014 and 2018. We are profitable and have over 600 clients."

Case Scenario

PowerInbox's ability to increase revenue without headcount growth was unusual. "We are efficient. We have no headquarters and no staff functions. Everyone is a doer and works remotely. We are organized by function: sales, product, technology, operations. To manage these functions, we promote individuals to both manage and do work," he said. Measuring performance and communicating how well people were meeting performance targets was crucial. "We set annual company targets that are broken down into quarterly targets split by departments. For example, we have volume targets for the sales team and product delivery targets for the product team. We report out weekly and all employees have visibility on our financial and key performance indicators (KPIs). With transparency we believe we can get alignment across the team. Our teams meet weekly across all departments and there are additional channels to help ensure folks are aligned," he said. Putting so much responsibility on such as small team meant that some people left. "It's usually clear from the performance of the individual as well as the feedback received from peers where there are performance gaps. At PowerInbox, we do 90-day and full-year reviews so employees know where they stand vis-à-vis their goals. It is rare for us to make a replacement decision that's a surprise for anyone involved," according to Kupietzky. PowerInbox had ambitious goals. "We want to double our business in the next 12 months. Since we want to maximize the opportunity, we may not be profitable. We might acquire to build a new product line. If we do an IPO it will be a funding event, rather than an endpoint."

Case Analysis

PowerInbox appeared to have been unable to raise enough capital to hire more people. Yet the company claimed to be growing extremely quickly and to be profitable. Its CEO said its profitability was due in part to keeping its expenses low by shunning costly office space, avoiding management and executive positions, and holding everyone accountable for achieving goals every three months. The scrutiny was intended to assure that those who stayed with the company were making a clear contribution to PowerInbox's growth goals.

Principles

Founders seeking to hold people accountable for winning initial customers should bear in mind the following dos and don'ts:

- **Do**

    - Articulate clear corporate goals.

    - Encourage functions to meet performance targets that are under their control and linked to the corporate goals such as bringing in new customers, boosting customer retention, and increasing net promoter score.

    - Assess and improve the effectiveness of the performance management process.

- **Don't**

    - Apply so much pressure to achieve goals that people burn out.

Stage 2: Building a Scalable Business Model

Success Case Study: Qubole Aims at IPO with $75 Million in Capital After Doubling Two Years in a Row

Introduction

A privately-held provider of data analytics software, Santa Clara, California-based Qubole, was growing fast: two- to three-fold per year, according to a September 2018 interview with Ashish Thusoo, CEO, who cofounded the company in 2011. Qubole described itself as a big data activation platform. Thusoo said, "Qubole is the largest cloud agnostic big-data-as-a-service company and provides the infrastructure needed for analytics programs. Our hundreds of customers include Warner Music Group, Activision Blizzard, NetApp, Lyft, and Box. We process over an exabyte of data per month." To fuel its growth Qubole raised another $75 million. After its latest $25 million in capital, raised in November 2017, Qubole shook up its management structure. Kevin Kennedy joined as Chief Operating Officer and Mohit Bhatnagar took on the role of Senior Vice President of Products.

Thusoo and his cofounder both joined Facebook in 2007 and replaced what he called its "antiquated data warehousing infrastructure that had been built in the 1990s for structured business data. We started the big data movement. It took months to get it working, but between 2007 and 2011 we built an infrastructure that made it possible for any employee to access and use data for new products, security, fraud, and monetization." They started Qubole to "bring the template for hypergrowth companies like Facebook and Google to the enterprise. We asked companies what was holding them back from using machine learning to do advanced analytics. They said, 'We have no expertise and no platform.' We delivered a cloud-based unified platform that runs on AWS, Microsoft Azure, and Oracle Cloud," explained Thusoo.

Case Scenario

Qubole offered customers a better value than rivals' products. As Thusoo said, "Customers find our SaaS platform to be faster and more cost efficient. It takes Cloudera and Hortonworks 6 to 18 months to get customers up and running. We wash away the friction." Qubole's organization grew fast. "Between 2011 and 2018, our headcount increased from 2 to 320 people. 50% are in R&D and 50% do go-to-market: sales, marketing, and field engineering. We have over 200 customers in many verticals. We doubled in 2017 and in 2018. We are trying to capitalize on a huge opportunity by investing in certain functions. It takes less than a quarter to close deals in the fast-moving tech market but two to three quarters in the more thoughtful enterprise market," he said.

Qubole held different functions within the company accountable for different metrics. As Thusoo explained, "We measure our go-to-market on the topline. We ask, how many people do we need to meet our sales targets? What is the ratio of support people we'll need? How good is the lead funnel from marketing? What are our conversion ratios? Our R&D measures are different: What products do we need next year? What is our two- to three-year vision? Where will growth come from as technology evolves? How can we be best of class as we support new clouds? How can we boost sales from cloud and technology partners such as Snowflake and Talend?" To reach its goals, Qubole created cross-functional teams around strategic initiatives that were "growth oriented," he said. They included demand generation, product, sales, and solutions engineering. In September 2018, Qubole aspired to a "liquidity event, hopefully soon," although Thusoo "didn't fret about it."

Case Analysis

With 200 customers, 320 employees, and $75 million in capital, Qubole doubled its revenues each year in 2017 and 2018 and hoped to go public. Its CEO demonstrated the ability to bring on new executives, set ambitious goals for the company, and hold different functions accountable for specific, controllable outcomes that would help the company achieve its growth goals—and potentially enable Qubole to go public.

Less Successful Case Study: StreamSets Grows Rapidly in Competitive Market While Trying to Make Its Business Model Scalable

Introduction

It is an impressive accomplishment for a four-year-old startup to be growing rapidly in a very crowded market while seeking to make its business model scalable. Many questions come to mind in considering such a company: Is it wise to target a market so crowded with incumbents and upstarts? Is it possible for such a company to grow quickly and earn a profit or does the need for growth require the company to set its price below its costs? Can such a company ever hope to become profitable or can it only try to make its processes more efficient to lower its cash burn rate? Addressing such questions was the challenge facing Girish Pancha, who earned a BS and MS in Electrical Engineering from Stanford and Penn, respectively, and rose to Chief Product Officer at Informatica. Pancha started San Francisco-based data integration middleware supplier StreamSets, which he told me in a September 2018 expected 2018 recurring revenue to rise 200% while its headcount increased 50%. Data integration middleware let "enterprises manage their data performance in the same way they use application performance management

(APM) and network product management (NPM) to manage applications and networks," Pancha said. The $28.5 billion market was helmed by the biggest players, IBM (21.5% market share) and Oracle (11.1%), which grew more slowly in 2017 than the industry. And two challengers were coming up very fast: Salesforce, with 6.3% market share, grew 31.9% and Amazon, with a mere 2.9% share, enjoyed 119% growth.

Yet StreamSets, which by 2018 had raised a total of $67.5 million (including $35 million in September 2018) said it tripled its revenues in 2017. The reason for its growth was that StreamSets saved enterprise customers time and money, boosted their productivity, and offered protection from hackers, Pancha said. StreamSets offered "peace of mind for a company's chief data officer worried about security and corrupted data" coupled with a "10x increase in developer productivity and guaranteed service level agreements around data flow." StreamSets charges customers not on the number of users but on the complexity and size of customer's applications, and it beat rivals like IBM because "we focus on a specific problem and keep it simple while incumbents say they can do it but can't deliver. They send busloads of people. We send one engineer who does a 30-minute demo. Customers rave at the simplicity of our product," said Pancha.

Case Scenario

StreamSets was seeking a path to profitability. "We have three tactics to make our business model scalable. We increase our sales productivity. We add to our sales capacity, putting teams into new territories to get new logos. We land and expand, selling more products to our existing customers. By adding more capabilities over the last nine months we have more customers who buy over $1 million a year," he said. The company focused on its Magic Number. "If I can generate an incremental dollar of recurring revenue for every dollar in sales and marketing expense, I will do it. One reason this works is that StreamSets has a proactive customer success group that makes sure that its customers are succeeding with the product. Of our roughly 100 paying customers, 50% of our business is renewed annually and 50% is multiyear," explained Pancha. StreamSets was organized by function. "We have about 110 or 120 employees and are unusual because a year ago I decided to align sales, marketing, and customer success under a single leader, our President. Engineering and technical support report to our cofounder and Chief Technology Officer, and three other functions, general and administrative and product, also report to me," he said.

Pancha held people accountable for many specific metrics. "Product has five milestones: ideation, validation, roadmap, vision, and scope. Product development, which reports to the CTO, is charged with developing product specifications and making upgrades to the product as it scales and helping sales to close deals. Presales and marketing develop the lead pipeline and customer presentations. The partnerships and alliances team works with product to build relationships with partners like Azure. And customer success unearths problems and gets the product team involved to solve them," he said.

Case Analysis

StreamSets was growing rapidly, an impressive accomplishment in a highly competitive market, thanks to its ability to offer customers more value than the large incumbents. With 100 customers and about 110 employees, StreamSets was working on creating a scalable business model. StreamSets developed clear performance measures for its business functions and appeared to be in a good position to test their effectiveness as it grew. As of September 2018, it was unclear whether the company would be able to hurdle all the challenges mentioned above so it could go public or be acquired.

Principles

Founders seeking to hold people accountable for building a scalable business model should bear in mind the following dos and don'ts:

- **Do**

    - Upgrade the top executive team with people who have scaled their function successfully.

    - Set and gain consensus on a handful of corporate objectives.

    - Encourage each function to set and meet key performance indicators linked to objectives.

- **Don't**

    - Impose objectives without gaining consensus from those who will be charged with achieving them.

    - Hold functions accountable for outcomes they can't control.

    - Assume that people will understand how they will be measured without telling them explicitly.

Stage 3: Sprinting to Liquidity

Success Case Study: With $207.5 Million in Capital, WalkMe Sprints to a 2019 IPO

Introduction

San Francisco-based startup WalkMe offers what it called a Digital Adoption Platform (DAP) to make technology much easier for end users to operate. Simply put, WalkMe's DAP aspired to "transform the way users interact with technology as GPS changed the way people drive," according to the company. WalkMe's market opportunity was to solve a problem that caused most digital transformations to fail: that people lacked the training to use the technology.

Although WalkMe was founded in 2011, it was not until 2013 that it realized it should focus on digital transformation. In a September 2018 interview, cofounder and President Rephael Sweary said, "Digital transformation is a new way to do business and a way to use technology to make organizations more efficient. For example, if an employee asks her manager to take a vacation day, the manager must check with HR to see if the employee is eligible. Digital transformation would speed up the process." WalkMe's DAP anticipated what people were trying to do with the technology and gave them step-by-step guidance so they could achieve their goal. It shortened processes from 10 clicks to three, said Sweary. While he was unwilling to provide details of the company's revenues or growth, it was doing something right. That's because by September 2018, WalkMe had raised a whopping $207.5 million, including a $40 million Series F funding that closed in September 2018. At that time, WalkMe had 2,000 corporate customers, including over 30% of the Fortune 500, and 660 employees in seven offices in the U.S., Europe, and Asia Pacific. WalkMe was then valued at "over $1 billion as business continued to 'grow rapidly.'"

Case Scenario

The company was organized into three parts: 200 people in engineering, 200 in sales, and the rest in customer success and other functions. As Sweary said," WalkMe is revenue and product driven. We align the key performance indicators of the functions to the goals for the company. Customer success helps customers see that they are getting value from the product, asking them how much they use the product and what else they need. This helps drive engineering to decide which features to develop." WalkMe's culture was based on three values: growth, efficiency, and customers. "We are very transparent and every week I send out an email that reports on our progress on each value. For growth, we measure net new customers, average selling price (ASP), and annual recurring revenues (ARR). To track efficiency, we measure the time it takes to cross sell and whether ARR exceeds customer acquisition costs. For customers, we track how much they are using the product and growing ASPs," he said. WalkMe encouraged functions to work together, for example, in product development. As Sweary said, "The people in sales, engineering, and customer success know each other and they know how to pass the baton. And marketing generates demand from online channels, PR, and conferences. It's measured by the opportunities it creates for the sales team."

By September 2018, WalkMe was trying to stay private to build a more efficient business model while getting bigger. "We want to build barriers to entry while we are still a private company. We will make upfront investments to get into new markets. We are preparing for liquidity," he said. The new funding, which Sweary said was *to avoid a cash flow crunch, would help it sprint to an early 2019 IPO. But he did not provide a specific estimate of WalkMe's total addressable market. "The market is huge. It could be $10 billion or $100 billion. Our biggest competitor is corporate technology training," said Sweary.*

Case Analysis

WalkMe was creating a new market by making technology easier for untrained business people to operate. The goal was to provide corporations with a higher return on their investment in so-called digital transformation. WalkMe's service anticipated what users were trying to accomplish and walked them through the steps to required to get there. Along with winning 2.000 corporate customers, hiring 660 people, and raising over $200 million in capital, WalkMe operated an effective system to hold different functions accountable as it sprinted to an IPO.

Less Successful Case Study: With $90 Million in Capital, Panzura Forges a Scalable Business Model and Targets a 2020 IPO

Introduction

A 10-year-old company lost its founder after eight years and hired an HP executive to take charge of the company. And by September 2018, it looked to be two years away from an IPO. That's the story behind Campbell, California-based Panzura, a hybrid cloud data management platform supplier which had raised $90 million. Panzura helped companies to analyze what it called unstructured data, such as three-dimensional images, 4k video, and Internet of Things. Panzura, which targeted the $68 billion cloud data management industry, said it had "more than doubled its revenues, bookings, and headcount from 100 to over 200, and expected to go public in the next 18 to 24 months," according to my September 2018 interview with its CEO. Patrick Harr. Randy Chou, who was previously a software security architect at Aruba Wireless Networks, founded the company in 2008 but left in February 2016. Before joining Panzura in May 2016, Harr spent five years as a general manager at Hewlett Packard Enterprise where he presided over its cloud business, which enjoyed over 12-fold revenue growth to $1.5 billion during his tenure.

Case Scenario

Panzura was growing much faster than rival NetApp because its product did more for customers at a lower price. As Panzura said, its product consolidated, managed, and provided insight into unstructured data in the cloud, and was 70% cheaper to own and operate than NetApp and others. Panzura was organized into three functional departments: 45% of its people worked in engineering, 45% in what Harr called go-to-market, meaning marketing and sales, and the other 10% was in general and administrative functions like human resources and finance. The key line functions were measured differently. As Harr explained, "Engineering is about innovation. There's always someone up and coming, and you must maintain the innovative edge. Go-to-market is focused on revenue growth and customer satisfaction, measured by the Net Promoter Score (NPS). Ours is a very high 83. We also measure the rate at which leads are converted into sales." Panzura was working to make its business processes more efficient as it grew. "The average $50,000 enterprise deal takes 7.4 months to close and the average customer takes 16.8 months from the time they learn of a product to buying. We want to reduce that by using a digital selling process. We are making a heavy push on social media and email marketing to get people to try our Vision.ai service. Normally when you have a freemium model, only 2% buy the premium version; we are now above 15%. We have the right product to meet demand in the market today," he said. Panzura hoped to go public in a few years. "There is $68 billion worth of spend, according to IDC. We are substituting for the $12 billion to $15 billion network attached storage market where NetApp is a leader. Our target is to go public in 18 to 24 months," Carr said.

Case Analysis

Panzura had been around for a decade and was still working on making its business model scalable. Yet its product offered customers a valuable service at a much lower price than products offered by incumbents. With $90 million in capital, it was struggling to speed up its sales process, yet it had clearly defined metrics with which to hold its functions accountable. It remained to be seen whether Panzura would be able to sustain its growth, become profitable, and generate enough revenue to go public.

Principles

Founders seeking to hold people accountable for sprinting to liquidity should bear in mind the following dos and don'ts:

- **Do**

    - Set ambitious growth goals.

    - Hold functions accountable for performance on controllable factors such as lower customer acquisition costs, higher net promoter scores, higher prices, increased customer retention, and higher revenue per customer.

    - Assess and improve the effectiveness of the company's performance monitoring process.

- **Don't**

    - Expect improved performance on key metrics without changes to strategy and business processes.

    - Launch new strategies to boost efficiency without hiring experts in the key skills needed to be successful.

Stage 4: Running the Marathon

Success Case Study: Kronos Goes Public, Goes Private, and Keeps Growing

Introduction

Often, fast-growing startups that go public and keep growing remain publicly traded thereafter. This is particularly true of technology companies since most of them need access to the stock market to finance their continued growth. The reason is that technology companies often invest most of their capital in growth opportunities, either by cutting prices to gain market share or to generate new revenue streams either from internally-developed products or acquisition. After being publicly traded for a while, most CEOs learn how to handle the responsibilities, most notably communicating every quarter with investors and complying with regulations. However, some CEOs become frustrated with those responsibilities and seek the opportunity to access capital while returning to private ownership. In so doing, they seek a fairer valuation for their shares and more time to generate investment returns. This comes to mind in considering the story of Lowell, Massachusetts-based workforce and human capital management software maker Kronos, which San Francisco's Hellman & Friedman took private in 2007 for $1.8 billion. Since then, it grew from $500 million in revenue to about $1.4 billion, according to my September 2018 interview with CEO Aron Ain.

Case Scenario

Kronos went private to help it keep growing in a way that better suited the CEO's style and in so doing it held people accountable for acting according to its values of employee engagement, management effectiveness, and innovation. Kronos went public in 1992 with revenues of $59 million but it was taken private in 2007. In the subsequent 11 years, Kronos's value increased from $1.8 billion to $6.5 billion. Ain, a Hamilton College economics graduate who started with Kronos back in 1979, sold Kronos because he thought it was under-valued as a public company. As he said, "We were growing at 7% to 9%, our earnings before interest, taxes, depreciation, and *amortization was increasing 10% to 12%, and we were valued at only $1.2 billion in the public market. We got multiple bids for $1.8 billion. Hellman & Friedman owns 50% of the company, Blackstone has 25%, and Singapore's GIC owns 22%." Ain vastly preferred being owned by private equity investors. "I only have two or three shareholders; we agree on a strategy that will require at least $100 million investment and take several years to pay off. They tell me to spend it as quickly as possible to get a return sooner. We've grown from about $500 million before the buyout to a fiscal 2019 revenue target of $1.5 billion and from about 3,000 to nearly 6,000 employees," he said.*

Ain believed that Kronos's relationships with people were a key to its success. Kronos held people accountable for specific measurements of the strength of those relationships. As he explained, "We have a unique view on our relationships with people. We believe in employee engagement. Great people want to stay here. They have choices, they work hard, and our culture engages them." Kronos, which was organized functionally (e.g., sales, service, engineering, human resources, and marketing), had a clearly defined culture. As Ain said, "We believe in an engaged workforce and our rate of engagement, measured by a survey in which 92% of employees participate, has increased from 65% in 2005 to 87%. We value effective management and we've developed a manager effectiveness index (MEI) that correlates positively with employee engagement. And we emphasize innovation throughout our operations, both in our product and service. For example, one of our customer service employees in Australia came up with an idea to reduce the Kronos installation time by 40% using best practices. The MEI puts a high value on low ego, trust, and collaboration." As he said, "Managers with the highest MEI care about people, engender trust, overcommunicate, partner with their team to support the company's goals, and ask their people about their career goals and ambitions. It is a privilege to lead people and the impact managers have on the team is huge."

After 40 years there, Ain seemed very happy as CEO of a private-equity-backed Kronos. "I am a lucky duck. I keep doing this because I love what I do. My job is hard intellectually. In navigating changing technology, there are too few people to make difficult choices. I love working with our people and our customers."

Case Analysis

If a CEO can sustain a company's growth, take it public, and keep it growing after the IPO, it has a better chance of realizing its vision of changing the world. Kronos was able to do that but decided that it would be better able to continue its growth by going private. Ain's unique management approach, which held people accountable for acting according to its values of employee engagement, management effectiveness, and innovation, helped the company to achieve its growth goals.

Less Successful Case Study: Snap Burns Through Cash, Its Stock Falls, As Its Efforts to Hold People Accountable Fall Short

Introduction

Going public before building a scalable business model can doom a company. After all, during times when an economic bubble is expanding, the combination of a very popular consumer service built by spending far more than a company generates in revenue can enable a company to go public. However, unless that company can prove that it can sustain that growth and become profitable, investors may abandon the company. The CEO's challenge is to plan and monitor the company's achievement of the right key performance indicators and hold people accountable for meeting the goal of profitable growth. Simply tracking the right variables is not enough; to gain investor confidence, the CEO must deliver improved results by managing people effectively.

This comes to mind in considering Venice, Calif.-based social media service Snap. Weirdly, Snap, with about 158 million users and 88% of its revenue coming from U.S. advertising, referred to itself as a camera company. Between 2015 and 2017, Snap's revenues grew from $59 million to $825 million while it lost money in each year and its negative free cash soared from $335 million to $827 million. And by the second quarter of 2018, Snap had $1,570 million worth of cash, having burned through $250 million during the quarter. Snap's stock fell about 69% from its all-time high the day of its March 2017 IPO to $8.48 a share on September 29, 2018.

The problem underlying these losses and the declining stock price was that Snap had gone public before creating a scalable business model. More specifically, as Wharton professor Gad Allon explained in a June 2018 interview, successful scaling means that as a company grows, its costs drop and the value to customers of its product increases. For example, since Snap outsourced computing, it was adding costs as it added new features. As Allon said, "Snap is adding new features that are heavy in terms of computing power. For example, adding 'ears' to people on photos is more expensive than one may imagine. Snap outsources all of its computing to Google, which means that as Snap adds more features, its cost is bound to go up in the aggregate and on a per customer basis." Indeed, the numbers illustrated Allon's observation because its ratio of sales, general, and administrative expenses to sales kept rising as it grew: from 3 in 2015 to 4.4 in 2017. Moreover, Snap's business was easy to copy. Facebook subsidiary Instagram took a mere six months to copy Snap's Story feature (a way to share photos or videos for 24 hours in a narrative format). Allon argued that "Snap creates customer value but as long as [the social networking industry is] dominated by Facebook and Instagram, Snap needs to chase and retain its customers using costly endeavors." Due to its inability to generate positive cash flow, Allon believed that Snap could be rescued only if Facebook were to be regulated or "Apple or Google, which never managed to develop a social network, were to acquire Snap."

Case Scenario

Snap CEO Evan Spiegel was tracking many of the right metrics; however, he failed to hold people accountable for improvement in the most important measures. In Snap's second quarter 2018 conference call, Spiegel, his CFO Tim Stone, and his Chief Strategy Officer, Imran Khan, were happy to provide details on measures where they believed Snap had done well. For example, they discussed rising revenues and monthly active users. They also provided information about rising costs, negative cash flow, and sharply declining prices and numbers of daily active users. And despite numerous questions from analysts for a forecast of Snap's number of daily active users or revenue per user, Spiegel, Stone, and Khan stuck with their refusal to offer forecasts.

These disturbing numbers were preceded by Spiegel's sunny perspective on Snap's culture. As he said, "[We] are optimistic about the opportunities ahead as we continue to improve our team, reinforce our culture, and invest in innovation. We have focused a lot of our time and effort this past year on developing our team, culture, and leadership that we need to rapidly scale our business. Our team is passionate about our mission to contribute to human progress by empowering people to express themselves within the moment, learn about the world, and have fun together. And we've redesigned our performance management processes to incorporate our values of being kind, smart, and creative. For us, it's not just about the work that we do, it's about the way that we do it."

All the sunshine that Spiegel shared with analysts was in stark contrast to the reality inside Snap for most of its brief history. By August 2018, daily usage had begun to decline. A redesign introduced in late 2017 was rejected by users, sending its daily user count down three million between the first quarter of 2018 and the second one. And Spiegel was largely to blame for the Snap's problems, such as missing revenue estimates for four of the six quarters since its IPO and losing or replacing the heads of engineering, finance, hardware, legal, product, and sales. Snap employees complained that Spiegel was dictatorial and secretive. Since they worked in small, unconnected office buildings, employees did not know what the company was doing and were shocked to learn that they would not received cash bonuses because Snap had not achieved its goals, which had never been communicated with employees. In December 2017, Snap started trying to remedy the problem. Stone told people that Snap's goals included improving employee performance, boosting the number of daily average users, revenue growth, user time spent on the app, and making a profit. Meanwhile, Spiegel tried to professionalize its executives by requiring them to participate in coaching sessions with Stephen Miles, read management books, and spend more time with board members such as former Procter & Gamble CEO A.G. Lafley.

Sadly, Spiegel's efforts to redesign Snap's performance management processes to fit with its values of being kind, smart, and creative were not paying off for Snap investors. Indeed, the company was falling short on the most measurable of the five priorities that Stone articulated: its daily average users were going down and the company was far from being sustainable. By November 2, 2018, Snap stock had tumbled 75% from its IPO high of $27. Without a path to profitability, it was unclear whether Snap's business would survive.

Case Analysis

Snap went public without a sustainable business model and its founder and CEO was outmatched by the challenges of running a public company. He ignored competition from Instagram, disregarded the relatively low value that the company provided advertisers (its primary source of revenue), did not communicate with employees, and failed to articulate the company's goals or hold its people accountable for achieving them. When Spiegel finally realized that all this was a problem, he was mesmerized by a management guru who sent him and his people to workshops. Rather than measure employee performance relative to values of being kind, smart, and innovative, Snap might have been better off holding people accountable for the company's top priorities.

Principles

Founders seeking to hold people accountable for running the marathon should bear in mind the following dos and don'ts:

- **Do**
  - Set long- and medium-term goals and communicate them broadly.
  - Link performance measures to key values.
  - Reward people who improve organizational effectiveness.

- **Don't**
  - Dictate to others and hold key information within a small group.
  - Cut bonuses, claiming goals were not achieved when the goals were not communicated.
  - Ignore loss of market share and customer engagement.

Holding People Accountable Success and Failure Principles

To hold people accountable at each scaling stage, CEOs must follow the principles summarized in Table 7-1.

Table 7-1. Summary of priciples for holding people accountable for successes and failures

Scaling Stage	Dos	Don'ts
1: Winning the first customer	Articulate clear corporate goals.	Apply so much pressure to achieve goals that people burnout.
	Encourage functions to meet performance targets that are under their control and linked to the corporate goals such as bringing in new customers, boosting customer retention, and increasing net promoter score.	
	Assess and improve the effectiveness of the performance management process.	
2: Scaling the business model	Upgrade the top executive team with people who have scaled their function successfully.	Impose objectives without gaining consensus from those who will be charged with achieving them.
	Set and gain consensus on a handful of corporate objectives.	Hold functions accountable for outcomes they can't control.
	Encourage each function to set and meet key performance indicators linked to objectives.	Assume that people will understand how they will be measured without telling them explicitly.
3: Sprinting to liquidity	Set ambitious growth goals.	Expect improved performance on key metrics without changes to strategy and business processes.
	Hold functions accountable for performance on controllable factors such as lower customer acquisition costs, higher net promoter scores, higher prices, increased customer retention, and higher revenue per customer.	Launch new strategies to boost efficiency without hiring experts in the key skills needed to be successful.
	Assess and improve the effectiveness of the company's performance monitoring process.	
4: Running the marathon	Set long- and medium-term goals and communicate them broadly.	Dictate to others and hold key information within a small group.
	Link performance measures to key values.	Cut bonuses by claiming goals were not achieved when the goals were not communicated.
	Reward people who improve organizational effectiveness,	Ignore loss of market share and customer engagement.

Are You Doing Enough to Hold People Accountable?

Holding people accountable increases the chances that a startup can meet its growth goals and gives management early warning of problems, ideally in time to correct the course. As the company grows, the corporate objectives and the key performance objectives for each function change. And the best CEOs assess and evaluate the company's performance management system to make it a more useful tool for keeping the company on course to achieve its goals. To test whether your company is doing enough to hold people accountable, ask these four questions:

- Did you build an executive team charged with setting goals, monitoring progress to the goals, analyzing variances, and correcting course?

- Do you collaborate with your executive team to set corporate goals?

- Do functions hold themselves accountable for achieving controllable performance indicators that contribute to achieving corporate goals?

- Do you operate effective systems to generate timely and accurate data to assess the company's progress in pursuit of corporate and functional objectives?

Conclusion

Holding people accountable effectively is an element in a cluster of scaling levers that enable a company to implement its growth strategy for turning an idea into a large company. Underlying the process of holding people accountable is the notion that a leader must communicate clear, specific goals and encourage each function in the company to identify and take responsibility for achieving controllable performance metrics that contribute to corporate objectives. Chapter 8 will focus on the final execution scaling lever: coordinating processes.

Coordinating Processes

CEOs organize people into departments by function and hold them accountable for corporate goals. While such functional specialization boosts efficiency in each department, it could also motivate leaders of each function to gain more resources by taking them from other departments. Unless CEOs create and manage processes to encourage departments to work together, the disadvantages of specialization can overwhelm the advantages. Simply put, leaders make the best use of a company's talent by first differentiating and then integrating. And to scale their companies, CEOs must achieve corporate goals through four business processes:

- **Adding new customers:** Every quarter the CEO sets goals for growth in the number of new customers. To achieve the goals, CEOs must encourage departments to act as follows:

    - **Engineering** develops products that customers want to buy.

    - **Marketing** generates interest in the company and its products, and siphons out all but the most interested prospective purchasers.

    - **Sales** provides the most interested potential customers with a proof of concept and wins hopefully many of these competitive face-offs.

© Peter S. Cohan 2019
P. S. Cohan, *Scaling Your Startup*, https://doi.org/10.1007/978-1-4842-4312-1_8

- **Increasing revenue per customer:** Companies need to retain almost all their customers and encourage them to buy more. To do this, the CEO must coordinate three departments to do the following:

  - **Customer success** calls new customers to evaluate how they are using the product, identifying which product functions they find useful, which are not, which don't work right, and which should be added.

  - **Engineering** incorporates this feedback into new versions of the company's product.

  - **Sales** contacts customers before their contract expires to encourage them to renew and to purchase the new products that company built in response to their feedback.

- **Hiring and motivating top talent:** Rapidly growing companies must retain their best talent and hire new talent to tackle the challenge of sustaining rapid growth. To achieve this critical aim, CEOs must manage a process that anticipates the number of people the company will need to hire in each department based on the company's revenue growth goals. Each department must work with human resources to identify, interview, and hire excellent candidates to fill these roles. At the same time, departments must assess their people, identify the top performers, and make sure they're motivated and paid enough to keep them happy at the company.

- **Scaling the culture globally:** The CEO is unable to make all the business decisions in a global company. Scaling the culture is a way for the CEO to create an environment in which talented people can make those decisions in a way that's consistent with the company's values. To achieve these aims, CEOs must communicate regularly with the company's employees around the world. To that end, CEOs should

  - Send weekly corporate emails to share details of the company's operations.

  - Require all employees of a global company founded, say, in France to speak English in all business communications.

  - Hold quarterly all-hands meetings to celebrate employees who embody the company's values.

As a company's corporate objectives evolve, so must its coordinating processes. To create new processes, eliminate old ones that have outlived their usefulness, and revive existing ones, CEOs must take the steps detailed in Figure 8-1.

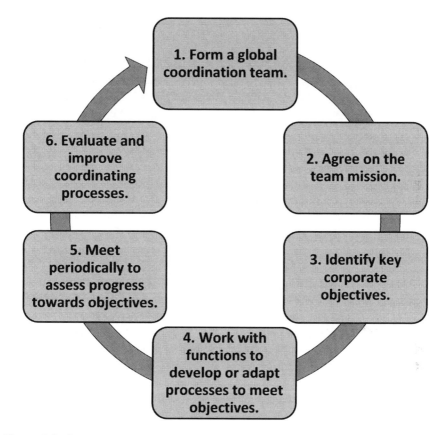

Figure 8-1. Six steps to coordinating processes

These steps include

1. **Form a global coordination team.** The CEO must first assemble a team of key functional executives. The team should consist of the heads of sales, engineering, marketing, service, finance, and human resources.

2. **Agree on the team mission.** The team should meet to agree on its purpose. A good mission for the team might be to create and improve processes to coordinate functions to achieve the company's evolving goals.

3. **Identify key corporate objectives.** After the team has agreed on its mission, the CEO should suggest a set of three to five corporate objectives. These might include specific revenue growth goals, new product initiatives, and plans to expand into new countries. Such corporate objectives would evolve in response to changing customer needs, new technologies, and other factors.

4. **Work with functions to develop or adapt processes to meet objectives.** The heads of the functions should propose processes for coordinating their efforts to meet corporate objectives. Four such processes were outlined above.

5. **Meet periodically to assess progress towards objectives.** The CEO may delegate to the Chief Operating Officer responsibility for making sure that each of the coordinating processes is operating according to a schedule. The COO will will work closely with the heads of the functions to keep the processes on track.

6. **Evaluate and improve coordinating processes.** The CEO should reevaluate the business process each quarter or each year, depending on how well the company is meeting its goals. If the company is meeting its goals, then the processes may be fine but could be made more effective through minor tweaks. If the company is not meeting its goals, the processes might need more radical updating. And if the company changes its corporate objectives, some processes might need to be eliminated and other new ones created.

Takeaways for Stakeholders

Coordinating processes is a shared responsibility of the CEO, the heads of key functional departments, and a company's employees. Here are the imperatives for each of these stakeholders:

- **CEO**
    - Work with the executive team to set corporate objectives.
    - Establish coordinating processes to achieve corporate objectives.

- Supervise the coordinating processes or delegate that supervision to the Chief Operating Officer.
- Evaluate and improve the effectiveness of the coordinating processes.
- **Functional executives**
  - Take responsibility for achieving departmental performance indicators.
  - Define roles of employees in processes.
  - Collaborate across departments and identify improvement opportunities.
- **Employees**
  - Understand and perform activities required to achieve departmental goals.
  - Assess the effectiveness of the departmental process.
  - Make recommendations on how to improve the process.

Coordinating Processes Success and Failure Case Studies

In this section, I offer case studies of coordinating processes used by successful and less successful startups at each scaling stage, analyze the cases, and extract principles for helping founders to coordinate processes at each stage.

Stage 1: Winning the First Customers

To win its first customers, startup CEOs must coordinate engineering, marketing, and sales. Engineering must partner with early adopter customers, who are in effect design partners, to develop a version of the company's product that satisfies those customers' unmet needs. Marketing must generate interest in the product among potential customers and screen out all but the most promising leads. Sales must participate in competitive bidding processes and prevail often enough to meet the company's growth goals.

As a coordinator of the process of winning the startups' first customers, the CEO must monitor each function's activities, offer advice to overcome impediments, and encourage cross-functional communication. For example,

- **Engineering <> Marketing:** Engineering and marketing ought to discuss what product features the early adopters find the most valuable and why. This will help marketing to identify which groups of customers might be most interested in the product. For a product sold to enterprises, such customers might be more clustered in specific industries or sizes of companies.

- **Product Management <> Sales:** Product management helps sales to close deals by providing updates on product development plans, often in front of potential customers. Sales also tells product management about what product features are of most interest to potential customers.

- **Product Management <> Engineering:** Product management also takes this input from sales and works with engineering to identify the highest priority opportunities for enhancing current products and developing new ones.

- **Sales <> Marketing:** Sales should talk with marketing to share which kinds of leads are most effective and which do not work so that the company can improve the quality of the lead generation process.

- **Sales <> Engineering:** For smaller companies that chose not to create product management roles, sales should communicate with engineering about its challenges and successes in selling the products. These conversations should yield insights about what features help the sales people to close deals, which do not help, and which features are missing,

Success Case Study: Arcadia Data Plans for Growth As It Adds Blue Chip Customers

Introduction

To win its first customers, a startup's most important task is to solve the right problem much better than rivals do. The right problem is one that both causes potential customers significant "pain," the solution of which represents a large market, and that your company is better equipped to solve than rivals. If your company builds a better product, it will be easier to sell to win initial customers and, if those initial customers are happy with the product, to win more customers. To achieve this goal, the CEO must manage a process of setting goals, anticipating the resources needed to achieve those goals, monitoring progress, and taking prompt action to repair any deviations from the plan. This comes to mind in considering San Mateo, California-based business analytics service Arcadia Data, which I discussed in Chapter 7.

Case Scenario

A crucial process that CEO Sushil Thomas managed was the marketing/sales funnel aimed at generating broad interest in Arcadia Data's products and systematically filtering out all but the best sales leads, which its account representatives would try to turn into new customers. This process engaged people from marketing, inbound sales, and field sales departments. Here are the six stages of Arcadia Data's marketing/sales funnel:

- **Collect new names from inquiries or conference attendees.** *Arcadia Data's marketing sought to generate interest in its products. To do that well, marketing identified which groups of potential customers to target. Marketing hosted conferences, got articles written in relevant media outlets, and conducted social media and email marketing campaigns to interest potential customers in the company.*

- **Send company and product information electronically.** *Arcadia Data's marketing department automatically emailed documents and videos to potential customers who expressed interest in the company. Marketing analyzed the responses to what Thomas called electronically-qualified leads generated by these emails: the people who opened the emails, clicked on the videos, and read the documents.*

- **Contact electronically-qualified leads by telephone.** *Arcadia Data's telesales force contacted the electronically-qualified leads and asked them about their job responsibilities, why they were interested in the company's products, whether they were considering purchasing products from other companies, and when they expected to make a purchase decision. When those conversations went well, telesales considered them qualified leads.*

- **Forward telesales-qualified leads to the account executive in the right territory.** *Arcadia Data's telesales contacted the manager of the territory or a specific account executive and shared the information they learned from their conversations.*

- **Evaluate whether to bid on the deal.** *If the telesales-qualified lead sounded promising, the account executive designated it a sales-accepted lead. For each of them, the account executive spoke with the potential customer to assess whether the project was real, who the executive sponsor(s) were within the company, and the project budget. If these details suggested that there was a good opportunity for the company, the sales executive deemed it what Thomas referred to as a sales-qualified lead.*

- **Win the bid.** *For each sales-qualified lead, Arcadia Data assigned resources to develop a proof of concept for the potential customer. If the customer decided that this proof of concept was better than that of the competitors, it asked for Arcadia Data's proposed terms and checked references. If all that checked out, Arcadia Data won the bid.*

Arcadia Data continued to improve its sales/marketing funnel. For example, over time the company learned what conversion rates (e.g., at Stage 2, how many people who received social media messages or email would turn into electronically-qualified leads) to expect at each stage. What's more, the company made sure it had the right number of telesales people and account executives to follow up on leads and turn the best ones into paying customers. Its marketing department also learned from failure: how to target its social media and email campaigns to surface a higher proportion of electronically-qualified leads; how telesales could boost the number of leads they qualified that turned into paying customers; and when the company lost to competitors, whether the loss was due to fielding the wrong product at too high a price or whether the failure was due to the company's need to strengthen its reputation.

Case Analysis

Arcadia Data was adding customers rapidly because it offered them a better product. Moreover, its CEO was doing an excellent job of sustaining the company's growth by managing a formal business planning process: setting specific corporate and departmental goals, tracking actual progress towards the goals, and acting to correct deviations from plan. Moreover, Arcadia Data's process of attracting potential customer interest and siphoning off all but the best sales leads seemed to be setting the stage for the company to build a scalable business model in the future.

Less Successful Case Study: Molekule Builds a Better Air Purifier but Struggles to Meet Demand

Introduction

What happens to a company that identifies a groundbreaking idea to solve a huge medical problem, but the chief inventor takes 20 years to build a working prototype of the solution? And once that prototype is built, can the inventor's son and daughter, who have no prior management experience, build and manage a company to satisfy the swell of demand for the product once it is available to the public? These are the questions that come to mind in considering San Francisco-based air purifier provider Molekule.

When he was a baby, Dilip Goswami suffered from asthma and allergies. After 20 years of work, his father, University of Florida mechanical engineer and veteran energy researcher Yogi Goswami, built a prototype of an air purifier that could relieve Dilip's symptoms. It also formed the basis of Molekule (cofounded in 2014 by CEO Dilip), which took on Honeywell and Dyson in the $33 billion air filter market. Since launching in May 2016, Molekule had been working hard to make enough of its air purifiers to keep up with demand. Its $799 product (annual air filter subscriptions cost $129) had sold out seven times by September 2018. Molekule's product worked better than standard high efficiency particulate air (HEPA) filters, which were invented in the 1940s. As *Fast Company* wrote "Molekule is the world's first air purifier that destroys pollutants at the molecular level. Its process, called photoelectrochemical oxidation (PECO), involves shining light onto a filter membrane that has been coated with proprietary nanoparticles, triggering a reaction that breaks down pollutants of any size, including allergens, mold, bacteria, viruses, and carcinogenic volatile organic compounds that concentrate in indoor air."

The market potential for the PECO-based product was significant. In addition to helping Dilip, Molekule's product also helped Jaya Rao, Yogi Goswamis' daughter, who was the company's cofounder and COO. As Rao told me in a September 2018 interview, "I moved to Tampa and suffered from migraine headaches. I used the prototype my father had developed and a week later my headaches went away." Molekule helped people in California affected by wildfire smoke in the summer of 2018. Moreover, in August 2018, the company saw a market opportunity in reaching the 80 million Americans with allergies and the 25 million asthma sufferers. My math (I multiplied the total number of allergy and asthma sufferers by Molekule's prices) suggests that these two groups of customers represent a total addressable market of $83.9 billion in air purifiers and another $13.5 billion in filters.

Case Scenario

Molekule, which had raised $13.4 million in capital by October 2018, began ship-ping the product in July 2017. As Rao said, "We've sold tens of thousands of the devices, more than we originally imagined. We've grown from 11 people to 72 to meet demand for the product, which we sell directly to the consumer. We manufacture through a partnership with Foxconn in China."

Molekule's 72 people were organized by function, and collaboration across these functions was crucial. As Rao explained, "we were mission driven from our earliest days. We sit in the interviews with every new hire. And we want to create teams of scientists that collaborate with each other. Dilip and I are siblings who collaborate, which is good and bad. But we fill in the gaps. Dilip started working on the core technology; he is deeper into the technology and is continuously innovating. I communicate with customers because the scientists have trouble getting across the benefits of the product to customers. We have leaders for each of our functions: manufacturing, engineering, R&D, marketing, and customer service. We want to have a flow of value and information across the functions. We need everyone to collaborate because it leads to better outcomes."

Case Analysis

Molekule took decades to build a product to realize its vision of building a breakthrough in the air purifier industry. While there is a huge market for its product, it is unclear whether the brother and sister who are managing the company have the know-how to turn the company into a large company that will realize its mission. Certainly, the vagueness of the description that Rao provided of its coordinating processes does not inspire confidence that Molekule would be able to scale the company efficiently. As of October 2018, it was unclear whether the company would be able to raise enough capital and attract the management talent needed to realize the company's vision.

Principles

Founders seeking to coordinate processes to win initial customers should bear in mind the following dos and don'ts:

- **Do**
    - Create a formal business planning process.
    - Use a marketing/sales funnel to increase sales efficiency.
    - Assess and improve coordinating processes.

- **Don't**
  - Assume that enforcing the right culture is sufficient to sustain rapid growth.

Stage 2: Building a Scalable Business Model

As they seek to sustain rapid growth while becoming more efficient, startups must manage cross-functional processes that bring in new customers, retain existing ones, boost average revenue per customer, and reduce costs. For first-time founders, managing such processes successfully is a significant challenge. Successful startups should approach the challenge with intellectual humility and an eagerness to learn from those who have succeeded in similar situations. With the right mental attitude, such CEOs can make the most of their efforts to build networks of advisors among other CEOs and investors. Moreover, if they can hire functional executives who have had prior success building scalable business models, such founders can learn how to establish and operate such processes effectively.

Success Case Study: Algolia Outdoes Google in Business Search As It Grows Along a Path to Profitability

Introduction

Between 2015 and 2018, I took undergraduate students to visit startups in Paris each spring. Our visits there highlighted a handful of startups that seemed to be coping with their challenges. However, we did not see any companies that had recently raised significant amounts of capital or were aggressively seeking to hire people. However, in May 2018, we visited with a company that was founded in Paris; our visit featured recent college graduates from around the world who had recently joined the company, and they were all speaking to the audience of American students in English. The company in question was Algolia, a San Francisco-based provider of enterprise search services. In an October 2018 interview with Algolia cofounders, I learned that behind its rapid growth was a product that better served its business customers and a willingness to learn the Silicon Valley approach to growing a startup, coupled with its intent to hire the best talent globally and to move towards profitability.

Algolia, which was founded in 2012 in Paris and had raised a total of $74 million by October 2018, was growing fast. According to my October 2018 interview with cofounders CEO Nicolas Dessaigne and CTO Julien Lemoine, by September 2018, its customer count had grown 38% to 5,700 businesses since the start of 2018; annual recurring revenue was expected to more than double to between $40 million and $50 million by year-end, up from $1 million in 2014, $10 million in 2016, and $20 million in 2017; and headcount was expected to soar 33% to 300 by year end from 200 in 2017 and 60 the year before. Algolia was targeting the enterprise search market that was expected to reach $8.9 billion by 2024, according to Grandview Research. And Dessaigne said that this number excluded a significant segment: marketplaces and other business-to-consumer search.

Case Scenario

Algolia was growing rapidly for three reasons: its product was a better solution for businesses; its cofounders were schooled in the Silicon Valley approach to startup growth; and its process for hiring talent was helping to fuel its continued growth as it became more profitable on its path to an IPO. Before meeting Algolia, I thought that Google had the search market sewn up. But there was one segment of the market that Google had abandoned: the business of helping consumers search through a company's online product catalog. Google was good at bringing users to a website but once there, customers relied on the websites' own search functions to find products. Some companies built their own engines; others used open-source software, such as Elasticsearch; and Algolia, which charged clients for its service, rather than selling ads and collecting user data, was rapidly gaining market share by supplying a service that hunted the client's website and swiftly offered consumers relevant results.

Algolia's cofounders had been exposed to the Silicon Valley approach to startups via their participation in the famed startup incubator Y Combinator. As we saw in May 2018, Algolia used English in all its offices and sought U.S. clients from the beginning. Dessaigne and Lemoine were in their first time as startup leaders and they were learning some important lessons about how to scale. As Dessaigne said, "We would view an IPO as a funding event. We want to keep the company independent so it can achieve its full potential. It is not about the money, it's about learning. And one thing we are focused on is finding the right talent in functions like sales, customer success, marketing, and engineering. As you grow bigger, the roles become more specific. For example, we hire account executives for small and medium-sized businesses, middle-market with industry specializations, and enterprise. When we feel the pain, we hire. It's very humbling. What do we need to learn? Who do we need to hire? We learn from other companies at our stage of development. The reason talent would want to work at Algolia was not the same in October 2018 as it was in its early days." As Lemoine explained, "We tell candidates to join us for the adventure. The market has unrealized potential; we've only tapped 1% of it so far. The entrepreneurial talent we hired in the early days would not join us today. Now we are hiring for a narrower scope. We need experienced people now who have seen this before."

Algolia was not profitable. As Dessaigne said, "Like many fast SaaS companies our stage, we invest in growth over short term profit. That growth is sustainable and will lead to higher profits in the future." Algolia was keeping a close eye on the IPO of another company in the business search industry, Elastic, which commercialized open-source software for search and data analytics. Elastic enjoyed 79% revenue *growth in the July 2018-ending quarter to $56.6 million and a net loss of $18.6 million. And its stock price soared 94.4% on its first day of trade, October 5, 2018. Would Algolia sustain its growth rate long enough to go public in 2020?*

Case Analysis

Unlike other Parisian startups I've visited, Algolia was growing rapidly on a path to profitability. In addition to providing a better solution to the problem of business search, its growth was attributable to the intellectual humility of its cofounders. This mindset enabled them to fill in the gaps in their knowledge and experience as they tried to sustain an annual doubling of revenue, hire the talent needed to sustain that growth pace, and make its operations more sustainable. Algolia was growing mostly due to the competitive superiority of its product, almost in spite of its less-than-fully developed business processes. While it appeared to be eager to hire and motivate talented people around the world and efficiently bring in new customers, retain existing ones, and sell them more. Algolia's leaders seemed to be learning how to coordinate its processes efficiently.

Less Successful Case Study: After Eight Years, Kinetica Hires a New CEO to Jump-Start Its Growth

Introduction

There's no guarantee that a company's founder has what it takes to build a large company. In fact, some 60% of founders do not survive their Series D round of venture funding. This comes to mind in considering San Francisco-based database supplier Kinetica. Founded in 2009, Kinetica raised $50 million in June 2017, bringing its total funding to $63 million. Six months later, Kinetica's board replaced cofounder and CEO Amit Vij with Paul Appleby, an experienced sales executive. Kinetica said that its technology "combined artificial intelligence and machine learning, data visualization and location-based analytics, and the accelerated computing power of a GPU [graphical processing units made by the likes of Nvidia to run video games] database." Kinetica built relationships with companies and technology partners to bring this idea to life. Kinetica's customers came from industries including healthcare, energy, telecommunications, retail, and financial services. And its technology and marketing partners included NVIDIA, Dell, HP, and IBM.

The brains behind Kinetica were Vij and his Kinetica co-founder, Nima Negahban. As *Fortune* wrote, "They worked at the United States Army Intelligence and Security Command and the National Security Agency creating a system to track and capture terrorists in real time. The U.S. Postal Service has used Kinetica since 2014 in a system that optimizes routes and tracks packages." Vij lost the top spot at Kinetica to Appleby in December 2017.

The company was looking for "sales momentum" and Kinetica director Ray Lane seemed to think Appleby fit the bill. Appleby most recently served as President, Worldwide Sales and Marketing at BMC Software (and previously as an executive at Salesforce, C3 IoT, and Siebel Systems). As Lane said in December 2017, "2017 has been a breakout year for Kinetica, doubling headcount while it onboards and grows new customers and partners around the globe. There is considerable demand today for Kinetica's speed and capabilities produced by its native GPU-accelerated, in-memory architecture. Paul recognizes the strategic nature of the enterprise data challenges Fortune 2000 companies face and how Kinetica can accelerate real-time insights from any data sources, regardless of volume, velocity, and structure. Paul's proven experience leading global growth teams, plus the drive to take Kinetica to the next level, makes him a unique choice for Kinetica."

Case Scenario

Appleby delivered growth. As he said in a September 2018 interview, "At the beginning of the year we had 70 to 80 people and now we have 110. In the first half of 2018, we grew bookings 156% and the number of net new customers by 190%. A significant number of our existing customers are expanding their relationship with Kinetica. We could grow [with a scalable business model]." To get Kinetica to the next level, Appleby organized the company by function. "We're an innovation-driven company, and most of our employees, two-thirds of the company, are engineering and innovation-focused. Almost half of our employees are based out of our Arlington, Virginia engineering office. Our administrative, finance, and marketing functions are San Francisco-based, and our sales team is distributed across Europe, Asia, and the United States," he said. Appleby believed that everyone who worked with a company, including its leadership, employees, and partners, should be "aligned to a common set of strategic goals and objectives. As such, creating an environment where all parties felt ownership of the company strategy and alignment to that is a top priority. Our objectives span product, ecosystem, customer success, and culture. We use them to formulate our employees' MBOs [Management by Objectives], and to guide our company direction holistically."

He chaired Kinetica's Executive Leadership Team (ELT) which included executives from its "product development, customer success, sales, marketing, and finance [functions]. ELT meets regularly to plan, track, and execute on our key objectives. Every member of the team has detailed dashboards that map to key metrics that measure progress towards our objectives." Kinetica held everyone accountable for results. "On a quarterly basis, our executive team determines key outcomes we want to achieve, in accordance with our strategic objectives. These leaders then meet with their teams and determine MBOs for each employee that help us meet those objectives. The MBOs change each quarter, but they are always formulated to meet our strategic goals," Appleby told me, "Everybody in the company knows how their success will be measured. As he said, "We link metrics and objectives by following the Objectives & Key Results (OKR) model used by Facebook, Amazon, and Salesforce. The metrics, or key results, are in place at company, departmental and individual levels to gauge progress. Each employee has a specific set of measurable, quarterly MBOs that act as the metrics to track progress towards our company objectives."

Kinetica's MBOs seemed much more specific and measurable than its goals/objectives, which were meant to inspire. For example, Appleby said one of the company's objectives was "change the world by helping companies innovate and transform in the post-big data world." Two MBOs associated with that objective seem to drive people to find good sales leads and achieve high customer retention. The first MBO was "identify the number of companies that are tackling new initiatives. This gives us an indication that companies can use our technology to drive their business forward as we enter the extreme data economy." The second was to achieve "high customer retention rates [which] give us a way to show we're delivering value and are critical to our customers' business," he said.

Case Analysis

In less than a year after having taken over as CEO of Kinetica, Appleby had demonstrated his ability to accelerate the company's revenue growth. Moreover, he had established clear goals, a clearly articulated process for making people accountable, and the hope that Kinetica's organization would be able to achieve the ambitious goals he set. However, Kinetica's processes for bringing in new customers, retaining and selling more to existing customers, and making its operations more efficient were unclear in October 2018.

Principles

Founders seeking to coordinate processes to build a scalable business model should bear in mind the following dos and don'ts:

- **Do**

    - Establish a process for understanding customer pain and building products that relieve that pain better than competitors' products.

    - Manage the process of attracting, motivating, and retaining the best talent for key jobs.

    - Maintain intellectual humility and a deep commitment to admitting areas of ignorance and building professional networks to close the knowledge gaps.

- **Don't**
  - Hold on too long to a technical CEO who lacks the ability to set aggressive growth goals and drive the company to achieve them.

Stage 3: Sprinting to Liquidity

Success Case Study: JFrog Sprints to Liquidity with a Scalable Business Model

Introduction

A startup that helped software developers to deliver software updates to customers was growing so rapidly after a decade in operation that investors valued it at over $1 billion as the company sprinted to liquidity. The company solved a common problem: almost everything people did at home or work was powered by software. But not too long after getting that software, it stopped working as well as it should. How so? Hackers exploited its weaknesses, it took too long to open pages or to respond after a user clicked on a button, it didn't work right when a user bought a new device or installed a new app, and if the user tried to retrieve things from the cloud, it took too long before responding. Delivering software as a service, in which fixes were sent to users a few times a day, helped solve these problems. But the software developers had a big problem of their own: the process of creating and updating software was fraught with problems: it was expensive, slow, and vulnerable to hackers. Not surprisingly, there was a big business, dubbed DevOps (short for development operations), to solve this problem. It was a $50 billion market populated by some big companies like Google, Microsoft (which acquired GitHub for $7.5 billion), and Amazon as well as many smaller companies such as Atlassian, which has enjoyed an 88% rise in its stock as of October 2018.

And one of those, 10-year-old Mountain View, California-based JFrog, raised a whopping $165 million on October 4, 2018 to continue outpacing these big rivals. JFrog's so-called liquid software allowed its customers to deliver code in the form of binaries so they could distribute it regularly behind the scenes without impinging on the user experience. JFrog, which had raised a total of $226.5 million and was valued way north of $1 billion in October 2018, had grown rapidly in the previous two years. Between January 2016, when it raised its $50 million Series C funding, and October 2018, JFrog said its sales had grown over 500%. It had more than 4,500 customers, including more than 70% of the Fortune 100—including Amazon, Facebook, Google, Netflix, Uber, VMware, and Spotify. JFrog was popular with developers. The company said it added 100 new corporate customers a month and its so-called Bintray binary hub, a place to store, monitor, and send the collection of 1s and 0s, images, sounds, and compressed versions of other files that make computer hardware do its magic, was used by 700,000 open source community projects distributing more than 5.5 million unique software releases that generate over three billion downloads a month.

Case Scenario

JFrog, which had operations in Israel, North America, Europe, and Asia, had grown its staff considerably since it was founded in 2008. According to my October 2018 interview with cofounder and CEO, Shlomi Ben Haim, "We had under five people in 2008 and today we have 400. In 2012, revenues were $2 million, and we will end 2018 with $100 million in revenues."

Along with its rapid growth, the company had been profitable since 2014. As Ben Haim explained, "We have been cash flow positive since 2014. We did it because we built an efficient funnel [a marketing process to filter out efficiently all but potential customers eager to buy the product]. We did it with zero field sales people. It was all inbound leads converted to buyers by inside sales people. It works because developers don't like salespeople; they test our product, like it, and adopt it. Developers saw that we are solving their pain; our product became viral."

JFrog's people were organized by function, with people in R&D, sales and marketing, and customer success. "JFrog values customer happiness, not satisfaction. We have less than 3% churn. We listen well to our community, which sends us tickets suggesting how to improve the product. We are best of breed on what matters most to the community rather than trying to do everything, as some competitors do. We solve the most urgent customer pain and then launch it," he said. With its October 2018 capital infusion, JFrog planned to add talent to fuel global expansion. Ben Haim explained, "We plan to grow organically offices around the world, offering a platform with seven solutions. We will build an enterprise field sales force and use the professional services company we acquired. We also plan to acquire companies in the landscape of our technology." The company said it had a bright future. "Our revenue growth rate is not coming down. We will reach $1 billion in revenue by 2025. An IPO would be a milestone. We are built to last and an IPO is a tool to get there."

Case Analysis

A decade after its founding, JFrog was clearly sprinting to liquidity. With $100 million in revenue, ample capital, and a business model that enabled it to grow profitably, which had been working since 2014, in October 2018 JFrog was aiming to go public within a few years. JFrog coordinated several important processes that enabled it to grow profitably; most notably, its product development process yielded product improvements driven by direct feedback from its users and the company managed an efficient marketing funnel that produced inbound leads without field sales people—a powerful combination.

Less Successful Case Study: After 10 Years, Virtual Instruments Is Growing at 20% While Hoping to Be Acquired

Introduction

Some CEOs describe their venture backers as patient. But after holding on for a decade, even the most patient venture capitalists can be excused for their eagerness to realize a return on their investment. Such impatience can prompt investors to turn their back on a startup, asking for more capital if its CEO can't deliver sufficiently rapid revenue growth due to having saturated a small market. Lacking cash, such a CEO would need to shut down or merge. And if the CEO of that merger partner was run by an executive who had previously sold companies that he had led, the investors might be willing to pour in more capital to target a larger market. That is the labyrinthine story of San Jose, California-based Virtual Instruments, a provider of "application-centric infrastructure performance monitoring." Founded in 2008, it had raised $96.5 million by October 2018.

That incarnation of Virtual Instruments was formed in 2016 when it merged with Load Dynamix, of which Philippe Vincent was CEO. Vincent, a native of France with an MS in Mechanical Engineering from Berkeley and a Harvard MBA, spent 10 years at Accenture where he rose to partner. In 2007, he started as Chief Operating Officer of Big Fix software, a provider of intelligent monitoring of devices and infrastructure for security and compliance issues, which IBM bought for $400 million in July 2010. In 2012, he became CEO of Load DynamiX, which had raised about $19.3 million to simulate and monitor corporate storage workloads. In April 2016, Load DynamiX merged with Virtual Instruments, whose product tapped the flow of information through network equipment (such as Fibre Channel and Ethernet). They merged for two reasons: first, Virtual Instruments had run out of room to grow in its core fibre channel market, which led its investors to turn down another round of investment. Second, customers were installing products from both companies (LoadDynamiX used Virtual Instruments' product) and wanted them to work together. At the time of the merger, Virtual Instruments' VirtualWisdom product analyzed the performance of a company's computing infrastructure, but it was unable to simulate production workloads in its lab, which was where LoadDynamiX's technology fit in.

Case Scenario

Virtual Instruments grew following the merger, yet it was still refining its processes for product development and marketing. Vincent wanted to accelerate revenue growth from about 20% to above 30%; however, he hinted that being acquired was a more likely outcome than going public. Under Vincent's leadership, Virtual Instruments has grown since the merger. In an October 2018 interview, he said, "We merged to invest in innovation and to reposition around a larger total addressable market. At the time of the merger, we had 140 employees and we now have 210 plus engineering contractors. We spent 2016 and part of 2017 enhancing the product. In the four quarters since we began selling the product, we have grown in the mid-20% growth rate. We went from 0 to 60 in a year and in 2017 had 173% growth rate in new customers. We are planning on $75 million in revenue for 2018. We expect to boost our growth rate to at least 30% in the future.

Vincent saw a $20 billion addressable market for Virtual Instruments. "Gartner says that the performance and availability space will reach $4.8 billion in 2018, growing to $6.13 billion in 2022. When you add infrastructure monitoring to application monitoring, the business of AppDynamics [which Cisco Systems acquired for $3.7 billion in January 2017 just after it filed for an IPO], to workload automation, you get $20 billion," he explained. Virtual Instruments won business because it gave companies a single tool built to automate the data center. As Vincent said, "The analogy is to look at the way Google built self-driving cars. Instead of using legacy technologies that solved parts of the problem and trying to make them work together, Google built an integrated system specifically for self-driving cars. We do the same for the data center. VirtualWisdom monitors the entire infrastructure and analyzes and optimizes the performance, utilization, and health of IT infrastructure within the context of the applications running on it." There was evidence that customers preferred VirtualWisdom to similar products from VMWare, CA, and IBM. Gartner Peer Insights found that of 12 verified reviews by customers, VirtualWisdom (with 4.7/5.0 rating) came out ahead of Computer Associates (4.0 rating), IBM (4.3 rating), and VMware (4.5 rating).

To accelerate its growth, Virtual Instruments was working on its product and improving the way it marketed and sold that product. "The first version of our app-centric version of VirtualWisdom hit the market in April 2018 and it has been adopted well by big customers. We must learn how to take it to market. We are learning," he said. Virtual Instruments had a multi-pronged marketing strategy. "We are holding a three-day bootcamp so our sales people can understand the value proposition of our new product, focusing on the gaps in competitors' products and describing how our product closes those gaps. We are partnering with channels and application performance monitoring vendors, VMWare, and change management vendors like ServiceNow," according to Vincent. By October 2018, Virtual Instruments seemed to me to be looking for an acquisition partner. As Vincent explained, "We don't know about an IPO. AppDynamics filed for an IPO and Cisco bought it. It's a $20 billion market and Cisco is building a portfolio through acquisition. Splunk could bring our approach to the hybrid cloud. We believe our principles will carry our growth." Vincent helped to build BigFix, which IBM acquired. It looks to me like he could sell Virtual Instruments to Cisco or IBM.

Case Analysis

Virtual Instruments expected to reach $75 million in revenue by the end of 2018, and if it could maintain its 20% revenue growth rate, it would be able to reach $100 million in revenue by 2020, 12 years after it was founded. Since $100 million is the informal threshold for taking a company public, were Virtual Instruments to reach that size, it would have reached an important benchmark for success. Yet compared to JFrog, Virtual Instruments was lagging in important ways: its revenue growth rate was much slower, it did not have well-developed processes for setting and achieving goals, it was probably not profitable since its sales force was still learning how to sell its product, and it was unclear whether it would be able to gain enough market share to accelerate its revenue growth rate.

Principles

Founders seeking to coordinate processes to sprint to liquidity should bear in mind the following dos and don'ts:

- **Do**
    - Establish a process for understanding customer pain and building products that relieve that pain better than competitors' products.
    - Operate a selling process that enables the company to grow rapidly and profitably.
    - Maintain intellectual humility and a deep commitment to admitting areas of ignorance and building professional networks to close the knowledge gaps.
- **Don't**
    - Develop new products without involving the sales force.
    - Add products through a merger before building an efficient marketing and sales process.

Stage 4: Running the Marathon

For a company to go public, it usually needs at least $100 million in revenue and to sustain growth of at least 30% a year. Before a company goes public, many founders describe the IPO as a funding event. However, this statement downplays the amount of preparation required to make the company successful after it goes public. After all, a public company CEO must report to shareholders each quarter and make sure that the company complies with all the requirements of being a publicly-traded company. Being public puts pressure on a company to beat investors' expectations for revenue and profit growth and to increase its forecasts for future quarters every three months. In order to accomplish that, the CEO must create and run processes that make the company's quarterly results as predictable as possible.

Such processes include the four mentioned at the beginning of this chapter. But after a company goes public, there is one process that often sits above the rest in importance: financial forecasting and reporting. Setting up such a system must begin years before the company goes public so that when public reporting becomes mandatory, its system will have been tested and improved so it will work effectively. Fortunately for companies, there are many services available to support this planning and reporting process. Yet the systems will only work if the data provided to these systems, both the financial goals and the assumptions that underly them (e.g., the number of new customers, the anticipated revenue per customer, the customer retention rates), reflect what people in the business believe are realistic, yet ambitious goals. It is not difficult to imagine that a founder who started a company based on product innovation skill might find it less than appealing to spend time managing this process. Indeed, many founders who remain CEO after a company goes public may choose to delegate this process to a Chief Operating Officer or Chief Financial Officer.

Success Case Study: Okta Goes Public and Keeps Revenue Growing Faster Than 50%

Introduction

If a company can go public and keep growing rapidly thereafter, investors are likely to bid up its value. Underlying such a company's ability to increase its stock price are processes that reliably yield faster-than-expected growth each quarter. If the company continues to exceed investor expectations for both the most recent quarter and the next one, its stock is likely to keep rising. Sustaining such growth depends on careful management of all seven growth levers discussed in this book. This comes to mind in considering San Francisco-based identity management services provider Okta. In a nutshell, Okta kept companies from letting unwanted people access their computer systems. Okta provided its Okta Identity Cloud, which "lets companies securely connect the right people to the right technology, improving security, employee productivity, and user experience."

Okta's stock price responded favorably to its expectations-beating results. As of October 2018, Okta had a record of growth, which as of October 4, 2018 had propelled its stock up by 150% since its April 2017 IPO. Since 2015, its revenues had grown at an 85% annual rate from $41 million in 2015 to $260 million in 2018. It had generated negative free cash flow in each of those years, burning through $37 million worth in 2018. In September 2018 Okta posted better-than-expected results and its shares popped 16%. More specifically, on September 6, 2018 Okta reported a 57% rise in revenues to about $95 million, nearly $10 million more than analysts anticipated, and its loss of 15 cents a share was four cents lower than expected, according to Investors.com. Okta's forecast for the quarter ending in October also beat expectations. Its revenue forecast of $96.5 million was $7.5 million more than analysts expected while its loss forecast of 11 cents to 12 cents was about six cents better than expectations.

Case Scenario

Okta's expectations-beating growth came from a product that kept it ahead of its evolving customer needs and its ability to set and achieve ambitious goals for revenue growth and hiring to deliver on those goals. As CEO Todd McKinnon explained in a September 2018 investor call, "Our customer-first focus impacts everything we do: how we design and develop our technology; how we go to market; how we service our customers every day. So as we look at our long-term product strategy, we strive to anticipate what will solve our customer's business pain points today and over time." Turning that idea into tangible outcomes was the job of Charles Race, Okta President, Worldwide Field Operations. Since joining Okta in November 2016, he had been responsible for "growing Okta's addressable market, building a world class delivery capability built on customer and partner success, and driving revenue growth [globally]. [He oversees] worldwide sales, customer success and support, partner ecosystems, field marketing, professional services, and business operations," according to the company.

One way that Okta executed its strategy was to plan rigorously. As Race explained in an October 2018 interview, "Six months ahead [of the next fiscal year] we use a planning process we call Vision, Methods, Targets. [On my team,] we plan for consolidated growth by product, customer, and expansion into distinct markets. We set metrics such as annual recurring revenue growth, renewal rates, introduction of new product functionality, and adding new partners, and we decide how much of our budget to spend on achieving them." Okta ranked opportunities so it would feel confident that it could achieve its ambitious growth goals. "We allocate quotas across geographies, prioritizing opportunities based on the growth rate, our competitive position, and the resources we have there. Our go-to-market strategy varies by customer group. We sell to a 100-person company using digital sales, work with partners for small and medium enterprises, and assign field sales people to Global 2000 companies," he said. Okta's partner program was very broad. According to Race, "We have technology alliances with Google, Amazon, and VMWare; we go to market with vendors like SailPoint which complement our offerings; we work with systems integrators such as Accenture and Deloitte; we partner with resellers like Active Cyber and CDW; and in countries where we don't have a presence we work with indirect channels."

To grow fast enough, Okta sought to bring in new customers and to sell more to existing ones. As he said, "Once we acquire a customer we ask how we can upsell. Our customer success people make sure that customers are getting value; they find out what product functions they're using and which they're having trouble deploying. We consider what we can sell by customer segment and by product. We have goals for increasing revenue from existing customers and allocate marketing resources to achieve them." Okta also anticipated the talent it would need to hire and retain to achieve these goals. "We have a software-as-a-service model, which requires us to plan two three quarters out. And we need lead time to recruit and get up to speed the direct sales and technical resources we think we will need to meet our objectives," he explained. Because it was growing "57% year on year," Okta faced an ongoing challenge of hiring enough people with the right skills in the right places and getting them on board in time to minimize the chaos. "To keep growing at that rate, we need to either double the quotas or half the territories [Okta did the latter]. And we hire new people to cover the new territories. That means our new and current sales people get new territories and it takes time for them to get up to speed. Our first quarter is not as productive," said Race.

Okta believed that it had unlimited growth potential, Race concluded, "We are at the intersection of three megatrends: cloud, mobile, and Internet of Things. To tap that unlimited potential, we have to align our product strategy to international growth opportunities."

Case Analysis

Okta enjoyed a successful IPO and kept growing faster than investors expected thereafter due to three factors: its product stayed ahead of its customers changing needs, its CEO had hired a skilled executive to manage the processes of setting and achieving ambitious revenue goals, and its ability to hire, motivate, and retain top talent to sustain that growth. Okta's ability to continue to beat expectations would depend on whether these processes would function even more effectively as the company grew.

Less Successful Case Study: ForeScout Technologies Pays the Price for Lowering Its Growth Expectations

Introduction

There is a dark side to taking public a rapidly-growing company that is consistently unprofitable. If it is unable to sustain expectation-beating growth for the current and future quarters every three months, investors will sell the stock, driving its price down substantially. Even if a company delivers faster-than-expected growth for the recently completed quarter, investors will punish the company should it simultaneously lower its forecast for the current and/

or future reporting periods. Investors not only punish such a company in the immediate aftermath of a disappointing report, they also stand ready to punish its shares even more if the company does not resume the desired pattern of beating and raising each quarter. If a company does not recover quickly from a bad quarter, investors will question not only its strategy and talent pool, but the company may also need to look at whether its coordinating processes need repair.

This comes to mind in considering San Jose, California-based ForeScout Technologies, an Internet of Things (IoT) security company that let companies track the growing number of devices connecting to their networks. ForeScout went public in October 2017 and its shares had risen 44% as of October 3, 2018. In its second quarter 2018 report, ForeScout beat analysts' expectations but lowered its guidance for the quarter. Its revenues were up 35.2%, over $4 million more than analysts expected, while it reported negative EPS of $0.18, which was 19 cents less bad than expected. But not only did ForeScout report negative EPS, it burned through cash, posting a free cash flow margin of negative 12%. The biggest problem for ForeScout was that it lowered its revenue growth forecast. CFO Chris Harms said in an August 2018 investor conference call that the company expected to report 13% revenue growth and a net loss of 11 cents a share. And for the full year, revenue was expected to rise 25% while ForeScout expected EPS of negative 11 cents a share (all figures at the midpoint of the forecast range). Investors did not like this report much; its shares lost 14% of their value in the week following the conference call.

Case Scenario

Was ForeScout's lower growth forecast a result of focusing on a trend that had peaked? The trend in question was General Data Protection Regulation (GDPR), a European data privacy requirement that forced companies to invest in new technology to avoid paying significant fines for being out of compliance with GDPR, which went into effect in 2018. ForeScout believed that GDPR-like regulation was spreading around the world and would create opportunity for ForeScout to provide companies with real-time data on what was connected to their networks. As CEO Mike DeCesare said in an August 2018 investor conference call, GDPR is driving companies to protect data on corporate networks, a challenge that companies can't meet unless they know what devices are connected to them. And he believed that the growth in such new devices is growing fast. These include, "nontraditional IoT devices on campus, wired and wireless networks like security cameras, televisions, HVAC controllers, and phones," he said.

ForeScout hoped that its coordinating processes would help it improve its competitive position. DeCesare, who joined ForeScout in 2015 from Intel/McAfee, believed that as a public company ForeScout ought to raise its game due to the added scrutiny. "After an IPO, your data becomes public. How much you spend on

R&D, sales and marketing, and G&A as well as days sales outstanding and cash is subject to a higher level of scrutiny. This forces you to inspect yourself more carefully and to do better," he said in an October 2018 interview. ForeScout's primary goal was to maintain a high growth rate. "We set goals for R&D, sales and marketing, and G&A functions all premised on the corporate goal of high top-line growth. Since the IPO we have been growing at least 30% a quarter. To get there, we need new logos, we need to boost the revenue coming from each customer, and we need to hire and motivate new talent," he said.

To bring in new customers, ForeScout's engineering, marketing, and sales functions needed to collaborate effectively. As DeCesare said, "Thanks to companies like Salesforce and Facebook, customers expect us to be much more agile, updating our product frequently, and making it easy to use, like Facebook. Engineering must work with customers to quickly evaluate and streamline the product. Marketing is responsible for identifying which 500 of the Global 2000 are the best prospects. Marketing gets the product into the hands of their key people so they can test drive the product. This surfaces opportunities for sales, which participates in bake-offs and closes deals." To boost the ratio of total revenue from a customer to the amount earned in the original sale, ForeScout coordinated engineering, marketing, and sales. "We sell more as customers add more devices to their networks. We want customers to be successful with our product and we track product quality through our net promoter score, which is in the high 70s," he said.

Bringing in talent was another crucial process for enabling ForeScout to grow. "Salary and bonus are our biggest costs. We have grown our employee base 80% in the last four years. We want to minimize unwanted attrition and we are as careful about last 100 people we hired as the first 100. I am pushing the hiring decisions down to executives, but I still approve every offer because I want to see the level of talent our managers are bringing in. We need to make sure every person is a good fit and we must reward, recognize, and not lose our top performers," said DeCesare.

Case Analysis

ForeScout was growing rapidly before it went public. However, in August 2018 it announced that growth would slow down considerably in the quarter ending September 2018. The company's CEO had succeeded in taking the company public two-and-a-half years after he joined as CEO. He was managing important coordinating processes such as signing up new customers; keeping customers satisfied so they would renew their contracts and buy more of ForeScout's services; and hiring, motivating, and retaining top talent. Because ForeScout forecast a growth slowdown, investors slashed by over 10% the value of the company. By October 2018, it remained uncertain whether ForeScout had the right strategy, talent, and processes needed to get itself back on the path of regularly exceeding investor expectations and raising guidance every three months.

Principles

Founders seeking to coordinate processes to run the marathon should bear in mind the following dos and don'ts:

- **Do**
    - Manage a product development process that keeps the company ahead of rivals in anticipating customer needs and building new products to meet them.
    - Delegate growth planning to a Chief Operating Officer.
    - Operate a rigorous process for hiring, motivating, and retaining top talent.
- **Don't**
    - Depend too heavily on unsustainable growth trends.

Coordinating Processes Success and Failure Principles

To coordinate processes at each scaling stage, CEOs must follow the principles summarized in Table 8-1.

Table 8-1. Summary of the principals for coordinating processes

Scaling Stage	Dos	Don'ts
1: Winning the first customer	Create formal business planning process. Use a marketing/sales funnel to increase sales efficiency. Assess and improve coordinating processes management process.	Assume that enforcing the right culture is sufficient to sustain rapid growth.
2: Scaling the business model	Establish a process for understanding customer pain and building products that relieve that pain better than competitors' products. Manage the process of attracting, motivating, and retaining the best talent for key jobs. Maintain intellectual humility and a deep commitment to admitting areas of ignorance and building professional networks to close the knowledge gaps.	Hold on too long to a technical CEO who lacks the ability to set aggressive growth goals and drive the company to achieve them.
3: Sprinting to liquidity	Establish a process for understanding customer pain and building products that relieve that pain better than competitors' products. Operate a selling process that enables the company to grow rapidly and profitably. Maintain intellectual humility and a deep commitment to admitting areas of ignorance and building professional networks to close the knowledge gaps.	Develop new products without involving the sales force. Add products through a merger before building an efficient marketing and sales process.
4: Running the marathon	Manage a product development process that keeps the company ahead of rivals in anticipating customer needs and building new products to meet them. Delegate growth planning to a Chief Operating Officer. Operate a rigorous process for hiring, motivating, and retaining top talent.	Depend too heavily on unsustainable growth trends.

Are You Doing Enough to Coordinate Processes?

Coordinating processes increases the chances that a startup can meet its growth goals and helps the company to learn and improve its efficiency and effectiveness. As the company grows, the company should develop and refine processes for attracting new customers; developing new products that anticipate evolving customer needs; retaining existing ones and selling them more; boosting sales and marketing efficiency by operating a marketing/sales funnel; setting growth goals; and hiring, motivating, and retaining talent to achieve the goals. To test whether your company is doing enough to coordinate processes, ask these four questions:

- Did you build an executive team charged with creating and operating processes to achieve corporate goals?

- Did you engage your functional executives in identifying the mission and objectives of these coordinating processes?

- Do you monitor the effectiveness of the coordinating processes?

- Do you improve processes that are still essential, eliminate ones that are no longer worth performing, and create new processes to meet new objectives?

Conclusion

Coordinating processes is an essential lever for uniting a company in pursuit of corporate objectives. As a startup goes from an idea to a public company and beyond, it needs to add more coordinating processes, enhance the ones it has created in the past, and eliminate ones that no longer serve an important purpose. All these processes are focused in some way on sustaining a high level of growth. In the first stage of scaling, the most important process coordinates the efforts of marketing, engineering, and sales to develop a product that customers are eager to buy. As the company grows, it must build an efficient process for attracting new customers, retaining existing ones, and providing a broader array of products that yield higher revenues for each customer. As a company sprints to liquidity and goes public, it must ultimately operate a reliable process for planning and achieving aggressive growth goals, while hiring, motivating, and retaining the talent needed to achieve those goals. Chapter 9 concludes the book by presenting a CEO action agenda for startup scaling.

Implications for Leaders

What's Next?

If you've read this far, you should have a better understanding of the four stages of scaling and the seven scaling levers you can pull at each stage to turn your idea into a large publicly-traded company that keeps growing rapidly. Chapters 2 through 8 described methodologies for how to exercise each of the scaling levers plus case studies of successful and less successful companies and key principles for applying the levers at each scaling stage. But how can you apply these ideas to your startup? To answer that, I'll conclude by presenting a set of general principles to bear in mind as you grapple with the challenges of scaling your startup and a tool you should use called the scaling quotient to assess your startup's strengths and opportunities for improvement so you can sustain your company's growth.

The Seven Principles of Scaling

The case studies we've seen suggest seven principles of scaling. You should think of these principles as North Stars that keep you heading in the right direction as you encounter the challenges you must overcome to turn your startup idea into a large, rapidly-growing company. Here are the seven principles.

Stay Intellectually Humble

Of all the scaling principles, one stands above the rest. It's an idea I thought was brilliantly described in Yuval Harari's book, *Sapiens*, which I read in 2018. Harari's point was that one simple change in mindset unlocked most of humanity's greatest accomplishments. The change? Instead of taking the answers supplied by religious institutions as the undisputable source of truth, people started

© Peter S. Cohan 2019

P. S. Cohan, *Scaling Your Startup*, https://doi.org/10.1007/978-1-4842-4312-1_9

admitting when they didn't know something and did experiments to try to discover the answers. What I find interesting is that plenty of CEOs act as though they are the sole source of all knowledge and truth. This mindset is like a straitjacket constraining a startup's full potential. That's because such a CEO also feels crushing pressure to always appear to be in control and is unwilling to delegate important tasks to others. Changing this mindset to one of intellectual humility is the one easy-to-articulate but hard-to-accomplish change that can unlock a founder's full potential for success. In Chapter 4, we saw how that mindset permeates Amazon, as articulated in its Day One philosophy which keeps Amazon from getting complacent and focuses the company on listening to its demanding customers and continuing to give them more. It is only by staying ahead of the customers' changing needs that Amazon can continue to reinvent itself.

Target Blue Oceans

Startups that struggle to grow quickly have picked the wrong markets. Such markets either do not resolve important customer pain or are crowded with competitors. In Chapter 8, we saw an example of this. JFrog, a company that delivers software updates, picked a blue ocean and enjoyed rapid, profitable growth in the wake of that choice. JFrog was targeting what it saw as a $50 billion opportunity with a product that was essential to the growing trend towards providing software as a service. It was very popular with developers because its product worked much better than that of its rivals and could be sold without fielding a huge sales team. As a result, by 2018 JFrog was enjoying 500% sales growth and had been cash flow positive since 2014. JFrog exemplifies the notion that a founder with the right mindset will come up with hundreds of potential ideas and analyze them rigorously, focusing on problems that pass four tests:

- They are very big sources of customer pain.
- There are no available products that solve the problem well.
- The company has the skills to build an excellent solution that the customer values.
- The market potential is well over $1 billion.

Keep Betting on New Growth Trajectories

It is very satisfying for a founder to enjoy growth by meeting the needs of the startup's initial market. But companies that succeed initially can only sustain their success if they realize that such growth opportunities eventually mature. To sustain growth, successful founders must always be anticipating that their existing markets will mature and must bet on new growth opportunities with enough vigor to make the transition from a declining product to a growing one. In Chapter 2, we examined the case of data warehousing service Snowflake, which increased its customer count by 300% in 2018. As it grew, Snowflake bet on new growth trajectories, targeting new customer segments as it saturated the growth opportunities from its first ones. In 2015, Snowflake sold to companies in the entertainment, media, online gaming, and technology industries that were already using Amazon's AWS cloud service; it more recently sold to traditional enterprise customers—companies in financial services, manufacturing, oil, and gas, and retail—that were converting from on-premise to the cloud.

Create and Scale a Growth Culture

Some company cultures scale better than others. And since culture comes from the founder's values, success or failure can be a very personal thing. The key point for a growth culture is to create an environment that attracts innovators who dedicate themselves to solving customer problems so well that the company has a great reputation. This reputation will help the company bring in new customers and keep existing ones. Yet such reputations are difficult to sustain. Founders must encourage people to keep close tabs on how well customers are using the product, fix problems, and identify unmet needs that can be the basis for new products. In Chapter 4, we looked at ezCater, a Boston-based business catering platform that was valued at $700 million when it raised capital in June 2018. ezCater's culture put a premium on people who were passionate about inventing new products that customers were eager to buy and thereafter gave those customers excellent service so they would keep buying over a long period of time. If the people loved working for the company and the customers loved its products and services, then the customers would become its most compelling evangelists. As ezCater CEO Stefania Mallett said, "My cofounder and I are tinkerers. We ask, 'Can we make it go faster?' We come up with hypotheses, build a model, try it, track it, and learn from what works and what doesn't. We try to stay ahead of the curve rather than lag it. This growth mindset is at all levels of the company and it means that everyone shares responsibility for achieving growth."

Hire Functional Experts to Scale Your Processes

Founders will not make the journey from idea to public company unless they reinvent the company's organization. The most important thing they must do is to hire heads of key functions like sales, engineering, marketing, and human resources who have previously built successful companies. Such leaders will know how to design and run their departments in ways that get more efficient as the company grows. Such scalable processes are essential as a company sprints to an initial public offering. In Chapter 5, we studied Redis, a rapidly-growing Silicon Valley and Israel-based provider of an open source database, which was adapting its organization to keep up with the growth in demand. Redis struggled to attract top talent before it introduced a product, so it hired the best people it could and "everyone did everything," according to CEO Ofer Bengal. However, once its product was widely adopted, Redis was able to formalize functional departments like sales, marketing, and engineering, and the company attracted experienced executives who had run these functions in companies that had enjoyed successful outcomes.

Win New Customers Efficiently

The most impressive founders I've spoken with have developed the right match between their product's benefits and the needs of customers. And that's not all: they also know how to get their product to market in a way that does not involve sales people. Instead, such founders let potential customers try their product for free. Once they get value from the product, such users become the most effective internal evangelists for the product. And that makes selling far more efficient. As we saw in Chapter 8, Arcadia Data, a business intelligence service provider that was growing at 500% in 2018, developed a disciplined process for attracting leads and siphoning out all but the ones with the highest chance of becoming customers. Not only was its sales/marketing funnel effective, but Arcadia Data worked hard to improve it based on its analysis of what was working and what needed to be improved. For example, the company made sure it had the right number of telesales people and account executives to follow up on leads and turn the best ones into paying customers.

Retain Your Current Customers and Sell Them More

Finally, the most successful entrepreneurs are great at keeping existing customers. The key to doing this successfully is making sure that customers are using your product after they buy it. To do so, companies must assign people to work with their customers to find out what parts of the product they're using, which they are not, and what bugs they are encountering. Such interactions fix problems, make customers eager to renew, and help identify unmet needs that can become new products that customers will want to buy. Arcadia Data was also good at customer retention and boosting revenue per customer. It retained customers because it gave them more value than competing products did. For instance, its competitors required customers to spend between $50 million and $100 million to purchase hardware to run its systems and to spend another $2 million to $3 million for software and staffing. Arcadia Data did not require these large investments and could provide analytical results in 15 minutes, compared to the five hours it took competing products. Arcadia Data also had a rigorous process for planning and evaluating its business, in which it estimated revenue and headcount in sales, marketing, and engineering in its four channels: inbound, outbound, partners, and upselling to existing customers. One key to Arcadia Data's ability to sell more to existing customers was to encourage its engineers to talk to customers and customer service people to help them build new products that customers would want to purchase. Through these conversations, engineers learned what changes customers needed and what bugs to fix. Arcadia Data tracked its bug-fix rate, the customer churn rate, and the upsell rate. And the company introduced a new version every six to eight weeks.

Can You Scale Your Startup? Calculating Your Scaling Quotient (SQ)

Chapters 2 through 8 presented methodologies to help founders to apply the seven scaling levers. But the chapters leave important questions unanswered, such as

- **Which scaling lever should a founder pull first and how does the answer vary by scaling stage?** While I addressed which scaling levers should be pulled at each stage in Chapter 1, there are many right answers to this question. One approach is that when a company is getting started, the first thing to do is to create a sustainable growth trajectory, beginning with finding the right match between the company's product and unmet customer needs. As a company reaches the second stage, hiring executives who have built scalable business models takes center stage.

- **Which scaling levers should a founder pull second, third, and so on?** Although I discussed this in Chapter 1, there are also many answers to this question. For example, in the first stage, hiring, promoting, and letting people go comes second, as does raising capital. As a company approaches an IPO and thereafter, holding people accountable, creating growth culture, and coordinating processes take on greater importance.

- **How can a founder decide whether to remain as CEO to tackle the next stage of scaling?** ThoughtSpot's CEO offered a good set of questions to address this issue, which he answered every six months based on anonymous feedback:

  - Do I feel bogged down or not?

  - Am I having fun?

  - Do people respect me or are they following orders?

  - Are we hitting our goals?

  - Are good people staying and doing well?

An insatiable appetite for learning is critical for a founder trying to turn an idea into a $10 billion company. That's because each founder and startup faces unique challenges that require specific solutions. Founders must craft these solutions themselves, but they ought to form networks of CEOs and others who have overcome similar challenges. Such networks can offer valuable feedback and help founders manage the uncertainty and stress of what can often be the lonely job of leading a fast-growing startup.

To get your journey started, I suggest assessing your startup. More specifically, you should identify your startup's strengths and opportunities to improve how well it manages the seven scaling levers. To do this, you should calculate your startup's Scaling Quotient (SQ), a number between 0 and 100, which gives you a quick way to identify whether your startup is ready for the next stage of scaling. The SQ is calculated by scoring a startup from *5 = best in class* to *1 = worst in class* on the answers to the readiness questions listed at the end of Chapters 2 through 8. Below are the key questions for assessing your startup's ability to manage the seven scaling levers:

- **Creating a sustainable growth trajectory**

  - Is your startup solving a problem that is so painful that potential customers would be willing to pay for an effective solution?

  - Do you know which growth vectors your startup will follow to get big and keep growing at each of the stages of scaling?

  - Does your company continue to invest in new growth opportunities to sustain its rapid growth at each stage?

- **Raising growth capital**

  - Do you have or are you creating customers who will happily refer you to others?

  - Is your product targeting very large markets?

  - Can your company offer so much value to customers that it will gain significant market share?

  - Do you have a team of experienced executives with prior experience in taking a company public?

  - Does your company have the discipline to set and exceed ambitious quarterly goals for growth and profitability?

- **Creating growth culture**

  - Have you articulated your startup's values?

  - Are your startup's values consistent with your beliefs and what will attract and motivate employees to create products that customers love?

  - Do you consistently behave in ways that embody your startup's culture?

  - Do you use the startup's culture to hire, promote, and let people go?

- **Redefining job functions**

  - Are you adapting your organizational structure to your evolving business strategy?

  - Are you splitting organizational responsibilities to limit managers' span of control to six or seven direct reports?

  - Are you holding key executives accountable for results and giving them freedom to redefine their roles as the company grows?

  - Are you eliminating roles that cost more than the value they create?

- **Hiring, promoting, and letting people go**
  - Have you articulated a clear vision and values that inform the process of hiring, promoting, and letting people go?
  - Are you weighing the advantages and disadvantages of promoting from within to fill a new executive or management role?
  - If a strong contributor does not fit the requirements of a new role, do you help the person find a new job or manage them respectfully out of the company?
  - If you hire from the outside for a new role, do you evaluate whether the candidate embraces the company's vision and values, has the skills needed to do the job as it evolves, and will take responsibility for achieving the company's goals?
- **Holding people accountable**
  - Did you build an executive team charged with setting goals, monitoring progress to the goals, analyzing variances, and correcting course?
  - Do you collaborate with your executive team to set corporate goals?
  - Do functions hold themselves accountable for achieving controllable performance indicators that contribute to achieving corporate goals?
  - Do you operate effective systems to generate timely and accurate data to assess the company's progress in pursuit of corporate and functional objectives?
  - Are you assessing and improving your company's performance management process?
- **Coordinating processes**
  - Did you build an executive team charged with creating and operating processes to achieve corporate goals?
  - Did you engage your functional executives in identifying the mission and objectives of these coordinating processes?

- Do you oversee the functioning of these coordinating processes or delegate them to the chief operating officer?

- Do you monitor the effectiveness of the coordinating processes?

- Do you improve processes that are still essential, eliminate ones that are no longer worth performing, and create new processes to meet new objectives?

You should calculate your startup's SQ for its *current scaling stage* and estimate the potential SQ for its *next scaling stage*. To calculate your startup's current SQ, conduct interviews to answer these questions with customers, employees, investors, other CEOs, and professors. You should analyze the results of the interviews and reach conclusions about how well your company performs on these questions relative to your competitors. Using the SQ framework presented in Table 9-1, you should assign a score between 5 and 1 to your conclusion on your startup's answer to each question and summarize the reason behind each score. Once you've calculated your current SQ by dividing your company's total score on the 28 questions by the maximum score of 140, you should develop a similar framework that enables you to assess how well your startup might score on the most significant questions on the scaling levers in the next stage of scaling.

Table 9-1. Scaling Quotient Framework (Scoring Key: 5=Excellent, 4=Very Good, 3= Good, 2=Fair, 1=Poor) The maximum number of points for each scaling lever is in parentheses below.

Scaling Levers and Questions	Company Score	Score Rationale
Creating a sustainable growth trajectory (15)		
Solving the right problem		
Sequencing growth vectors		
Investing in new growth opportunities		
Raising growth capital (25)		
Creating reference customers		
Targeting large markets		
Providing more value to customers than rivals do		
Fielding an experienced executive team		
Setting and achieving stretch goals		

(continued)

Table 9-1. (continued)

Scaling Levers and Questions	Company Score	Score Rationale
Creating growth culture (20)		
Articulating values		
Using values to attract talent		
Acting in accordance with values		
Using values to hire, promote, and let people go		
Redefining job functions (20)		
Adapting organizational structure		
Limiting managerial span of control		
Giving leaders freedom and responsibility		
Eliminating wasteful functions		
Hiring, promoting, and letting people go (20)		
Articulating clear vision and values		
Promoting from within vs. outside hiring		
Letting go those who don't fit future needs		
Assessing the cultural fit of outside hires		
Holding people accountable (20)		
Creating a performance management team		
Collaborating to set corporate goals		
Aligning functional goals with corporate ones		
Using a system to track progress towards goals		
Coordinating processes (20)		
Creating a process management team		
Engaging functions in setting process goals		
Evaluating process effectiveness		
Reinventing processes		
Your company's score		
Maximum possible score	140	
Scaling Quotient (your score/maximum)		

Founders seeking to calculate their startup's SQ may need help. A starting point could be to examine the SQs of other startups. I am developing an SQ database that could be useful for founders seeking to assess their readiness for the next stage of scaling. Once you've developed the SQ for your current and next stage of scaling, you are in a better position to act. You should be able to identify which strengths can help you scale and which weaknesses you should seek to bolster, possibly by developing your own skills or by hiring executives with strong experience in these areas. The SQ can be a helpful tool for CEOs considering whether to continue or hire a replacement as they anticipate the next stage of scaling.

Conclusion

Most entrepreneurs go into battle with the cry of building a company that will change the world. Very few get there. The few that do excel at scaling their startup from an idea to a $10 billion company. By applying the lessons of this book, you have a better chance of really building a company that changes the world. And even if you can't take your company to this promised land, the principles, processes, and lessons from the case studies presented in this book can help you get closer than you otherwise would have.

Notes

Chapter 1: Introduction

[1] Peter Cohan, "This $280 Million Founder Pulls Six Levers to Scale from Idea to $1 Billion," *Inc.*, March 6, 2018, https://www.inc.com/peter-cohan/this-280-million-founder-pulls-6-levers-to-scale-from-idea-to-1-billion.html

[2] Peter Cohan, "This $280 Million Founder Pulls Six Levers to Scale from Idea to $1 Billion," Ibid

[3] Peter Cohan, "This $280 Million Founder Pulls Six Levers to Scale from Idea to $1 Billion," Ibid

[4] Julia Boorstin, "From rule-breakers to rule-makers: How Uber, Airbnb and other star start-ups scale up for success," *CNBC*, May 22, 2018, https://www.cnbc.com/2018/05/22/how-uber-and-other-star-start-ups-scale-up-for-success.html

[5] Peter Cohan, "Scaling Expert On Finding The Next Bezos, Zuckerberg," *Forbes*, June 6, 2018, http://www.forbes.com/sites/petercohan/2018/06/06/hbs-scaling-expe...bezos-zuckerberg/

[6] Peter Cohan, "Wharton Scaling Expert On Why Snap, Blue Apron Are In Danger," *Forbes*, June 6, 2018, http://www.forbes.com/sites/petercohan/2018/06/06/wharton-scaling-...on-are-in-danger/

[7] Peter Cohan, "Stanford Expert Highlights Reasons To Like Amazon And Netflix," Forbes, June 6, 2018, http://www.forbes.com/sites/petercohan/2018/06/06/stanford-expert-...azon-and-netflix/

© Peter S. Cohan 2019
P. S. Cohan, *Scaling Your Startup*, https://doi.org/10.1007/978-1-4842-4312-1

[8] Peter Cohan, "8 Keys To Changing The World According to Harvard Business School," Inc., June 14. 2018, https://preview.inc.com/peter-cohan/8-keys-to-changing-world-according-to-harvard-business-school.html

[9] Peter Cohan, "8 Keys To Changing The World According to Harvard Business School," Ibid.

[10] Ranjay Gulati, Alicia DeSantola, "What Is Scaling?" Harvard Business Review, March 2016, https://hbr.org/2016/03/start-ups-that-last

[11] Peter Cohan, "MIT Prof's Brilliant Solutions to the Nine Toughest Startup Problems," Inc., June 9, 2018, https://www.inc.com/peter-cohan/mit-profs-brilliant-solutions-to-nine-toughest-startup-problems.html

Chapter 2: Creating Growth Trajectories

[1] Peter Cohan, "Disciplined Growth Strategies," Apress (February 2017)

[2] Peter Cohan, "4 Pincers for Crushing Your Competition," *Entrepreneur*, April 22, 2015. http://www.entrepreneur.com/article/245019

[3] Paul Stukel, "Why merely satisfy if you can go for the thrill?," *President and CEO Magazine*, April 16, 2013, http://www.presidentandceomagazine.com/opinion/4707-why-merely-satisfy-when-you-can-go-for-the-thrill.html

[4] "Platform.sh," *CrunchBase*, accessed July 4, 2018, https://www.crunchbase.com/organization/platform-sh#section-overview

[5] Peter Cohan, "2 CEOs Reveal How They Got Their First Customers and Raised Capital," Inc., July 2, 2018, https://www.inc.com/peter-cohan/2-ceos-reveal-how-they-got-their-first-customers-raised-capital.html

[6] Peter Cohan, "2 CEOs Reveal How They Got Their First Customers and Raised Capital," Inc., Ibid.

[7] "Harmon.ie," *CrunchBase*, accessed July 4, 2018, https://www.crunchbase.com/organization/harmon-ie#section-overview

[8] "Yaacov Cohen," LinkedIn profile, accessed July 4, 2018, https://www.linkedin.com/in/yaacovc/

[9] Peter Cohan, "2 CEOs Reveal How They Got Their First Customers and Raised Capital," Inc., Ibid.

[10] Peter Cohan, "2 CEOs Reveal How They Got Their First Customers and Raised Capital," Inc., Ibid.

[11] Peter Cohan, "You Won't Believe How These Growth Strategies Are Propelling 3 Startups to IPO," Inc., April 4, 2018, https://www.inc.com/peter-cohan/you-wont-believe-how-these-growth-strategies-are-propelling-3-startups-to-ipo.html

[12] Peter Cohan, "You Won't Believe How These Growth Strategies Are Propelling 3 Startups to IPO," Ibid.

[13] Lucia Maffei, "Threat Stack Lays Off 'Less Than 10%,' Says Headcount 'Will Be Unchanged'," BostonInno, October 22, 2018, https://www.americaninno.com/boston/bostinno-bytes/threat-stack-lays-off-less-than-10-says-headcount-will-be-unchanged/

[14] "Actifio," *CrunchBase*, accessed July 5, 2018, https://www.crunchbase.com/organization/actifio#section-recent-news-activity

[15] Peter Cohan, "500% Growth Makes Actifio History's Swiftest Storage Start-up, Forbes, October 8, 2012, https://www.forbes.com/sites/petercohan/2012/10/08/500-growth-makes-actifio-historys-swiftest-storage-start-up/

[16] Peter Cohan, "500% Growth Makes Actifio History's Swiftest Storage Start-up, Forbes, October 8, 2012, Ibid.

[17] Peter Cohan, "500% Growth Makes Actifio History's Swiftest Storage Start-up, Forbes, October 8, 2012, Ibid.

[18] Peter Cohan, "500% Growth Makes Actifio History's Swiftest Storage Start-up, Forbes, October 8, 2012, Ibid.

[19] Peter Cohan $1.1 Billion Startup Recovers from Bad Advice on Managing 'Disruption' Jul 13, 2016, https://www.inc.com/peter-cohan/11-billion-startup-recovers-from-bad-advice-on-managing-disruption.html

[20] Peter Cohan $1.1 Billion Startup Recovers from Bad Advice On Managing 'Disruption' July 13, 2016, Ibid.

[21] Garry Kranz, "Actifio copy data management sales help turn a profit," TechTarget, July 12, 2017, https://searchstorage.techtarget.com/news/450422558/Actifio-copy-data-management-sales-help-turn-a-profit

[22] Garry Kranz, "Actifio copy data management sales help turn a profit," Ibid.

[23] Chris Mellor, "Whatever they're putting in Actifio's water, we'd like some too. Sheesh!," The Register, August 8, 2018, https://www.theregister.co.uk/2018/08/08/actifio_funding_round_f

[24] Peter Cohan, "Startup Raised $180M To Take On Tableau Software In $18B Analytics Market," Forbes, October 23, 2017, https://www.forbes.com/sites/petercohan/2017/10/23/startup-raised-180-million-to-take-on-tableau-software-in-4-billion-data-visualization-market/

[25] Peter Cohan, "Caltech Grad Grows Startup As Ex Punk Rocker Barrels Towards 2019 IPO," *Inc.*, May 8, 2018, https://www.inc.com/peter-cohan/caltech-grad-grows-startup-as-ex-punk-rocker-barrels-towards-2019-ipo.html

[26] Peter Cohan, "Caltech Grad Grows Startup As Ex Punk Rocker Barrels Towards 2019 IPO," *Inc.*, May 8, 2018, https://www.inc.com/peter-cohan/caltech-grad-grows-startup-as-ex-punk-rocker-barrels-towards-2019-ipo.html

[27] Peter Cohan, "Snowflake Computing is Beating Oracle in $15 billion data warehousing market," *Forbes*, June 15, 2018, https://www.forbes.com/sites/petercohan/2018/06/15/1-5b-snowflake-computing-is-beating-oracle-in-15b-data-warehousing-market/

[28] Peter Cohan, "Snowflake Computing is Beating Oracle in $15 billion data warehousing market," Ibid.

[29] Peter Cohan, "Snowflake Computing is Beating Oracle in $15 billion data warehousing market," Ibid.

[30] Peter Cohan, "Snowflake Computing is Beating Oracle in $15 billion data warehousing market," Ibid.

[31] Ron Miller, "Snowflake scoops up another blizzard of cash with $450 million round," TechCrunch, October 11, 2018, https://techcrunch.com/2018/10/11/snowflake-shovels-another-blizzard-of-cash-with-450-million-round/

[32] "amazon business description," Morningstar, accessed July 7, 2018, https://www.morningstar.com/stocks/xnas/amzn/quote.html

[33] "Jeff Bezos," Biography, accessed July 7, 2018, https://www.biography.com/people/jeff-bezos-9542209

[34] "Amazon Startup Story," Fundable, accessed July 7, 2018, https://www.fundable.com/learn/startup-stories/amazon

[35] Makeda Easter and Paresh Davem, "Remember when Amazon only sold books?," LA Times, June 18, 2017, http://www.latimes.com/business/la-fi-amazon-history-20170618-htmlstory.html#

[36] "Amazon-JPMorgan-Berkshire Health Care Venture Names Atul Gawande As CEO," Bloomberg News, June 20, 2018, https://www.investors.com/news/amazon-jpmorgan-berkshire-health-care-venture-ceo-atul-gawande/

[37] Ingrid Lunden, "Amazon buys PillPack, an online pharmacy, for just under $1B," Techcrunch, June 28, 2018, https://techcrunch.com/2018/06/28/amazon-buys-pillpack-an-online-pharmacy-that-was-rumored-to-be-talking-to-walmart/

[38] Peter Cohan, "3 Reasons To Gag On Blue Apron's IPO," *Forbes*, June 2, 2017, https://www.forbes.com/sites/petercohan/2017/06/02/3-reasons-to-gag-on-blue-aprons-ipo/

[39] Peter Cohan, "Wharton Scaling Expert on Why Snap, Blue Apron Are In Danger," Forbes, June 6, 2018, https://www.forbes.com/sites/petercohan/2018/06/06/wharton-scaling-expert-on-why-snap-blue-apron-are-in-danger/

[40] Alex Konrad, "Blue Apron's Got Big Plans For Dinner -- But So Do Its Hungry Rivals," Forbes, October 14, 2015, https://www.forbes.com/sites/alexkonrad/2015/10/14/inside-blue-apron-and-the-meal-kit-rush/

[41] "Blue Apron 2018 10-K," sec.gov, accessed July 8, 2018, https://www.sec.gov/Archives/edgar/data/1701114/000155837018000955/aprn-20171231x10k.htm

[42] "Blue Apron 2018 10-K," Ibid.

[43] Peter Cohan, "3 Reasons To Gag On Blue Apron's IPO," Ibid.

[44] Jason Del Rey, "Blue Apron is stuck in a dangerous cycle that has nothing to do with Amazon," Recode, August 11, 2017, https://www.recode.net/2017/8/11/16127050/blue-apron-q2-earnings-warehouse-issues-linden-new-jersey-matt-salzberg

[45] Jon Russell, "Blue Apron gets a much-needed boost with Jet.com partnership," TechCrunch, October 29, 2018, https://techcrunch.com/2018/10/29/jet-com-blue-apron/

Chapter 3: Raising Capital

[1] Peter Cohan, "How Much Money Should You Raise for Your Startup? Here's How to Find Out in 5 Steps," Inc., July 25, 2018, https://www.inc.com/peter-cohan/how-much-money-should-you-raise-for-your-startup-heres-how-to-find-out-in-5-steps.html

[2] Peter Cohan, "Hungry StartUp Strategy," Berrett-Koehler (2012)

[3] For insight into how to decide which offer to accept, see Faisal Hoque, "What Every Entrepreneur Should Know Before Taking Any Outside Investment," *Fast Company*, December 16, 2014, https://www.fastcompany.com/3039508/what-every-entrepreneur-should-know-before-taking-any-outside-investment

[4] Peter Cohan, "Sell Signal? Startup Snags Big Contract From Splunk," *Forbes*, July 6, 2018, https://www.forbes.com/sites/petercohan/2018/07/06/sell-signal-startup-snags-big-contract-from-splunk/

[5] Peter Cohan, "Sell Signal? Startup Snags Big Contract From Splunk," Ibid.

[6] Peter Cohan, "Sell Signal? Startup Snags Big Contract From Splunk," Ibid.

[7] Peter Cohan, "Sell Signal? Startup Snags Big Contract From Splunk," Ibid.

[8] "MapD," Crunchbase, accessed July 19, 2018, https://www.crunchbase.com/organization/mapd#section-overview

[9] Peter Cohan, "Startup Aiming at Oracle, IBM in $70B Market Fits What VCs Want," Forbes, July 17, 2018, https://www.forbes.com/sites/petercohan/2018/07/17/startup-aiming-at-oracle-ibm-in-70b-market-fits-what-vcs-want/

[10] Peter Cohan, "Startup Aiming at Oracle, IBM in $70B Market Fits What VCs Want," Ibid.

[11] Peter Cohan, "Startup Aiming at Oracle, IBM in $70B Market Fits What VCs Want," Ibid.

[12] Bernice Landry, "MapD Rebrands as OmniSci; Maintains its Data Optimization Focus," RTInsights, October 10, 2018, https://www.rtinsights.com/mapd-rebrands-as-omnisci-maintains-its-data-optimization-focus/

[13] Peter Cohan, "Varsity Tutors Raised $107M To Take On $38B Worth of Public Companies In $100B Market," Forbes, July 19, 2018, https://www.forbes.com/sites/petercohan/2018/07/19/varsity-tutors-raised-107m-to-take-on-38b-worth-of-public-companies-in-100b-market/

[14] Peter Cohan, "Varsity Tutors Raised $107M To Take On $38B Worth of Public Companies In $100B Market," Ibid.

[15] Peter Cohan, "Varsity Tutors Raised $107M To Take On $38B Worth of Public Companies In $100B Market," Ibid.

[16] Peter Cohan, "Varsity Tutors Raised $107M To Take On $38B Worth of Public Companies In $100B Market," Ibid.

[17] Peter Cohan, "Tipalti Simplifies Global Payment Complexity," Forbes, October 2, 2012, https://www.forbes.com/sites/petercohan/2012/10/02/tipalti-simplifies-global-payment-complexity/

[18] Peter Cohan, "3 Growth Insights Helped This CEO Raise $50 Million," Inc., February 14, 2018, http://www.inc.com/peter-cohan/3-growth-insights-helped-this-ceo-raise-50-million.html

[19] Peter Cohan, "IBM and Oracle Could Buy Growth From These 4 Startup CEOs Who've Raised $192M," Forbes, July 15, 2018, http://www.forbes.com/sites/petercohan/2018/07/15/ibm-and-oracle-c...hove-raised-192m/

[20] Peter Cohan, "3 Growth Insights Helped This CEO Raise $50 Million," Inc., Ibid.

[21] Peter Cohan, "Startup Nibbles $20 Billion Market Away From IBM, Oracle, SAP," *Forbes*, July 10, 2017, https://www.forbes.com/sites/petercohan/2017/07/10/startup-nibbles-20-billion-market-away-from-ibm-oracle-sap/

[22] "Cloud Unicorn Anaplan Hires Red Hat Exec as CEO," Reuters, January 10, 2017, http://fortune.com/2017/01/10/cloud-financials-unicorn-anaplan-hires-ceo/

[23] Deborah Gage, "Business Software Maker Anaplan's CEO Steps Down," Wall Street Journal, April 27, 2016, https://www.wsj.com/articles/business-software-maker-anaplans-ceo-steps-down-1461760716

[24] Peter Cohan, "Startup Nibbles $20 Billion Market Away From IBM, Oracle, SAP," *Ibid.*

[25] Peter Cohan, "3 Successful Leaders Reveal Their Growth Strategies," Inc., May 7, 2018 https://www.inc.com/peter-cohan/3-successful-leaders-reveal-their-growth-strategies.html

[26] "Series F - Anaplan," Crunchbase, accessed July 21, 2018, https://www.crunchbase.com/funding_round/anaplan-series-f--7fc43287#section-overview

[27] Peter Cohan, "With $300M In Capital, Anaplan Is Taking $100M+ Bite Out Of IBM, Oracle in $20B Market," *Forbes*, July 21, 2018, https://www.forbes.com/sites/petercohan/2018/07/21/with-300m-in-capital-anaplan-is-taking-100m-bite-out-of-ibm-oracle-in-20b-market/#5db90f942de1

[28] "Anaplan's stock opens 43% above IPO price," Marketwatch, October 12, 2018, https://www.morningstar.com/news/market-watch/TDJNMW_20181012365/mw-anaplans-stock-opens-43-above-ipo-price.html

[29] Peter Cohan, "SentinelOne To Take $100M in 2019 Revenue from Symantec," *Forbes*, April 30, 2018, https://www.forbes.com/sites/petercohan/2018/04/30/sentinelone-to-take-100m-in-2019-revenue-from-symantec/

[30] "SentinelOne," Crunchbase, accessed July 21, 2018, https://www.crunchbase.com/organization/sentinel

[31] "Tomer Weingarten," Crunchbase, accessed July 21, 2018, https://www.crunchbase.com/person/tomer-weingarten#section-overview

[32] Peter Cohan, "SentinelOne To Take $100M in 2019 Revenue from Symantec," *Ibid.*

[33] Stephanie Yang, "Cyber-Security Company Sentinel Labs Raises $2.5M," TechCrunch, August 7, 2013, https://techcrunch.com/2013/08/07/cyber-security-company-sentinel-labs-raises-2-5m/

34 "SentinelOne raises $70M Series C," PitchBook, January 26, 2017, https://pitchbook.com/newsletter/sentinelone-raises-70m-series-c

35 Jonathan Shieber, "SentinelOne Raises $25 Million To Attack Security Threats At The Kernel," TechCrunch, October 13, 2015, https://techcrunch.com/2015/10/13/sentinelone-raises-25-million-to-attack-security-threats-at-the-kernel/

36 Mike Butcher, "SentinelOne raises a $70M C round to tackle multiple-vector cyber-attacks," TechCrunch, January 25, 2017, https://techcrunch.com/2017/01/25/sentinelone-raises-a-70m-c-round-to-tackle-multiple-vector-cyber-attacks/

37 Reuters Staff, "Cyber firm SentinelOne raises $70 million bringing total to over $110 million," Reuters, January 25, 2017, https://www.reuters.com/article/us-tech-cyber-sentinelone/cyber-firm-sentinelone-raises-70-million-bringing-total-to-over-110-million-idUSKBN1591EY

38 Peter Cohan, "SentinelOne To Take $100M in 2019 Revenue from Symantec," Ibid.

39 Liana B. Baker, "Under threat: Cyber security startups fall on harder times," Reuters, January 17, 2018, https://www.reuters.com/article/us-cybersecurity-startups-analysis/under-threat-cyber-security-startups-fall-on-harder-times-idUSKBN1F62RW

40 For how to fix the problem of negative cash flow, see Peter Cohan, "How to Make Your Business Profitable in Five Steps," Inc. July 26, 2018, https://www.inc.com/peter-cohan/how-to-make-your-business-profitable-in-5-steps.html

41 Peter Cohan, "Talend CEO Expects Strong Growth, Free Cash Flow," Forbes, July 13, 2018, https://www.forbes.com/sites/petercohan/2018/07/13/talend-ceo-expects-strong-growth-free-cash-flow/

42 Peter Cohan, "Talend CEO Expects Strong Growth, Free Cash Flow," Ibid.

43 Peter Cohan, "Talend CEO Expects Strong Growth, Free Cash Flow," Ibid.

44 Peter Cohan, "Talend CEO Expects Strong Growth, Free Cash Flow," Ibid.

45 Peter Cohan, "Talend CEO Expects Strong Growth, Free Cash Flow," Ibid.

46 Peter Cohan, "Talend CEO Expects Strong Growth, Free Cash Flow," Ibid.

47 Michael Corkery, "Adobe Buys Omniture: What Were They Thinking?," Wall Street Journal, September 16, 2009, https://blogs.wsj.com/deals/2009/09/16/adobe-buys-omniture-what-were-they-thinking/

48 "Domo S-1A," June 18, 2018, sec.gov https://www.sec.gov/Archives/edgar/data/1505952/000162828018007944/domoincs-1a.htm

49 "Domo S-1A," Ibid.

50 Sramana Mitra, "From Unicorn to Unicorpse: Domo's Valuation Slashed Ahead Of IPO," *SeekingAlpha*, June 25, 2018, https://seekingalpha.com/article/4183873-unicorn-unicorpse-domos-valuation-slashed-ahead-ipo

51 "Domo S-1A," Ibid.

52 "Domo," Crunchbase, accessed July 22, 2018, https://www.crunchbase.com/organization/domo#section-ipo-stock-price. A March 2010 seed round raised $650,000; its May 2011 angel round totaled $10 million, its July 2011 Series A round, led by Benchmark Capital, raised $33 million and its January 2012 Series A round led by Institutional Venture Partners yielded another $20 million. Domo's March 2013 Series C round raised $60 million. TPG Growth led its February 2014 Series C round of $125 million. Blackrock led its April 2015 Series D round of $210 million. In March 2016, Domo's Series D round totaled $131 million and in April 2017, Blackrock led a Series E round of $100 million.

53 Ryan Lawler, "With Another $200M In The Bank, Josh James Finally Takes The Wraps Off Business Analytics Startup Domo," TechCrunch, April 8, 2015, https://techcrunch.com/2015/04/08/domo-finally-launches/

54 Alex Konrad, "Its Stock Up 30% After Diminished IPO, Domo's Defiant CEO Says It's Back On Track," Forbes, June 29, 2018, https://www.forbes.com/sites/alexkonrad/2018/06/29/domo-ceo-talks-ipo/

55 Dave Kellogg, "The Domo S-1: Does the Emperor Have Clothes?," Kellblog, June 2, 2018, https://kellblog.com/2018/06/02/the-domo-s-1-burn-baby-burn/

56 Marcus Baram, "It's worth remembering how Theranos first responded to the WSJ's exposé," Fast Company, March 14, 2018, https://www.fastcompany.com/40544465/its-worth-remembering-how-theranos-first-responded-to-the-wsjs-expose. After the Wall Street Journal first questioned Theranos's veracity, Holmes said, "This is what happens when you work to change things. First they think you're crazy, then they fight you, and then, all of a sudden, you change the world."

57 Alex Konrad, "Its Stock Up 30% After Diminished IPO, Domo's Defiant CEO Says It's Back On Track," Ibid.

Chapter 4: Sustaining Culture

[1] Entrepreneurial leadership – hiring people with entrepreneurial ability and helping them develop -- is one of four factors that enable large, rapidly-growing technology companies to sustain their market leadership. Peter S. Cohan, "The Technology Leaders: How America's Most Profitable High-Tech Companies Innovate Their Way to Success," (Jossey-Bass Publishers, 1997)

[2] Ben Horowitz, "Programming Your Culture," a16z.com, December 18, 2012, https://a16z.com/2012/12/18/programming-your-culture

[3] Chris McCann, "16 lessons on scaling from Eric Schmidt, Reid Hoffman, Marissa Mayer, Brian Chesky, Diane Greene, Jeff Weiner, and more," *Medium*, December 8, 2015, https://medium.com/cs183c-blitzscaling-class-collection/16-lessons-on-scaling-from-eric-schmidt-reid-hoffman-marissa-mayer-brian-chesky-diane-greene-3d6367e63a42

[4] Peter Cohan, "4 Types of Company Culture, Ranked From Best to Worst," Inc., August 9. 2018. https://www.inc.com/peter-cohan/4-types-of-company-culture-ranked-from-best-to-worst.html

[5] Chris Mellor, "Disaster-proofers merge: Axcient enclosed by eFolder," *The Register*, July 28, 2017, https://www.theregister.co.uk/2017/07/28/axcient_merges_into_efolder/

[6] Peter Cohan, "Silicon Valley's Culture Doctor," *Forbes*, November 4, 2011, https://www.forbes.com/sites/petercohan/2011/11/04/silicon-valleys-culture-doctor/

[7] Kevin Mercadante, "Twine Savings App Review – Saving and Investing for Couples," *DoughRoller*, July 6, 2018, https://www.doughroller.net/money-management/twine-savings-app-review/

[8] Peter Cohan, "Peter S. Cohan: A tale of innovation at two insurers," *Worcester Telegram & Gazette*, July 30, 2018, http://www.telegram.com/news/20180730/peter-s-cohan-tale-of-innovation-at-two-insurers

[9] Peter Cohan, "Peter S. Cohan: A tale of innovation at two insurers," Ibid.

[10] Peter Cohan, "Peter S. Cohan: A tale of innovation at two insurers," Ibid.

[11] Peter Cohan, "Peter S. Cohan: A tale of innovation at two insurers," Ibid.

[12] Peter Cohan, "Serial CEO's Five Surprising Lessons for Startup Success," Inc., October 7, 2016, https://www.inc.com/peter-cohan/serial-ceos-five-surprising-lessons-for-startup-success.html

[13] Peter Cohan, "How to merge your startup with a big company," *Worcester Telegram & Gazette*, September 4, 2017, http://www.telegram.com/news/20170904/wall-amp-main-how-to-merge-your-startup-with-big-company

[14] Peter Cohan, "Serial CEO's Five Surprising Lessons for Startup Success," Ibid.

[15] Peter Cohan, "Serial CEO's Five Surprising Lessons for Startup Success," Ibid.

[16] Peter Cohan, "How to merge your startup with a big company," Ibid.

[17] Peter Cohan, "How to merge your startup with a big company," Ibid.

[18] Peter Cohan, "3 Leadership Principles Propel This Boston Startup's Rapid Growth," Inc., April 18, 2018, https://www.inc.com/peter-cohan/successful-leadership-propels-this-boston-startups-rapid-growth.html:

[19] Matthew Lynley, "ezCater raises $100M as it looks to own office-catered meals around the world," *TechCrunch*, Jun 19, 2018, https://techcrunch.com/2018/06/18/ezcater-raises-100m-as-it-looks-to-own-office-catered-meals-around-the-world/

[20] Chris O'Brien, "Boston's ezCater raises $100 million to take its corporate catering platform international," Venture Beat, June 18, 2018, https://venturebeat.com/2018/06/18/bostons-ezcater-raises-100-million-to-take-its-corporate-catering-platform-international/

[21] Callum Borchers, "Boston-Based ezCater Expands into Europe With Acquisition of French Company," WBUR, July 24, 2018, http://www.wbur.org/bostonomix/2018/07/24/ezcater-buys-french-company

[22] Peter Cohan, "This MIT-Trained Female Founder's Secret to Reaching Success," Inc., August 4, 2017, https://www.inc.com/peter-cohan/3-secrets-of-this-mit-trained-female-founders-succ.html

[23] Peter Cohan, "3 Leadership Principles Propel This Boston Startup's Rapid Growth," Ibid.

[24] Peter Cohan, "3 Leadership Principles Propel This Boston Startup's Rapid Growth," Ibid.

[25] Peter Cohan, "This MIT-Trained Female Founder's Secret to Reaching Success," Inc., August 4, 2017, https://www.inc.com/peter-cohan/3-secrets-of-this-mit-trained-female-founders-succ.html

[26] "Threat Stack Named Top 5 Winner in Boston Business Journal 2016 Best Places to Work Competition," ThreatStack.com, accessed August 11, 2018, https://www.threatstack.com/press-releases/threat-stack-named-top-5-winner-in-boston-business-journal-2016-best-places

[27] Threat Stack Reviews, Glassdoor.com, July 24, 2018, https://www.glassdoor.com/Reviews/Threat-Stack-Reviews-E1038334.htm

[28] Peter Cohan, "CrowdStrike Raises $200M To Gain Share from McAfee, Symantec in $35B Market," Forbes, July 27, 2018, https://www.forbes.com/sites/petercohan/2018/07/27/crowdstrike-raises-200m-to-gain-share-from-mcafee-symantec-in-35b-market/

[29] Peter Cohan, "CrowdStrike Raises $200M To Gain Share from McAfee, Symantec in $35B Market," Ibid.

[30] "2017 Best Small & Medium Companies 34. CrowdStrike," Fortune, accessed August 12, 2018, http://fortune.com/best-medium-workplaces/crowdstrike-34/

[31] Peter Cohan, "CrowdStrike Raises $200M To Gain Share from McAfee, Symantec in $35B Market," Ibid.

[32] Peter Cohan, "Copper's Winning 60% Against Salesforce In $52B CRM Market," Forbes, August 8, 2018, https://www.forbes.com/sites/petercohan/2018/08/08/coppers-winning-60-against-salesforce-in-52b-crm-market/

[33] Peter Cohan, "Copper's Winning 60% Against Salesforce In $52B CRM Market," Ibid.

[34] Peter Cohan, "Copper's Winning 60% Against Salesforce In $52B CRM Market," Ibid.

[35] Peter Cohan, "Copper's Winning 60% Against Salesforce In $52B CRM Market," Ibid.

[36] "Copper Reviews," Glassdoor, July 25, 2018, https://www.glassdoor.com/Reviews/Copper-Reviews-E1024075.htm

[37] "Copper Reviews," Ibid.

[38] Peter Cohan, "Copper's Winning 60% Against Salesforce In $52B CRM Market," Ibid.

[39] Peter Cohan, "5 Ways That Amazon Keeps Its Lead in the $180B Cloud," Forbes, August 1, 2018, https://www.forbes.com/sites/petercohan/2018/08/01/5-ways-that-amazon-keeps-its-lead-in-the-180b-cloud/

[40] Peter Cohan, "5 Ways That Amazon Keeps Its Lead in the $180B Cloud," Forbes, August 1, 2018, https://www.forbes.com/sites/petercohan/2018/08/01/5-ways-that-amazon-keeps-its-lead-in-the-180b-cloud/

[41] Peter Cohan, "5 Ways That Amazon Keeps Its Lead in the $180B Cloud," Forbes, August 1, 2018, https://www.forbes.com/sites/petercohan/2018/08/01/5-ways-that-amazon-keeps-its-lead-in-the-180b-cloud/

[42] Peter Cohan, "5 Ways That Amazon Keeps Its Lead in the $180B Cloud," *Forbes*, August 1, 2018, https://www.forbes.com/sites/petercohan/2018/08/01/5-ways-that-amazon-keeps-its-lead-in-the-180b-cloud/

[43] Peter Cohan, "5 Ways That Amazon Keeps Its Lead in the $180B Cloud," *Forbes*, August 1, 2018, https://www.forbes.com/sites/petercohan/2018/08/01/5-ways-that-amazon-keeps-its-lead-in-the-180b-cloud/

[44] Peter Cohan, "5 Ways That Amazon Keeps Its Lead in the $180B Cloud," Ibid.

[45] Peter Cohan, "Will Nutanix's Rule Of 40 Propel Its Stock To $100?," Forbes, August 5, 2018, https://www.forbes.com/sites/petercohan/2018/08/05/will-nutanixs-rule-of-40-propel-its-stock-to-100/

[46] Peter Cohan, "Will Nutanix's Rule Of 40 Propel Its Stock To $100?," Ibid.

[47] Peter Cohan, "Will Nutanix's Rule Of 40 Propel Its Stock To $100?," Ibid.

[48] Peter Cohan, "Will Nutanix's Rule Of 40 Propel Its Stock To $100?," Ibid.

[49] Peter Cohan, "Will Nutanix's Rule Of 40 Propel Its Stock To $100?," Ibid.

[50] Peter Cohan, "Will Nutanix's Rule Of 40 Propel Its Stock To $100?," Ibid.

[51] Peter Cohan, "Will Nutanix's Rule Of 40 Propel Its Stock To $100?," Ibid.

Chapter 5: Redefining Job Functions

[1] Liz Gannes, "Sequoia Set to Lead $500M Valuation Round for Instagram," AllThingsD, April 6, 2012, http://allthingsd.com/20120406/sequoia-set-to-lead-500m-valuation-round-for-instagram/

[2] Evelyn Rusli, "Facebook Buys Instagram for $1 Billion," New York Times, April 9, 2012, https://dealbook.nytimes.com/2012/04/09/facebook-buys-instagram-for-1-billion/

[3] Assumes $501 billion stock market capitalization. "Facebook," Morningstar, accessed August 23, 2018, https://www.morningstar.com/stocks/xnas/fb/quote.html

[4] "Facebook stats," Facebook.com, accessed August 23, 2018, https://newsroom.fb.com/company-info/

[5] OEMs are typically well-established companies that incorporate a startup's product into their product

[6] "Stem Cell Basics II," National Institutes of Health, accessed August 30, 2018, https://stemcells.nih.gov/info/basics/2.htm

[7] Peter Cohan, "Square and MetLife Watch Out: Two Fintech Startups Target \$21T Markets," Forbes, August 14, 2018, https://www.forbes.com/sites/petercohan/2018/08/14/square-and-metlife-watch-out-two-fintech-startups-target-21t-markets/

[8] "Lingke Wang — Co-founder of Ovid Life," *IdeaMensch*, April 3, 2017, https://ideamensch.com/lingke-wang/

[9] Julie Verhage, "Robert Downey Jr., Jay Z, Durant Back Life Insurance Startup," Bloomberg, June 14, 2018, https://www.bloomberg.com/news/articles/2018-06-14/robert-downey-jr-jay-z-durant-back-life-insurance-startup

[10] Peter Cohan, "Square and MetLife Watch Out: Two Fintech Startups Target \$21T Markets," Ibid.

[11] Jeff Engel, "Communications Tech Firm Fuze Gulps \$104M, Eyes IPO in 2018," Xconomy, February 8th, 2017, https://www.xconomy.com/boston/2017/02/08/communications-tech-firm-fuze-gulps-104m-eyes-ipo-in-2018/

[12] Doherty was CEO of Manchester, NH-based domain name server operator, Dyn, from October 6, 2016 to January 2017 during which time it suffered a distributed denial of service attack two weeks after he joined and was sold to Oracle for \$600 million.

[13] Kelly J. O'Brien, "Cambridge-based Fuze gets a new CEO as co-founder steps aside," *Boston Business Journal*, Feb 16, 2017, https://www.bizjournals.com/boston/news/2017/02/16/cambridge-based-fuze-gets-a-new-ceo-as-co-founder.html

[14] Peter Cohan, "Fuze Raised \$484M To Take On Skype And WebEx In \$100B Market," Forbes, August 22, 2018, https://www.forbes.com/sites/petercohan/2018/08/22/fuze-raised-484m-to-take-on-skype-and-webex-in-100b-market/

[15] Peter Cohan, "Fuze Raised \$484M To Take On Skype And WebEx In \$100B Market," Ibid.

[16] Peter Cohan, "Fuze Raised \$484M To Take On Skype And WebEx In \$100B Market," Ibid.

[17] Lorna Garey, "Fuze Courts Resellers with New Partner Program, Professional Services," Channel Partners, February 6 2018, https://www.channelpartnersonline.com/2018/02/06/fuze-courts-resellers-with-new-partner-program-professional-services/

[18] Peter Cohan, "Fuze Raised \$484M To Take On Skype And WebEx In \$100B Market," Ibid.

[19] Peter Cohan, "Hired Challenges LinkedIn in $400 billion market for talent recruiting," Forbes, August 16, 2018, https://www.forbes.com/sites/petercohan/2018/08/16/hired-challenges-linkedin-in-400b-market-for-talent-recruiting/

[20] Peter Cohan, "Hired Challenges LinkedIn in $400 billion market for talent recruiting," Ibid.

[21] Peter Cohan, "Hired Challenges LinkedIn in $400 billion market for talent recruiting," Ibid.

[22] Peter Cohan, "Hired Challenges LinkedIn in $400 billion market for talent recruiting," Ibid.

[23] Peter Cohan, "Pendo Takes On Google And Adobe In $20B Product Engagement Software Market," Forbes, August 21, 2018, https://www.forbes.com/sites/petercohan/2018/08/21/pendo-takes-on-google-and-adobe-in-20b-product-engagement-software-market/

[24] Peter Cohan, "Pendo Takes On Google And Adobe In $20B Product Engagement Software Market," Ibid.

[25] Peter Cohan, "Pendo Takes On Google And Adobe In $20B Product Engagement Software Market," Ibid.

[26] Peter Cohan, "Pendo Takes On Google And Adobe In $20B Product Engagement Software Market," Ibid.

[27] Peter Cohan, "Redis Labs Growing 60%, Plans To Disrupt Oracle In $60B Database Market," Forbes, August 21, 2018, https://www.forbes.com/sites/petercohan/2018/08/21/redis-labs-growing-60-plans-to-disrupt-oracle-in-60b-database-market/

[28] Peter Cohan, "Redis Labs Growing 60%, Plans To Disrupt Oracle In $60B Database Market," Ibid.

[29] Peter Cohan, "Redis Labs Growing 60%, Plans To Disrupt Oracle In $60B Database Market," Ibid.

[30] Peter Cohan, "Redis Labs Growing 60%, Plans To Disrupt Oracle In $60B Database Market," Ibid.

[31] Peter Cohan, "Startup Wrestles With GE, Oracle And Microsoft In $25B Service Dispatch Market, Forbes, August 17, 2018, https://www.forbes.com/sites/petercohan/2018/08/17/startup-wrestles-with-ge-oracle-and-microsoft-in-25b-service-dispatch-market/

[32] Scott Bekker, "Vista Equity Partners Acquires Autotask," Redmond ChannelPartner, June 9, 2014, https://rcpmag.com/blogs/scott-bekker/2014/06/vista-acquires-autotask.aspx

[33] "Pitney Bowes To Acquire MapInfo For $408 Million," CNBC, March 15, 2007, https://www.cnbc.com/id/17627764

[34] Peter Cohan, "Startup Wrestles With GE, Oracle And Microsoft In $25B Service Dispatch Market, Ibid.

[35] Peter Cohan, "Startup Wrestles With GE, Oracle And Microsoft In $25B Service Dispatch Market, Ibid.

[36] Peter Cohan, "Invest In Companies Like Netflix That Do The Opposite Of What Clay Christensen Says," Forbes, July 14, 2014, https://www.forbes.com/sites/petercohan/2014/07/14/by-disrupting-disruption-netflix-reveals-new-investing-strategy/

[37] Cynthia Littleton and Janko Roettgers, "Ted Sarandos on How Netflix Predicted the Future of TV," Variety, August 21, 2018, https://www.nasdaq.com/article/ted-sarandos-on-how-netflix-predicted-the-future-of-tv-cm1010589

[38] Ashley Rodriguez, "Ten years ago, Netflix launched streaming video and changed the way we watch everything," Quartz, January 17, 2017, https://qz.com/887010/netflix-nflx-launched-streaming-video-10-years-ago-and-changed-the-way-we-watch-everything/

[39] Cynthia Littleton and Janko Roettgers, "Ted Sarandos on How Netflix Predicted the Future of TV," Ibid.

[40] "The Netflix revolution – Part I: History of Netflix," VDOcipher, accessed August 28, 2018, https://www.vdocipher.com/blog/2017/06/netflix-revolution-part-1-history/

[41] Todd Spangler, "Netflix Content Chief Says 85% of New Spending Is on Originals," New York Times, May 14, 2018, https://variety.com/2018/digital/news/netflix-original-spending-85-percent-1202809623/

[42] "Okta," Morningstar, accessed August 30, 2018, https://www.morningstar.com/stocks/xnas/okta/quote.html

[43] "Okta, SI/A," sec.gov, March 22s/1 3/27/17, https://www.sec.gov/Archives/edgar/data/1660134/000119312517096402/d289173ds1a.htm

[44] "Okta, SI/A," Ibid.

[45] "Okta, SI/A," Ibid.

Chapter 6: Hiring, Promoting, and Letting People Go

[1] Since firing happens relatively infrequently, the company may not have established a formal process. However, if a person has violated company policies, the process may be focused on documenting those violations. Whereas if the company needs to cut staff to save money, it will rank employees and dismiss the ones who are least effective. Finally, if the company expands the role of an individual who does not want to or lacks the skill to perform effectively, the company may seek to find a new position for the individual or encourage the person to seek employment elsewhere.

[2] Peter Cohan, "Cloudian Raises $94M More To Beat NetApp In $52B Storage Biz," Forbes, September 13, 2018, https://www.forbes.com/sites/petercohan/2018/09/13/cloudian-raises-94m-more-to-beat-netapp-in-52b-storage-biz/

[3] "Cloudian: Current Team," Crunchbase, accessed September 14, 2018, https://www.crunchbase.com/organization/cloudian#section-current-team

[4] Peter Cohan, "Cloudian Taking Customers from NetApp In $24B Market," Forbes, May 2, 2018, https://www.forbes.com/sites/petercohan/2018/05/02/cloudian-taking-customers-from-netapp-in-24b-market/

[5] "Cloudian Names Jon Ash Vice President Of Worldwide Sales," PR Newswire, Sep 25, 2014, https://www.prnewswire.com/news-releases/cloudian-names-jon-ash-vice-president-of-worldwide-sales-277054151.html

[6] "Storage provider Cloudian raises $94M," ROI Tech Services, August 29, 2018, http://www.roitechservices.com/storage-provider-cloudian-raises-94m/

[7] Peter Cohan, "Sapho Vies With Microsoft SharePoint To Boost Employee Engagement," Forbes, September 13, 2018, https://www.forbes.com/sites/petercohan/2018/09/13/sapho-vies-with-microsoft-sharepoint-to-boost-employee-engagement/#67a56e795afe

[8] Peter Cohan, "Sapho Vies With Microsoft SharePoint To Boost Employee Engagement," Ibid.

[9] Peter Cohan, "Sapho Vies With Microsoft SharePoint To Boost Employee Engagement," Ibid.

[10] Peter Cohan, "Sapho Vies With Microsoft SharePoint To Boost Employee Engagement," Ibid.

[11] "Marque Teegardin," LinkedIn, accessed September 14, 2018, https://www.linkedin.com/in/marque-teegardin-0385b/

[12] Peter Cohan, "Confluent Targets IBM, Oracle In $27B Middleware Market," Forbes, September 7, 2018, https://www.forbes.com/sites/petercohan/2018/09/07/confluent-targets-ibm-oracle-in-27b-middleware-market/

[13] Peter Cohan, "Confluent Targets IBM, Oracle In $27B Middleware Market," Forbes, Ibid.

[14] Todd Barnett, LinkedIn, accessed September 14, 2018, https://www.linkedin.com/in/tobarnett/

[15] "Confluent Expands Leadership Team With Four Key Hires as Stream Processing Initiatives Gain Enterprise Momentum," Confluent.io, July 14, 2016, https://www.confluent.io/press-release/confluent-expands-leadership-team-with-four-key-hires-as-stream-processing-initiatives-gain-enterprise-momentum/

[16] General Data Protection Regulation (GDPR) was a set of EU regulations to give consumers more control of their data online – for example, giving them the right to be forgotten. In 2018, companies that did business in the EU were scrambling to comply with these regulations. GDPR regulations penalizes privacy non-compliance with sanctions up to 4% of revenue, according to BigID.

[17] Peter Cohan, "BigID Takes On Varonis, Talend, Symantec In $19B Market," Forbes, September 6, 2018, https://www.forbes.com/sites/petercohan/2018/09/06/bigid-takes-on-sailpoint-varonis-talend-symantec-in-19b-market/

[18] Peter Cohan, "BigID Takes On Varonis, Talend, Symantec In $19B Market," Ibid.

[19] Peter Cohan, "BigID Takes On Varonis, Talend, Symantec In $19B Market," Ibid.

[20] Matt Hines, "CA to buy Netegrity for $430 million," CNET, October 6, 2004, https://www.cnet.com/news/ca-to-buy-netegrity-for-430-million/

[21] Nimrod Vax, LinkedIn, accessed September 15, 2018, https://www.linkedin.com/in/nimrodv/

[22] Scott Casey, LinkedIn, accessed September 15, 2018, https://www.linkedin.com/in/scottpcasey/

[23] Peter Cohan, "ThoughtSpot Raised $145M More To Target Tableau As It Barrels To IPO," Forbes, September 8, 2019, https://www.forbes.com/sites/petercohan/2018/09/08/thoughtspot-raised-145m-more-to-target-tableau-as-it-barrels-to-ipo/

[24] Peter Cohan, "ThoughtSpot Raised $145M More To Target Tableau As It Barrels To IPO," Ibid.

[25] Peter Cohan, "ThoughtSpot Raised $145M More To Target Tableau As It Barrels To IPO," Ibid.

[26] Peter Cohan, "ThoughtSpot Raised $145M More To Target Tableau As It Barrels To IPO," Ibid.

[27] "Social Media Marketer Vitrue Has Been Bought By Oracle For $300 Million," TechCrunch, May 23, 2012, https://techcrunch.com/2012/05/23/more/

[28] "Brian Blond," Crunchbase, accessed September 16, 2018, https://www.crunchbase.com/person/brian-blond#section-overview

[29] Peter Cohan, "Exabeam Wins 70% Of Splunk Faceoffs As It Targets 10% Market Share," Forbes, August 24, 2018, https://www.forbes.com/sites/petercohan/2018/08/24/exabeam-wins-70-of-splunk-faceoffs-as-it-targets-10-market-share/

[30] Peter Cohan, "Exabeam Wins 70% Of Splunk Faceoffs As It Targets 10% Market Share," Ibid.

[31] Peter Cohan, "Exabeam Wins 70% Of Splunk Faceoffs As It Targets 10% Market Share," Ibid.

[32] "Exabeam Initiates Sales Push with Hiring of Former Imperva SVP of Worldwide Sales Ralph Pisani," PR Newswire, July 8, 2014, https://www.businesswire.com/news/home/20140708005420/en/Exabeam-Initiates-Sales-Push-Hiring-Imperva-SVP

[33] Laura Barnes, "Exabeam appoints new CFO and Executive VP of engineering," PCR, November 2, 2018, https://www.pcr-online.biz/appointments/exabeam-appoints-new-cfo-and-executive-vp-of-engineering

[34] Peter Cohan, "Targeting $11B Market, SendGrid's A Fast-Growing Buy," Forbes, September 6, 2018, https://www.forbes.com/sites/petercohan/2018/09/06/targeting-11b-market-sendgrids-a-fast-growing-buy/

[35] Peter Cohan, "Targeting $11B Market, SendGrid's A Fast-Growing Buy," Ibid.

[36] Frederic Lardinois, "Twilio acquires email API platform SendGrid for $2 billion in stock," TechCrunch, October 15, 2018, https://techcrunch.com/2018/10/15/twilio-acquires-email-api-platform-sendgrid-for-2-billion-in-stock/

[37] Peter Cohan, "Targeting $11B Market, SendGrid's A Fast-Growing Buy," Ibid.

[38] "SendGrid Appoints Leandra Fishman as Senior Vice President of Sales and Customer Success," Sendgrid.com, August 15, 2016, https://sendgrid.com/news/sendgrid-appoints-leandra-fishman-as-senior-vice-president-of-sales-and-customer-success/

[39] Peter Cohan, "Targeting $11B Market, SendGrid's A Fast-Growing Buy," Ibid.

[40] Peter Cohan, "With $300M In Capital, Anaplan Is Taking $100M+ Bite Out Of IBM, Oracle In $20B Market," Forbes, July 21, 2018, https://www.forbes.com/sites/petercohan/2018/07/21/with-300m-in-capital-anaplan-is-taking-100m-bite-out-of-ibm-oracle-in-20b-market/

[41] "Anaplan, Form S-1," sec.gov, September 14, 2018, https://www.sec.gov/Archives/edgar/data/1540755/000119312518274158/d591366ds1.htm

Chapter 7: Holding People Accountable

[1] Some companies, such as Amazon, meet to review performance every week as we saw in Chapter 4.

[2] Peter Cohan, "Hungry Start-up Strategy: Creating New Ventures with Limited Resources and Unlimited Vision" Berrett-Koehler Publishers, (November 2012)

[3] Peter Cohan, "Startup Targets Tableau, IBM in $166B Business Intelligence Mart," *Forbes*, October 2, 2018

[4] Peter Cohan, "Startup Targets Tableau, IBM in $166B Business Intelligence Mart," Ibid.

[5] Peter Cohan, "Fast-Growing Startup Targets Google, Facebook in $50B Ad Market," September 11, 2018, https://www.forbes.com/sites/petercohan/2018/09/11/fast-growing-startup-targets-google-facebook-in-50b-ad-market/

[6] Peter Cohan, "Fast-Growing Startup Targets Google, Facebook in $50B Ad Market," Ibid.

[7] Peter Cohan, "Qubole Takes on Cloudera, Hortonworks in $50B Hadoop Market," Forbes, September 20, 2018, https://www.forbes.com/sites/petercohan/2018/09/20/qubole-takes-on-cloudera-hortonworks-in-50b-hadoop-market/

[8] Peter Cohan, "Qubole Takes on Cloudera, Hortonworks in $50B Hadoop Market," Ibid.

[9] Peter Cohan, "Qubole Takes on Cloudera, Hortonworks in $50B Hadoop Market," Ibid.

[10] Peter Cohan, "Qubole Takes on Cloudera, Hortonworks in $50B Hadoop Market," Ibid.

[11] Peter Cohan, "StreamSets Targets IBM, Informatica in $28.5B Middleware Market, Forbes, September 21, 2018, https://www.forbes.com/sites/petercohan/2018/09/21/streamsets-targets-ibm-informatica-in-28-5b-middleware-market/

[12] Peter Cohan, "StreamSets Targets IBM, Informatica in $28.5B Middleware Market," Ibid.

[13] Peter Cohan, "StreamSets Targets IBM, Informatica in $28.5B Middleware Market," Ibid.

[14] Peter Cohan, "WalkMe Raises $207.5M To Accelerate Corporate Digital Transformation," Forbes, September 27, 2018,https://www.forbes.com/sites/petercohan/2018/09/27/walkme-raises-208m-to-accelerate-corporate-digital-transformation/

[15] Peter Cohan, "WalkMe Raises $207.5M To Accelerate Corporate Digital Transformation," Ibid.

[16] Peter Cohan, "WalkMe Raises $207.5M To Accelerate Corporate Digital Transformation," Ibid.

[17] Peter Cohan , "Panzura Barreling Toward IPO In $68B Cloud Data Management Market," Forbes, September 22, 2018, https://www.forbes.com/sites/petercohan/2018/09/22/panzura-barreling-towards-ipo-in-68b-cloud-data-management-market/

[18] Peter Cohan, "Panzura Barreling Toward IPO in $68B Cloud Data Management Market," Ibid.

[19] Peter Cohan, "Kronos To Hit $1.5B In Revenue In $22.5B Human Capital Software Market," Forbes, September 27, 2018, https://www.forbes.com/sites/petercohan/2018/09/27/kronos-to-hit-1-5b-in-revenue-in-22-5b-human-capital-software-market/

[20] Peter Cohan, "Kronos To Hit $1.5B In Revenue In $22.5B Human Capital Software Market," Ibid.

[21] Peter Cohan, "Kronos To Hit $1.5B In Revenue In $22.5B Human Capital Software Market," Ibid.

[22] Peter Cohan, "Kronos To Hit $1.5B In Revenue In $22.5B Human Capital Software Market," Ibid.

[23] "Snap Balance Sheet," Morningstar, accessed September 29, 2018, http://financials.morningstar.com/balance-sheet/bs.html?t=SNAP&region=usa&culture=en-US

[24] Peter Cohan, "Snap Will Keep Falling Unless Apple or Google Buys It, Says Wharton Professor," Forbes, June 14, 2018, https://www.forbes.com/sites/petercohan/2018/06/14/wharton-prof-snap-will-keep-falling-unless-apple-or-google-buy-it/

[25] "Snap Inc. (SNAP) CEO Evan Spiegel on Q2 2018 Results - Earnings Call Transcript," SeekingAlpha, August 7, 2018, https://seekingalpha.com/article/4196142-snap-inc-snap-ceo-evan-spiegel-q2-2018-results-earnings-call-transcript

[26] "Snap Inc. (SNAP) CEO Evan Spiegel on Q2 2018 Results - Earnings Call Transcript," Ibid.

[27] Sarah Frier, "Nobody Trusts Facebook. Twitter Is a Hot Mess. What Is Snapchat Doing?" *BloombergBusinessweek*, August 22, 2018, https://www.bloomberg.com/news/features/2018-08-22/nobody-trusts-facebook-twitter-is-a-hot-mess-what-is-snap-s-evan-spiegel-doing

Chapter 8: Coordinating Processes

[1] Peter Cohan, "6 Things Your Marketing and Sales Teams Need to Know," *Inc.*, September 26, 2018, https://www.inc.com/peter-cohan/follow-these-6-essential-steps-to-turn-leads-into-paying-customers.html

[2] Peter Cohan, "Molekule Vies With Honeywell, Dyson In $33B Air Purification Market," Forbes, October 14, 2018, https://www.forbes.com/sites/petercohan/2018/10/14/molekule-vies-with-honeywell-dyson-in-33b-air-purification-market/

[3] Peter Cohan, "Molekule Vies With Honeywell, Dyson In $33B Air Purification Market," Ibid.

[4] Peter Cohan, "Molekule Vies With Honeywell, Dyson In $33B Air Purification Market," Ibid.

[5] Peter Cohan, "Molekule Vies With Honeywell, Dyson In $33B Air Purification Market," Ibid.

[6] Peter Cohan, "In $9B Business Search Market Algolia Tops Google," *Forbes*, October 6, 2018, https://www.forbes.com/sites/petercohan/2018/10/06/in-9b-business-search-market-algolia-tops-google/

[7] Peter Cohan, "In $9B Business Search Market Algolia Tops Google," Ibid.

[8] Peter Cohan, "In $9B Business Search Market Algolia Tops Google," Ibid.

[9] Peter Cohan, "In $9B Business Search Market Algolia Tops Google," Ibid.

[10] Peter Cohan, "In $9B Business Search Market Algolia Tops Google," Ibid.

11 Peter Cohan, "Kinetica Could Boost NVidia In $70B Big Data Market," Forbes, October 12, 2018, https://www.forbes.com/sites/petercohan/2018/10/12/kinetica-could-boost-nvidia-in-70b-big-data-market/

12 Peter Cohan, "Kinetica Could Boost NVidia In $70B Big Data Market," Ibid.

13 Peter Cohan, "Kinetica Could Boost NVidia In $70B Big Data Market," Ibid.

14 Peter Cohan, "Kinetica Could Boost NVidia In $70B Big Data Market," Ibid.

15 Peter Cohan, "Kinetica Could Boost NVidia In $70B Big Data Market," Ibid.

16 Peter Cohan, "JFrog Raises $165M To Outpace Google, Azure And AWS In $50B DevOps Market," Forbes, October 6, 2018, https://www.forbes.com/sites/petercohan/2018/10/06/jfrog-raises-165m-to-outpace-google-azure-and-aws-in-50b-devops-market/

17 Peter Cohan, "JFrog Raises $165M To Outpace Google, Azure And AWS In $50B DevOps Market," Ibid.

18 Peter Cohan, "JFrog Raises $165M To Outpace Google, Azure And AWS In $50B DevOps Market," Ibid.

19 Peter Cohan, "JFrog Raises $165M To Outpace Google, Azure And AWS In $50B DevOps Market," Ibid.

20 Peter Cohan, "Virtual Instruments Takes On IBM In $20B Market," Forbes, October 18, 2018, https://www.forbes.com/sites/petercohan/2018/10/18/virtual-instruments-takes-on-ibm-in-20b-market/

21 Peter Cohan, "Virtual Instruments Takes On IBM In $20B Market," Ibid.

22 Peter Cohan, "Virtual Instruments Takes On IBM In $20B Market," Ibid.

23 Peter Cohan, "Virtual Instruments Takes On IBM In $20B Market," Ibid.

24 Peter Cohan, "Virtual Instruments Takes On IBM In $20B Market," Ibid.

25 Peter Cohan, "Can Okta Keep Growing at 57%?" *Forbes*, October 5, 2018, https://www.forbes.com/sites/petercohan/2018/10/05/can-okta-keep-growing-at-57/

26 Peter Cohan, "Can Okta Keep Growing at 57%?" Ibid.

27 Peter Cohan, "Can Okta Keep Growing at 57%?" Ibid.

28 Peter Cohan, "Can Okta Keep Growing at 57%?" Ibid.

29 Peter Cohan, "Can Okta Keep Growing at 57%?" Ibid.

30 Peter Cohan, "Can ForeScout Technologies Keep Growing At 30%?" Forbes, October 4, 2018, https://www.forbes.com/sites/petercohan/2018/10/04/can-forescout-technologies-keep-growing-at-30/

31 Peter Cohan, "Can ForeScout Technologies Keep Growing At 30%?" Ibid.

32 Peter Cohan, "Can ForeScout Technologies Keep Growing At 30%?" Ibid.

33 Peter Cohan, "Can ForeScout Technologies Keep Growing At 30%?" Ibid.

Chapter 9: What's Next

1 Peter Cohan, "This Common Mental Block Is Holding You Back From Success," Inc., October 23, 2018, https://www.inc.com/peter-cohan/this-common-mental-block-is-holding-you-back-from-success.html

Index

© Peter S. Cohan 2019

P. S. Cohan, *Scaling Your Startup*, https://doi.org/10.1007/978-1-4842-4312-1

55584685R00164

Made in the USA
San Bernardino,
CA